CLAIMS TO MEMORY

Polygons: Cultural Diversities and Intersections
General Editor: **Lieve Spaas**, *Professor of French Cultural Studies,*
Kingston University, UK

CLAIMS TO MEMORY

Beyond Slavery and Emancipation in the French Caribbean

Catherine A. Reinhardt

Berghahn Books
New York • Oxford

First published in 2006 by

Berghahn Books
www.berghahnbooks.com

Portions of chapter 3 are adapted from my article "French
Caribbean Slaves Forge Their Own Ideal of Libery in 1789,"
in _Slavery in the Caribbean Francophone World: Distant Voices,
Forgotten Acts, Forged Identities,_ ed. Doris Y. Kadish, 2000, 19–38.

Chapter 4 was previously published as "Forgotten Claims to Liberty:
Free Coloreds in St. Domingue on the Eve of the First Abolition of
Slavery" in _Colonial Latin American Review_ 10, no. 1, 2001, 105–24.

Library of Congress Cataloging-in-Publication Data
A catalog record for this book
is available from the Library of Congress

British Library Cataloguing in Publication Data
A catalogue record for this book is available
from the British Library.

Printed in the United States on acid-free paper.

ISBN 1-84545-079-5 hardback

For my children
Cecilia and Nicolas

CONTENTS

LIST OF ILLUSTRATIONS

Acknowledgments

The turning point in the conception of this book was my first trip to Guadeloupe in 1999 to visit my in-laws. My discovery of the island ignited in me a renewed interest in the subject of my dissertation which I had completed the year before. I came across unexpected traces of the slave past everywhere I set foot and realized to what extent the memory of slavery constituted a problematic element of Guadeloupean society to this day. Particularly noteworthy was my visit of the *Musée du Rhum* that advertises a discovery of Guadeloupean history through the sugarcane plantations and rum production. Surprisingly, slavery is completely absent from the narratives of the museum displays. How is it possible that the principle actors of the story of sugarcane planting and harvest over a period of more than two hundred years have simply been left out? Awed by the bizarre way in which the memory of slavery is simultaneously remembered and forgotten, I decided to make this contemporary reality the cornerstone of my work.

As my project unfolded, many were the colleagues and friends who helped me progress. I would like to thank Thomas Buchanan, a Rockefeller Foundation Fellow at the University of Memphis at the time, whose careful reading of my dissertation, insightful comments, and firm belief in the validity of my argument, gave me the initial impetus to begin reframing my research and rewriting all the chapters. Doris Y. Kadish from the University of Georgia has encouraged my work on slave writings for many years and gave me the opportunity to publish the first results of my research. I would like to thank her especially for supporting my application for the National

Endowment for the Humanities Summer Fellowship. The 2001
NEH Summer Fellowship gave me the time, materials and support necessary to complete the photography project of sites of
memory in Martinique and Guadeloupe so essential to this
book. Without the active interest Caribbean historians and
writers including Myriam Cottias, Alain Yacou, and Gérard
Delvert as well as the staff of the *Office du Tourisme de la Martinique,* the *Conseil Général de la Martinique* and the *Maison du
Patrimoine de la Ville de Basse-Terre, Guadeloupe* took in my project, I would not have been able to compile the wealth of documentation that permitted the writing of the last chapter. In
particular, I would like to thank Maryse Condé who graciously
allowed me to interview her on two occasions in her home in
Guadeloupe. Our discussions greatly inspired my own writing.
Living in Guadeloupe and looking for sites of memory was
made particularly enjoyable by Lise Zacaïr's wonderful hospi-
tality. Joseph and Thierry Zacaïr shared with me their great
familiarity with the island to help me locate some well-hidden
sites of memory. I am particularly thankful to them.

Many thanks go to the staffs of the Bibliothèque Nationale
de France, the Archives Nationales de France, the Archives
d'Outre-Mer, the Archives Départementales de la Guadeloupe,
the Archives Départementales de la Martinique and the Inter-
library Loan Office at the University of California, Santa Barbara who worked with me to find the documentary evidence
needed for my project. Finally, I would like to thank Lieve
Spaas, the series editor of *Polygons,* for her initial encouragement
to submit my work, the outside press reviewer for his insightful comments and suggestions for improvement, and the edi-
torial staff at Berghahn Books, in particular Michael Dempsey,
for patiently working with me through the final stages of the
manuscript.

On a more personal note, I am most indebted to my husband Philippe Zacaïr. Were it not for our on-going and passionate discussions about Caribbean history, culture and
literature during the past ten years, this book could have never
existed. His perspective as a historian, combined with his personal experience as a Guadeloupean allowed me to approach
the French Enlightenment from a Caribbean point of view.
Throughout my dissertation and the writing of my book, he
has tirelessly encouraged me, believed in me and collaborated
with me. I thank him for his patience.

My deepest thanks go to my parents Annie and Viktor Reinhardt. Their unwavering belief in my ability to realize my

dreams has allowed me never to give up. Their personal invest-
ment at all stages of the project provided me with much support. Finally, the playfulness and joy of my children, Cecilia and
Nicolas, has made this long endeavor a pleasurable one.

Memories of Slavery

On 27 April 1848, the Second Republic abolished slavery in its French overseas colonies thus ending three centuries of African slave trade and forced plantation labor. One hundred fifty years later the government of the Fifth Republic for the first time organized extensive official celebrations to commemorate this historic event. The past was resurrected, invading the present with countless memories—though undoubtedly not the same for the French nation and for the formerly enslaved populations in the overseas *départements* of Guadeloupe, Martinique, French Guiana, and Reunion.[1]

The governmental commemorations of April 1998 were varied and all took place in France. President Jacques Chirac gave an opening speech, Prime Minister Lionel Jospin honored the abolitionary fervor of the small village of Champagney, various ministers presented plaques commemorating important abolitionary figures and French Caribbean artists were invited for a variety of artistic performances. The overseas domains also organized their own local commemorative functions including exhibitions, conferences, and theater productions as well as the inauguration of memorials. In Martinique, for instance, scenes of the slave trade were reenacted with the arrival of a slave vessel, the unloading of slaves, and the reconstitution of a slave market. In Guadeloupe, a flame honoring the memory of the *nèg mawon* (fugitive slave) passed from township to township during the entire year preceding the 150th anniversary and was returned to its starting point amid celebrations, dances, and traditional music.

The most revealing aspects of the commemoration lie in the articles of major French and French Caribbean newspapers such as *Le Monde, Libération, Le Figaro,* and *France-Antilles* written for the occasion. French and Caribbean writers, historians, politicians, and journalists debated the issues surrounding the memory of slavery in contemporary society, taking positions both for and against the anniversary celebrations. Who and what should be commemorated? The 1848 decree declaring the emancipation of black slaves in France's colonies? The French men, most importantly of course French abolitionist Victor Schœlcher, who made the signing of this decree possible? The three centuries of slave trade and plantation slavery that ended in 1848? The daily resistance and countless rebellions of blacks that continually destabilized the system of exploitation, rendering it unfeasible and thus ultimately contributing to its demise? The heroes who led their people in these struggles for freedom: Makandal, Boukman, and Toussaint Louverture from Saint Domingue; Louis Delgrès from Martinique; and Ignace and Mulâtresse Solitude from Guadeloupe, to name a few?

How to Commemorate the Abolition of Slavery

"Remembering together" is the etymological meaning of "commemoration" as the Guadeloupean historian Oruno D. Lara points out in an article of *France-Antilles* (1998b).[2] This type of memory presupposes the existence of a community sharing the same common memory of the past. As far as slavery is concerned, however, the nation is divided into communities that do not share the same history, or even a similar vision of its significance. The descendants of slaves entertain a radically different relationship to the past than do the French, for many of whom the history of slavery is a discovery rather than a memory. Since the slave trade and plantation slavery are absent from the official school curriculum, many are unaware of the economic, political, and social realities of this period.[3] As a result, the act of commemoration holds very different possibilities for the French and for French West Indians. For the former, 1848 can easily be reduced to a date symbolizing the accomplishments of the abolitionary movement, of the Second Republic, and of the Declaration of the Rights of Man. For the latter, the abolitionary decree is but one moment in a painful history they are often unable to face. The Guadeloupean historian René Bélénus (1998), who is fundamentally against the idea of commemoration, calls this date a "non-event in Guadeloupe." The abolition of slavery "is neither a man, nor a date, but a moment in history, a process," which was bound to occur. Bélénus would have preferred a day in memory of the slaves. Guadeloupean writers, artists, priests, and union leaders in general asked that the commemoration not reduce their history to one date:

> Commemorate, of course. Reveal the fruitful "triangular commerce," which enriched France and her slave-trading ports. Reveal two centuries of barbarism covered up by the humanists, the Enlightenment, the Church.... And not to forget that the celebrated abolition was already the second one, since the first one, accorded by the Convention in 1794 was revoked amid a bloodbath. Finally reveal the uprooting, the traumatism, the search for an identity (Cojean 1998a).

Celebrating 1848 one hundred and fifty years later was far from problematic for the people of the French Caribbean who feared that their history would be forgotten yet one more time. They denounced, for instance, the silencing of the first abolition of slavery in 1794. Its revocation by Napoleon in 1802 had a profound impact on Caribbean history, since it contributed to the radicalization of the Haitian Revolution, eventually leading to Haitian independence in 1804.[4]

The debate provoked by the 150th anniversary of the abolitionary decree turned the commemoration into an unprecedented moment of cultural and historical reflection for France and for her remaining overseas domains. This polemic brought into focus the most controversial aspects of the past that continue to haunt the memory of slavery in the present. In his monumental *Realms of Memory,* the French historian Pierre Nora (1996: xvii) calls moments, places, people, or objects that symbolize a community's memorial heritage "realms of memory." These symbolic spaces become realms of memory when they are characterized by an overwhelming presence of the past (16). Submerging the present with diverse attitudes toward the nation's slave past, the commemoration of 1848 is a realm of memory par excellence.

The articulation of this memory diverges considerably according to the historical standpoint assumed. From the official perspective of the government, the abolitionary decree was commemorated as a founding moment of the much-vaunted principles of equality, fraternity, and liberty. In his opening speech, President Chirac presented the abolition of slavery as a building block of the nation: "The abolitionary process was undertaken in a spirit of integration, helping to strengthen the unity of the nation." Emancipated, the former slaves became members of the nation that had formerly enslaved them. The freedom bestowed upon them further strengthened the principles upon which the nation's unity was constructed: "By ending an iniquitous situation, the promoters of the abolition of slavery did not only act in the name of humanity. They reinforced the foundations of democracy and of the Republic" ("L'humanisme" 1998). From the official perspective, the commemorated moment does not conflict with the nation's principles of equality. Chirac glosses over the long historical period preceding 1848—three centuries of slavery. Abolition becomes an unproblematic moment of France's history that is part of the legacy of universal freedom.

Celebrating the abolitionary decree as a symbol of France's commitment to freedom and democracy, the commemoration honored contributions of French individuals to the exclusion of Caribbean initiatives. The festivities organized in the small village of Champagney are striking in this regard. In the company of five ministers, Prime Minister Jospin paid tribute to the anonymous citizens of the village who included a plea against slavery in their *Cahiers de doléances* (grievances) presented to the king in March 1789. The earliest indication of the French population's concern for the fate of slaves, this episode became a symbolic moment in the nation's "fight against servitude" ("Lionel Jospin" 1998). It was, in a sense, celebrated as a precursory sign of the abolitionist trajectory. The act of commemoration did not, however, acknowledge that not one other *Cahier de doléances* thought slavery worthy of mention. In fact, the exceptional nature of Champagney's plea draws attention to the population's complete lack of interest in slavery on the eve of the French Revolution, rather than to the beginnings of abolitionary fervor.

One of the earliest French figures to be remembered during the commemoration was the historian and philosopher Abbé Raynal. His polemical work *Histoire philosophique et politique des établissements et du commerce des Européens dans les deux Indes*, published during the last decades of the eighteenth century, presents European colonial expansion in a critical light. Certain inflammatory passages of this work are believed to have fueled slave revolts in the French Caribbean. "The slaves revolted as they brandished his work," wrote a journalist (Vézins 1998) in an article of *Le Figaro*. According to her, Raynal was not only the hero of the revolted slaves, his work even inspired one of the most remarkable black leaders, Toussaint Louverture, whose bedside reading was nothing less than the *Histoire des deux Indes*. This provocative work, she held, "concentrates all the subversive seeds that could be found in the terrain of the Enlightenment." By glorifying Raynal, the author of this article rendered the memory of the slave revolts themselves secondary. They are overshadowed by the vaunted image of the Abbé Raynal. The portrayal of the Enlightenment as the primary source of abolition is quite common in articles written during the commemoration (Paringaux 1998 and Vidal 1998).

Lara (1998a) condemns the quest to explain the events of the Caribbean through the prism of French history. Toussaint Louverture, according to him, was not "an illustration of the benefits of the Enlightenment." Lara holds instead that the "start of a process of destruction of the system of slavery that propagates itself progressively throughout the Caribbean area" can be found in this geohistorical region as early as 1760. From the perspective of a historian who is critical of French historical thought, the 1998 commemoration sidestepped the powerful influence of Caribbean liberation movements.

In his monumental work, the French philosopher and historian Michel Foucault calls for a writing of history that is not subjugated to authoritative power. In *Power/Knowledge* (1980: 78–92), for instance, he opposes unitary historical knowledge to what he calls subjugated, low-ranking, marginal knowledges that have been buried and disguised. Foucault's writing project favors the struggle of these marginal knowledges against the coercive claims of a "true" knowledge. The abolition of slavery becomes part of a centralizing perspective of the past as long as the celebrated memory is limited to the glorification of France's egalitarian accomplishments; the traumatic experience of slave laborers is marginalized by such a tunnel vision.

The Enlightenment and the French Revolution are not points in a continuum, symbolizing France's linear progression toward fraternal nationhood. According to Nora (1996: 12–13), France's vision of its rooted past must be replaced by an experience of history in terms of its discontinuity. It is within a fragmented universe that pieces of the past must be glued together in a reconstructive effort. Nora's insight into the nation's relationship to the past also applies to the colonial situation. The actions and narratives by Frenchmen and black slaves eventually ending institutionalized exploitation do not form a single, unitary logic, subjugated to what Foucault calls "true"

knowledge. The slaves' struggle for freedom is not a direct consequence of Montesquieu's, Diderot's, or Raynal's denunciations of the slave regime—it is not an ideological outgrowth of
French thought: "history is nourished by a plurality of memories, a plurality of archives, and a diversity of documents" (Landi
1998).

A commemoration that does not restore the abolition within
its context of slavery and colonialism, as the French historian
Nelly Schmidt (1998) points out, not only fails to properly remember three hundred years of mass enslavement, it also ignores the vital component of the slaves' struggle for freedom.
In *Language, Counter-Memory, Practice,* Foucault (1977: 219)
argues that "popular movements ... are said to arise from
famines, taxes, or unemployment; and they never appear as
the result of a struggle for power, as if the masses could dream
of a full stomach but never of exercising power. The history of
this struggle for power and the manner in which power is ex-
ercised and maintained remain totally obscured." The power
of the middle class must always appear inaccessible to events
such as popular uprisings that completely disappear within the
continuity of the dominant power structure (221). Although
slavery does not exactly reproduce the class system that Foucault is referring to, it is governed by an organization that en-
genders similar results. The slaves' struggle for freedom disturbs
the power structure put in place by the colonizer. The collapse of
this system is, as a result, primarily attributed to the voluntary
actions of the colonizer, not to the power of slave rebellions.
Slaves are not represented as "makers" of historical events: history, by definition, is made in France. This is why the Martinican writer Edouard Glissant (1981: 100) takes up his people's
"non-history." Unable to see themselves in a historical dynamic constituted by events of their own making, the people
of the French Caribbean experience the past passively, as an
absence (130, 278).

In their reactions to the 1998 commemoration, French
Caribbean writers, historians, politicians, and journalists primarily emphasized the importance of remembering their slave
heritage. In particular, they brought into focus the power of
the slaves' struggle that made abolition inevitable. Alfred
Marie-Jeanne, the president of both the Martinican Indepen-
dentist Party and the Regional Council of Martinique, clearly
distinguished the celebrations on his island from those organized in France: "we do not celebrate the abolition of slavery!

We commemorate the antislavery insurrection. There is a difference. The Negroes did not wait for a divine liberator from metropolitan France to lead the revolt. The slaves conquered their freedom on their own" (Cojean 1998b). Marie-Jeanne deemed it necessary to empower the slave ancestors by remembering their fight against French domination. The Guadeloupean writer Daniel Maximin (1998) similarly underscored the relevance of the slaves' struggle in the commemorative context. It is necessary "to establish the reality of the fights, the struggles, the resistance and thus prevent ... 1848 from being interpreted as a liberal bestowal by humanistic deputies to poor, enchained slaves who have no conscience. [This must be done] without the temptation of condescension." Commemorating the slaves' active, voluntary, and autonomous engagement in their own history restores a sense of dignity and pride by empowering the people.

The course of the flame of liberty in honor of the *nèg mawon inconnu* (the unknown fugitive slave) exemplifies how Guadeloupeans commemorated their slave heritage. Runners passed a flame from township to township throughout the entire island for the duration of one year, ending in the spring of 1998. The arrival of the flame in each town was celebrated with traditional music and drums to evoke the means of communication used by slaves. Considering fugitive slaves as the principle actors of the abolition of slavery, the organizers of this commemorative event wanted to honor the memory of all the fugitive slaves the American continent had known during the three hundred years of slavery ("Une pensée forte" 1998). The most important aspect of this event was its popular appeal. It was meant to touch the people and incite them to participate in this active remembrance of the past ("L'hommage" 1997). A symbol of the slaves' fight against oppression, the "unknown fugitive slave" is one of the only anchors allowing the masses to proudly identify with their heritage. The struggle of their ancestors gives the people of the Caribbean an active role in a history their people forged throughout three centuries of slavery. In *El Siglo de las Luces,* the Cuban writer Alejo Carpentier beautifully conjures the power of the slaves' tradition of resistance: "If one were to make a spark correspond with each slave revolt, the American continent would constantly be flickering during the entire duration of Negro slavery" (qtd. in "L'hommage" 1997).

Memory and Forgetting

The West Indians' remembrance of their slave past is the central concern that emerges from the commemoration. Nonetheless, a "layer of silence" obstructs this memory (Cojean 1998a). With the abolition of slavery in 1848, the French Republic compelled the new citizens to forget their former enslavement (Cojean 1998b). Despite the numerous traces of slavery in their daily lives and in their mental makeup, the people had to forget a past replete with painful memories (Bélénus 1998). This systematic "silencing" of history, Glissant repeatedly points out in his *Discours antillais* (1981: 100, 130, 278), has erased the people's collective memory. And a people without memory are like a tree without roots, concluded Lucette Michaux-Chevry, president of the regional council of Guadeloupe, in her opening article of *France-Antilles: Supplément-Edition du 25 mai 1998* that was entirely dedicated to the commemoration.

The negation of history occurs not only in the context of slavery but also in that of colonialism in general as the Martinican psychiatrist, anticolonial writer, and activist Frantz Fanon (1991: 255–56) remarks in regards to Algeria. It is one of the determining characteristics of colonizers to wipe out all traces of the past prior to the period of colonization. The French philosopher Jacques Derrida (1996: 89) similarly shares his boyhood experiences as an Algerian Jew during which he saw the memory of his own community completely annulled and replaced by the history of the French nation. His handicapped memory, as he calls it, resulting from the amnesia he never had the courage and the force to resist, could only be remedied with the help of historical work he felt incapable of.

The memory of a people, according to Foucault (1976: 24–29), is the key to controlling their dynamism, their experience, and their knowledge of their struggles. This memory can be reprogrammed to contain a new framework that imposes upon the people an interpretation of the present. The Czech writer Milan Kundera (1980: 145, 234) observes this phenomenon in political relationships. Through organized forgetting, big powers deprive small countries of their national consciousness. As the people lose awareness of the past, they gradually lose themselves as a nation. After one hundred fifty years of controlled forgetting during which the former slaves were reprogrammed to see France as a generous, liberating mother, recollecting the past is a formidable challenge. The French West Indians' memory as a group is the key to this difficult process.

The French sociologist Maurice Halbwachs (1992: 182–83, 188) pioneered the concept of memory as a collective faculty. A group within a given society can reconstruct its past at any given moment by relying on the social memory of the group at large. However, society can only survive if there is sufficient unity among the different groups and individuals that comprise it. In order to achieve this unity, society erases from its memory those recollections that might separate groups and individuals too far from one another. The chosen recollections are rearranged in such a way as to reflect the consciousness that society has of itself in the present. Collective memory thus serves as a bridge between the store of recollections that provide a framework for the past and for the conditions in which society finds itself in the present. Once people or historical facts have permeated the memory of the group, they gain meaning as a teaching, a notion, or a symbol and become part of society's system of ideas.

When France abolished slavery for the second time in 1848, the new citizens of the colonies were to become entirely assimilated by a nation that adopted them as children. Incontestably, however, the distance separating the former slaves from the French could not have been greater. Nothing in the past united them and no common recollections could serve as a foundation for collective memory. Nonetheless, the unity for which the French Republic stood in the name of universalism had to be achieved. To this end, the recollections that were contrary to the ideal of equality, fraternity and liberty were to be systematically erased: the new citizens were to forget their enslavement under French dominion.

The Martinican historian Myriam Cottias (1998) speaks of the "politics of forgetting" in the article "La politique de l'oubli" of *France-Antilles: Supplément-Edition du 25 mai 1998.* Completely assimilated by the French Republic the colonies become part of an "imagined community" in the sense of political scientist Benedict Anderson. "In the name of political assimilation, the memory of slavery is forgotten so as to regenerate the colonies and integrate them into the nation." To successfully break with the past and with the memory of slavery, the Republic employed legal means. The new citizens were given family names they did not possess as slaves. An amnesty was declared in favor of the fugitive slaves who were asked to become members of a society that considered them as equal brothers. Finally, the instigators of rebellion prior to the announcement of the decree were officially pardoned by the State and a Mass was celebrated to calm the passions. It is not only the institution of slavery that was to be forgotten but also the slaves' violent struggle against the French nation. The pardon that was to cement the unity of the French nation was, however, not reciprocal. There was no mutual agreement between the new citizens and the State that the past be buried; the Republic simply dictated the erasure of three centuries of slavery from the official historical record of the nation.

In his *Imagined Communities,* Anderson (1991: 199–201) discusses the importance of forgetting in the process of community building. Parallel to Halbwachs, Anderson maintains that those events in a nation that set communities off against one another, for instance, fratricidal wars, must be tacitly forgotten by all. Even so, this implicit agreement between the communities guarantees that on the occasion of a commemoration, for example, the forgotten events need only be recalled in order for the communities to share a common knowledge of this past. In the case of slavery, this unspoken acknowledgment never took place. Despite the nation's proclaimed ideals of equality, the assimilated new citizens were never on equal footing with the French. Deemed problematic by the State, their entire history was replaced by that of the French nation. As a result, the foundation for a collective memory shared by the French and by descendants from slavery was never laid.

The French historian Louis Sala-Molins (1998) illustrates France's selective memory regarding her past. The State commemorates the 1598 Edict of Nantes, which granted Protestants the right to exercise their religion, as well as its 1685 revocation with all its disastrous effects. The latter is a part of the nation's forgotten recollections of fratricidal wars, of which society needs to only occasionally be reminded. The year 1685 is also the year Louis XIV promulgated the *Code Noir,* the first European document giving a judicial structure to the slave regime. The catastrophic consequences of this event for thousands of black slaves need not be recounted here. Nonetheless, the French State has never deemed this date worthy of commemoration. Instead, argues Sala-Molins, it is the abolitionary decree that is celebrated to commemorate France's generosity and to forget the preceding horrors. France—and this is why French West Indians are highly suspicious of the 1998 commemoration—has never integrated her slave past into the nation's history. The absence of slavery and the slave trade from the school curriculum exemplifies this lack. "We must construct the memory of our children and give them reasons to be proud of their slave ancestors," urges a Guadeloupean politician (Co-jean 1998a). One of the obvious ways to do this, suggests *Tras'Mémoires,* an intercommunal committee from Guade-loupe working to foster the memory of slavery among the pop-ulation, is to have chapters concerning slavery included in the Republic's history textbooks ("Tras'Mémoires" 1998).

Reconstructing the past is, according to Halbwachs, the func-tion of social memory. As a collectivity, West Indians can rely on the group's memory to recall previous experiences. Yet, since this collective memory has always been silenced it must somehow be conjured up before it can point the way to the past. Nora (1996: 7) calls such summoned memories realms of memory that emerge as "moments of history are plucked out of the flow of history, then returned to it—no longer quite alive but not yet entirely dead, like shells left on the shore when the sea of living memory has receded." The experience of slavery is plucked out of the historical consciousness of West Indians and becomes, to use Martinican writer Patrick Chamoiseau's (1998b) expression, an "obscure memory." In order to mobilize this painful past, to turn it into a realm of memory, to make it available for the collective memory of the people, slavery must become a part of "conscious memory." Chamoiseau associates "obscure memory" with the West Indians' difficulty in forming their own coherent community independently of France. He calls for a "collective catharsis" that would create such links and lead West Indian society to blossom (Chapelle 1998). To cease being the slaves of slavery, the people must experience a healthy memory of slavery, a memory that truly liberates (Chamoiseau 1998a).

"Prophetic Visions" of the Past

In this study, the 150th anniversary of the abolition of slavery serves as a point of articulation between present and past: be-tween the commemoration of slavery in the context of 1998 and the historical process shaping these memories. A realm of memory for French and French Caribbean communities, the commemoration generated numerous commentaries on slav-ery and abolition. For the first time, recollections were offi-cially brought out into the open as a consequence of the celebrations organized by the French government. Within the realm of the commemoration, the emblematic date of 1848—marking the Republic's generous humanism—was dismantled

by the penetrating analyses of French and Caribbean historians, politicians, writers, and journalists. While the State celebrated 1848 as a symbol of progress, numerous voices in France
and in France's overseas regions questioned the government's
uncritical perspective.[5]

The period spanning the late Enlightenment and the French
Revolution is crucial to the formation of the legacy of freedom
and equality. In a surprising way, the memory of France's long-
standing involvement in the slave trade is erased by the abolition of slavery in 1848. It appears as though France—the
liberating "mother"—had never been responsible for the enslavement of thousands of African slaves. What caused this bi-
ased remembrance? The ideological underpinnings of the
Enlightenment and the French Revolution are key to understanding this phenomenon. Powerful symbols of progress and
social justice, the French *philosophes* largely contributed to the
idea that the eighteenth century is at the origin of the nation's
advances. They are considered the ideological fathers of the
French Revolution, which in turn is thought to have brought
about the destruction of the slave regime. However, in the process of remembering the *philosophes,* the French Revolution, and
the abolition of slavery in 1848, the foundation of France's
wealth on the slave economy is passed over in silence. Forgotten is also the Caribbean dimension of this past. Agents of this
historical process, those who toiled for the economic benefit of
France disappear behind European ideologies of freedom and
equality.

An effective way to write about these forgotten memories is
to bring forward the intricacies of eighteenth-century narratives on slavery in the political context of the French Revolution and slave resistance. Using memory as a link between
past and present, this study examines focal points of the 1998
debate: enlightened thought, resistance, freedom, assimilation, and contemporary traces of slavery in the popular imagination. The five "realms of memory" are an inquiry into the
historical and cultural process that gave rise to the memorial
heritage of France and of the French Caribbean. They bring together some of the most divided perspectives, thereby allowing
multiple voices of the past to be heard.[6] This study is limited to
the second part of the eighteenth century for practical reasons.
Although a similar analysis of the first part of the nineteenth
century until the famous decree abolishing slavery in 1848
would complement this investigation, it is beyond the scope of
the present work.

I constituted the primary source material for the investigation of each realm of memory by voluntarily crossing the boundaries between human sciences. An extensive part of the sources include archives—the type of data typically used by historians. This work, however, is not a history of slavery. Instead, I use these documents in the framework of an interdisciplinary analysis. Most of the archival evidence consists of political pamphlets and letters by slaves, free coloreds,[7] and white colonial planters as well as legal documents by colonial administrators and French officials written during the last decades of the eighteenth century. Through literary analyses, these texts are compared to writings by the French *philosophes* and to plays staging the colonial situation in the Caribbean during the Enlightenment. Other primary sources include printed texts by various antislavery activists, mostly members of the *Société des Amis des Noirs*[8] as well as a number of court cases granting freedom to individual slaves. The eclectic body of sources comprised within each realm of memory brings out the ramifications of slavery and emancipation; even previously forgotten or obscured facets of this past come to light. This approach parallels Glissant's (1981: 133) vision of West Indian literary production today. Caribbean literature implicates all the human sciences as it nourishes, and is nourished by, historical reflection. This disregard for boundaries between categories of analytic thought allows elements of the past to be gleaned despite the silencing of the people's historical memory.[9]

The methodology is largely inspired by Glissant's theoretical exposition in *Introduction à une poétique du divers* (1996) on Caribbean literature, history, and culture. Aspects of Nora's and Foucault's theories complement this approach. The aim of this analysis is to take fully into account the specificity of historical formations amid former slave societies of the Caribbean. They do not—in contrast to European nations—have a genesis, upon which the founding myth of their communities can be built. To illustrate the opposition between European and Caribbean identity, Glissant (1996: 59) uses French philosopher Gilles Deleuzes's and French psychoanalyst Félix Guattari's notions of the unique root and the rhizome.[10] European and other occidental cultures have propagated the belief that all identity has one unique root to the exclusion of all other roots. This perspective is diametrically opposed to the experience of composite cultures, such as those of the Caribbean, which have emerged under very diverse ethnic, racial, historical, linguistic, and cultural influences. The identity of the latter can more closely be compared to a rhizome that spreads outward and encounters other roots during its growth (Glissant 1996: 23).

For the purpose of this study, Glissant's schema is adapted to the formation of collective memory under the slave regime of the eighteenth century. Each realm of memory is made up of ideologies, texts, and actions that are transformed through their mutual encounters. I call this evidence of the past rhizome-memories, since they do not form a unique historical root that might anchor the present memory of slavery to an origin. Rather, like rhizomes, these testimonies of the past spread widely and are continuously exposed to the transformative influence of other testimonies. They form the building blocks of a realm of memory that can never be fixed. Nora (1996: 15) maintains that realms of memory "thrive only because of their capacity for change, [and] their ability to resurrect old meanings and generate new ones along with new and unforeseeable connections." Rhizome-memories expose the connections, making it possible to analyze how the multiple voices of the past mold the historical process. This methodology allows such conflicting voices as the slaves', the colonial planters', and the *philosophes'* to be studied within the same contextual framework.

In a discussion about research on prisons, Foucault (1980: 38) emphasizes the importance of studying not only the discourses about prisons but also all the discourses that arise within the prison, including the voices of the prisoners, of the guards, of the administration, and of the institution's regulations and means of functioning. These discourses have to be brought together by making visible the strategic connections between them. The world of plantation slavery is in many ways similar to the institution of the prison. There are numerous regulations, laws, voices, and actions both inside and outside of this world that influence its smooth functioning or lack thereof. While each one of these forces affects institutionalized slavery to varying degrees, it is the relationship between them that constructs the memory of those who are implicated in the system.

During the past two decades, scholars have gradually intensified their inquiry into this forgotten past. Although the aim of this book is to contribute to this endeavor, I am well aware of the many obstacles rendering the recovery of the past difficult. The rare testimonies by slaves and emancipated slaves of the French Caribbean are the main barrier for my own work.

While there is a relative abundance of narratives by North American and to some extent also English Caribbean slaves, relatively few such written traces have been left in Saint Domingue, Guadeloupe, and Martinique. This lack of sources made my original aim of exclusively representing the slaves' viewpoint simply unfeasible. However, I came across so many eighteenth-century commentaries on slavery during my research that I saw the greatest potential in the integration of all these voices within one study. Slaves, people of color, white planters, colonial administrators, the *philosophes,* the *Société des Amis des Noirs,* French lawyers, and fictive slaves from plays tell stories of the past that reflect the network of ideologies forging the historical process. Since such a comparative analysis entails the concurrent use of literary, historical, political, and judicial material, I have had to bring out the uniqueness of each of these documents while knitting them together in a coherent whole. Although I clearly distinguish between factual and fictional primary sources, my questioning of these documents is rather similar. How do these diverse fragments of the past shed light on obscured memories of slavery? By combining factual and fictional traces of the past, I create a cultural space that allows memories of slavery to surface. The goal is not to reconstruct the past as it happened, so to speak, and therefore to limit the study to factual evidence. Rather, it is the dialogue between fact and fiction, between past and present that sheds light on obscured, silenced, forgotten, and even erased fragments of the slave past. It is at the interstices of these documents that memory can be found. Again, the final quest of this study is memory, not the elaboration of a "true" knowledge of the past.

Again, Glissant (1996: 86–87) proves inspirational for the conceptualization of my approach. He formulates the idea of a "prophetic vision of the past" that narrates the past but is not exclusively based on factual evidence. According to him, "the past must not only be recomposed objectively (or even subjectively) by the historian, it must also be dreamt prophetically for the people, the communities and the cultures whose past has been occulted." To illustrate his point, Glissant evokes a chapter of his novel *Le quatrième siècle* in which he had imagined two French government officials attributing last names to the recently emancipated slaves by using terms they found in encyclopedias and anthologies. Some time after the publication of his novel, he found that this chapter had been used as a reference in a scientific journal that specialized in onomastics: his literary invention had become a formal illustration of science. Glissant is convinced that systems of thought, as, for example, history, can no longer provide an exhaustive understanding of what is really taking place in the zones of contact and conflict between cultures. The recourse to imagination or to a prophetic vision provides insight where analytic systems of thought fail.

The cultural space of this study is inspired by Glissant's "prophetic vision of the past." Although I am not imagining the past like a creative writer, I am bringing together eclectic primary sources in an innovative way in order to expose memories left out by history. The cultural space is not produced by a system of thought but rather by a multiplicity of rhizome-memories, which through their contacts tell new and unpredictable stories of the past.

The contribution of this work to the field of studies on Caribbean slavery lies in the diversity of primary source material from the eighteenth and twentieth centuries, the interdisciplinary analysis of archival documents, and the cultural framing through memory. To my knowledge no such investigation—in particular concerning the French Caribbean—has yet been undertaken. At the crossroads of various disciplines, this investigation reveals connections between literary productions, political claims, historical events, and cultural phenomena that have generally gone unnoticed. Within this cultural space, this work does not record a chronological succession of events but rather a series of cultural impressions or snapshots bringing to life images of the past. The German philosopher Walter Benjamin (1969: 257) beautifully captures the ephemeral quality of the past as it is glimpsed in the present: "The true picture of the past flits by. The past can be seized only as an image which flashes up at the instant when it can be recognized and is never seen again ... every image of the past that is not recognized by the present as one of its own concerns threatens to disappear irretrievably." The fleeting quality of memory characterizes recollections of slavery. Fragments must be pieced together as images of the past flash up. This approach has the originality of reflecting Caribbean sociohistorical reality today—a reality emerging from what Chamoiseau (1998c) calls the people's "mosaic identity." The product of a cultural and historical heritage nourished by a range of racial, geographic, religious, artistic, and culinary roots, the peoples of the Caribbean reproduce the fragmentary nature of their past. By studying slavery as a cultural space of rhizome-memories, I hope to respect the idiosyncrasy of French West Indian cultural tradition. It is my aim to propose a vision of the past that brings out the subtlety and depth of Caribbean history and culture. Although my vision is by no means "prophetic," it does have the merit of offering a well-founded alternative to a Eurocentric view of the world.

While the body of my investigation is constituted by four chapters or realms of memory about the Enlightenment, the fifth realm of memory is a return to the memory of slavery in the present via the popular imagination of French West Indians. Chapter 1 investigates the ideology of universal freedom and equality through a comparative analysis of narratives on slavery by the *philosophes* and by the *encyclopédistes*, playwrights, white colonists, the royal court, and lawyers. By comparing the works of Montesquieu, Voltaire, Diderot, the Abbé Raynal, and Condorcet to other voices of the eighteenth century, I dismantle the causal relationship between the *philosophes* and French abolitionism. Scientific theories on race, letters and political pamphlets by colonial planters, memoirs by lawyers defending slaves in lawsuits against their masters, royal decrees regulating the control of slaves, and plays, all serve as counterpoints to the *philosophes'* perspectives. By bringing into dialogue these diverse eighteenth-century writings on race, slavery, humanity, and freedom, I reveal the inconsistencies of an age that actively justified the enslavement of Africans while vaunting ideological and humanitarian progress. The juxtaposition of the *philosophes* and anti-abolitionists, in particular white colonial planters, decidedly calls into question the received notion that the *philosophes* constituted an uncompromising front against slavery. As many of the *philosophes'* arguments found resonance among proponents of the slave regime and vice versa, the Enlightenment's celebrated abolitionism becomes a crumbling edifice.

Constructed around the figure of the maroon, chapter 2 is an inquiry into the question of self-liberation. The phenomenon of *marronnage* is often neglected in official histories and excluded as an abolitionary force.[11] Consequently, the slaves' agency within the system of slavery remains unacknowledged. The figure of the maroon is, however, one of the only anchor points allowing French West Indians to identify themselves as makers of their history; hence the recurrence of this theme during the commemoration in Guadeloupe and Martinique. Moreover, the voice of the maroon is largely present in eighteenth-century writings and colonists frequently addressed the pervasiveness of *marronnage.* The realms of the maroon elaborated in this chapter are based on a nonrestrictive use of the term *marronnage.* Rather than limiting myself to the formation of maroon bands in the mountainous regions of the islands, I include all forms of slave opposition or resistance within these realms.[12] After an initial historical contextualization contrasted with the emergence of the profoundly mythical dimension of the maroon, the chapter examines two themes dominating eighteenth-century narratives. On one hand, maroons are depicted as brutishly violent actors against the slave regime. On the other hand, they are thought to be fundamentally "civilizable" due to their superior power and intelligence. They are seen as the building blocks of a cooperative agreement between white plantation owners and the black masses. Both portrayals undermine the Caribbean tradition of resistance, thus contributing to its marginalization.

Chapter 3 brings together three different visions of freedom during the revolutionary period. The *Société des Amis des Noirs,* colonial planters, and slaves both fueled and opposed the increasing momentum toward freedom by disseminating letters and political pamphlets in France and in her Caribbean colonies. Through a comparative literary analysis of these documents I study the ways in which these interest groups influenced one another and shaped revolutionary changes on both sides of the Atlantic. The causes underlying both the 1794 abolitionary decree and the intense outbreak of slave revolts throughout the Caribbean during the late 1780s and early 1790s is subject to considerable debate among historians. While some hold the French Revolution directly responsible for these events, others insist that the tradition of slave revolts far predated the upheavals of 1789. Rather than take position one way or another, I study the diverse notions of freedom—expressed by the *Société des Amis des Noirs,* the planters, and the slaves—born from these exceptional circumstances. Together, they brought the question of freedom to the forefront of political thought at the turn of the century. The juxtaposition of multiple voices reveals the central role played by slaves in the eventual destruction of the slave regime. Interpreting the discourses and actions that affected them, slaves forcefully projected their vision of freedom through writings and revolts; their influence on the course of events in the Caribbean made change inevitable.

Chapter 4 is a study of the transformations that the politically and socially oppressed free coloreds experienced as a result of their new status as French citizens. In particular, it is the question of collective memory that is at stake in the evolving relationship to the mother country. The initial analysis is built on the arguments of race and class used by the people of color to vindicate their political rights. Their unique position as educated, wealthy slave and property owners gave the free coloreds a powerful economic status. Based on letters and political pamphlets by the free coloreds and white planters this chapter analyzes how race and class became stepping-stones for political representation. Once equality was granted in 1792, however, the free coloreds replaced their original demands for their due rights with expressions of overwhelming gratitude. The recurrent theme of assimilation exposes the powerful image of France as a source of liberty, equality, and fraternity even after three centuries of slavery. This new fraternal relationship, however, jeopardized the identity of the formerly oppressed since it required the active erasure of past injustices from their collective memory. The free coloreds' narrative on forgetting underscores the process of selective remembrance. The erasure of the past deplored today is in fact a phenomenon dating back to the last stages of the slave regime. Imposed by France, this attitude was also readily adopted by the formerly oppressed.

Chapter 5 is a result of fieldwork undertaken in Guadeloupe and Martinique to study contemporary traces of slavery in the popular imagination. The people's memory vividly exposes the continuing impact of enlightened thought, the omnipresence of the maroon as a symbol of liberation, the legacy of the French Revolution, and the consequences of assimilation. I apprehended the people's relationship to slavery through oral, material, and written manifestations of memory. Interviews with the local population, including historians and writers revealed the recent transformations in the people's perceptions, especially since the 150th commemoration of the abolition of slavery. The individuals interviewed deplored their compatriots' indifference to the slave past nourished by ignorance and denial. Nonetheless, they pointed to the current reappropriation of local history by the people as a positive sign that change was underway. This recent phenomenon can be observed in the numerous sites of memory erected during the past decade in Guadeloupe and Martinique. These include a large number of memorials recalling the horrors of the slave trade or honoring the legendary figure of the maroon. Murals depicting heroes and key episodes of French Caribbean history are among the

most graphic expressions of remembrance along with the politically charged symbol of the beheaded statue of Napoleon's
wife Josephine, smeared with red paint. Eighteenth-century remains from the slave period complement this material memory. Ruins of sugar and coffee plantations, for instance, are
invaluable sites of memory, especially when the slave quarters
are still visible. Other such places include aqueducts, steps, and
prisons constructed by slaves, as well as slave cemeteries. This
material memory—illustrated with original black-and-white
photographs—along with the inscriptions, legends, and cap-
tions describing these sites show how the people remember the
past. From total absence of memory, to a passive awareness of
the past and finally active claims to memory, popular imagination is simultaneously determined by a traditional perspective
on history and awakened by new currents of consciousness.
The encounter between the two gives rise to an unprecedented
identification with Caribbean history and culture. Current political events parallel these changes. The May 2001 union
worker strikes, aimed at instituting the date of the abolition of
slavery as an official holiday, are an example of such activism. Other examples are the Martinican, Guadeloupean,
and Guianese regional councils' attempt at redefining the
political status of these overseas regions. In the cultural and
political atmosphere of Guadeloupe and Martinique today,
the eighteenth-century realms of memory have become quite
alive again and invested with new meaning. Inspired by Guadeloupean writer Maryse Condé's *La Belle Créole* (2001), my
concluding words suggest an outlook upon the past that con-
structively envisions the future.

Notes

1. "On March 19, 1946 the Constituent Assembly, precursor to the
   Fourth Republic, voted unanimously to transform the Caribbean
   'Old Colonies' of Martinique, Guadeloupe, and Guiana, along
   with the Indian Ocean colony of Réunion, into *départements* (the
   equivalent of US states) of France. The vote had been spear-
   headed by France's elected overseas representatives to Paris (most
   notably the Martinican deputy/writer Aimé Césaire) and carried
   the virtually unanimous support of the populations in the
   colonies" (Miles 2001: 45).
2. All translations from French are the author's.
3. I verified this claim by looking for references to slavery or to the
   abolition of slavery in various history textbooks used by the state

education system at the middle and high school level. The slave trade and the abolition of slavery were briefly mentioned in only one of four textbooks I consulted: *Histoire/Géographie-4e, nouveau programme* (Klein and Hugonie 1998). In the other three textbooks I found absolutely no references to slavery, the slave trade, or the abolition of slavery: *Histoire/Géographie-4e, nouveau programme* (Ivernel 1998); *Histoire-Seconde* (Lambin 1996); and *Histoire-Seconde* (Quétel 1996).

4. For more information on how the revocation of the first abolition of slavery influenced the course of events in Saint Domingue, see Fick (1990: 204–36) and James (1989: 289–377).

5. It would be compelling to similarly analyze France's official commemoration of the bicentennial of Toussaint Louverture's death on 7 April 1803. Louverture died as Napoleon's prisoner in the Château de Joux in the region of the Franche-Comté. France's national commemoration was supported by the Ministry of Culture, sponsored by UNESCO and supported by many Caribbean and African countries and personalities (Norton 2003).

6. See Nora (1996: XXIV) and Marc Ferro (qtd. in Durand 2001: 303) for the notion of writing a history in multiple voices.

7. Free coloreds were of mixed African and European descent. They were also referred to as people of color or mulattoes. Though the term mulatto refers to the offspring of a white and black parent, this appellation was used interchangeably with the other ones. Though for the most part the people of color were emancipated and many of them were wealthy property and slave owners, free coloreds as a group had no political rights whatsoever.

8. During its brief existence from 1788 to 1791, the *Société des Amis des Noirs*—founded by Jacques-Pierre Brissot de Warville, an obscure public law specialist—gathered men and women from Parisian high society for the cause of freedom in France's slave colonies. It followed the model of the London Society for the Abolition of the Slave Trade, founded in 1787 by Thomas Clarkson.

9. See Fischer's (2004) recent interdisciplinary study of Haiti for a similar approach.

10. In one of the chapters of *Mille Plateaux* first published as a small volume under the title *Rhizomes*, Deleuze and Guattari establish a distinction between "root-thought" and "rhizome-thought." The unique root kills everything in its surroundings whereas the rhizome spreads out toward the encounter of other roots.

11. The French term *marronnage* denotes the act of running away from the plantation to become a fugitive slave or a maroon. Since there is no English equivalent, I will retain the French term.

12. My nonrestrictive use of the term maroon is inspired by Burton's work, *Le roman marron* (1997).

CHAPTER 1

REALMS OF THE ENLIGHTENMENT

In the context of African slavery, the period of the French Enlightenment is generally remembered as the founding moment of abolitionary ideology. In particular, the French *philosophes* Montesquieu, Voltaire, Denis Diderot, Jean-Jacques Rousseau, the Abbé Raynal, and Condorcet are believed to have been at the origin of a humanitarian process that undermined the slave regime and ultimately led to its demise. During the 150th anniversary of the abolition of slavery a journalist tellingly writes that the first abolition of slavery in 1794 was achieved through the "impetus given by the humanists" (Vidal 1998). Another journalist similarly links the abolitionary movement directly to the *philosophes'* unanimous condemnation of the African slave trade (Paringaux 1998). An exhibition organized on the same occasion by the Archives Départementales de la Guadeloupe (1998: 14–15) reserves a section to the *philosophes.* Passages of Voltaire's *Candide* ([1759] 1973) and Montesquieu's *De l'esprit des lois* ([1748] 1955) illustrate denunciations of the slave regime. The memory of slavery during the Enlightenment is still dominated by the belief in the transformative influence of the Age of Reason on inequality, injustice, and exploitation.

Historians of the beginning of the twentieth century retrace the history of slavery by representing the Enlightenment as the origin of antislavery thought. In his work *Montesquieu et l'esclavage*, Russell Parsons Jameson (1911) searches for the "true source of the moral energy," which led Montesquieu to take up the question of black slavery. Following in Jameson's footsteps, Edward D. Seeber (1937) begins his history of French antislavery opinion with Montesquieu whom he depicts as a sort of founding father of the movement. Although contemporary historians have since then developed a critical perspective toward the nature of the Enlightenment's antislavery ideology, the *philosophes'* writings are still often posited as a moment of origin. The problem with such univocal portrayals, as many critics have underlined, is that they mask the Enlightenment's contradictory heritage (Gauthier 2001). In particular, the diverse and often ambiguous elements of anti-abolitionism are not adequately taken into consideration. More importantly, local struggles against oppression born in the Caribbean basin are given at best a secondary role and are considered an outgrowth of the European movement. Yet, the powerful influence of slave revolts cannot be underestimated as American historian Julius Scott (1986) amply demonstrates in his dissertation "The Common Wind." He shows how revolt was an indigenous characteristic of Caribbean slave societies and was swept across different islands of the Caribbean, often independently of European influences.

In her provocative work *Anthropologie et histoire au siècle des lumières,* the French historian Michèle Duchet (1971: 138, 149) dismantles the univocal interpretation of antislavery literature by highlighting the internal contradictions of a humanism characterized as much by its own limitations as by its demands. She warns that expressions of sympathy vis-à-vis the slaves should not be the unique measure for the era's approach toward slavery. Rather, it is as multiple "humanisms" that eighteenth-century perspectives should be interpreted. Claims to the slaves' humanity were not necessarily an expression of altruism since they were often a result of economic interests. Despite the importance attributed to the Enlightenment as a precursor of abolitionism, the problem of slavery remained a marginal concern during the eighteenth century. Moreover, the slaves' racial difference and France's economic wealth due to the slave trade had a considerable impact upon the *philosophes'* denunciations, leading these thinkers to often fall short of contesting the legitimacy of the institution itself. The excesses of the slave regime generally became the focal point of attacks at the expense of a more uncompromising rejection of African slavery (Ehrard 1995). Contemporary historians and critics generally agree that the condemnations of slavery made during the Age of Reason and justice did not necessarily imply the advocation of racial equality or slave emancipation.[1] As the historian Robin Blackburn (1997: 590) points out, the philosophical Enlightenment was compatible with the continuing growth of the slave population in the sugar colonies. In fact, according to the historian Philip Curtin's (1969: 265) census, the eighteenth century was the most profitable period in the history of the slave trade with a summit reached between 1741 and 1810.

The ambiguities of Enlightenment attitudes toward slavery would lead one to be cautious of the notion that a unitary abolitionist ideology was born during the Age of Reason. Establishing a causal link between the *philosophes'* writings and abolition forgoes the complex network of ideological and physical struggles waged by the *philosophes,* the *Société des Amis des Noirs,* colonial planters and administrators, and most importantly, slaves and free people of color. What Pierre Nora (1996: 12–13) calls the nation's "cult of continuity" does not allow for such diverse voices of the past to be heard. French society's need to believe in progress is frustrated by the conflict around the institution of slavery: the opposition between humanism and exploitation. The Enlightenment embodies no unified momentum toward abolition but rather an erratic crisscrossing of forces that simultaneously destruct and augment one another. Nora calls this the fragmented and discontinuous universe of the past. Our memory is constructed from segments of these "microhistories." When one such segment or microhistory comes to dominate all the others, to marginalize their impact, this results in an atrophied memory, no longer adapted to the complex mosaic of what one might call "memory possibilities." As a single abolitionary force, the Enlightenment inscribes itself into people's memory in a linear fashion. This shrouds all the subtleties of the period; a period that saw revolutionary humanitarian ideologies clash with the greatest economic boom experienced by the French nation—and based on slave labor.

In an effort to break apart such a singular representation of the Enlightenment, this study of slavery in eighteenth-century thought is organized around Nora's concept of realms of memory. Realms of memory, according to Nora (1996: xvii), are entities or places that have become symbolic elements of a community's memorial heritage. The *philosophes* of the Enlightenment have come to represent all the "positive" facets of the slave past linked to the ending of cruelty, injustice, and exploitation. They symbolize the nation's memory of itself as the land of universal justice and equality. Nora's (1996: xviii) emphasis on investigating the whole spectrum of latent or hidden elements of national memory allows for a deep probing of the notion of memory. By focusing on the oppositional forces that constitute enlightened thought, I bring out hitherto omitted elements. As a result, the contradictions inherent to the *philosophes'* writings and the surprising overlap between their perspective and that of colonial planters become clearly apparent. Contrary to many representations of antislavery writings, the *philosophes* did not maintain a clear line of attack against the institution of slavery. Instead, they often appeared to contradict themselves, making it difficult to extricate their denunciations from their ambivalent feelings toward the race and civilization of Africans. According to the philosopher Tzvetan Todorov (1985–86: 372–73), incoherences even within the writings of the same author were typical of the age, making it difficult to determine whether or not the Enlightenment as a whole was pro- or antislavery.

To add to the ambiguous position of the *philosophes,* colonial planters and administrators often shared their condemnations of the institution's excessive cruelties, rendering the *philosophes'* humanism far more commonplace than is often believed. In the process of remembering the *philosophes'* thought, many of the contradictory passages of their writings have simply been left out. As a result, their work is often reduced to those excerpts that form a coherent and unified viewpoint. French schoolchildren, for instance, invariably study Voltaire's denunciation of slavery in *Candide*'s "Negro from Suriname" and Montesquieu's allegedly ironical indictment of the slave regime in *De l'esprit des lois.* They are not, however, exposed to more ambiguous passages by the same authors, thereby revealing their racial prejudice against Africans.

To uncover the full spectrum of memories of enlightened thought, I will fragment the unambiguous memory dominating France's historical narrative of slavery. Michel Foucault (1969: 36–37; 1977: 144–47) emphasizes the need "to dispel the chimeras of the origin," which do not reveal the truth about what we are. The search for an origin is characteristic of centralizing narratives. Coercively imposing a univocal discourse, these narratives marginalize those knowledges of the past that contradict its claims (Foucault 1980: 81–85). By breaking down the ideology of universal equality, freedom, and justice into the discourses of the *philosophes,* playwrights, the royal court, colonists, and lawyers, I destabilize the singular memory of the Enlightenment. Out of the fabric of these competing memories arises the full spectrum of the French and Caribbean memorial heritage.

Blackness in French Thought

During the eighteenth century, a variety of forces influenced the relationship between race and slavery. Both noble and savage, the African was born as a figure of exoticism in the European literary imagination with English writer Aphra Behn's novel *Oroonoko,* published in 1688 and translated into French by La Place in 1745. To a large extent reflecting French attitudes toward Africans, literary renditions of blacks across the centuries paralleled their growing importance in the French imaginary. While the original mythical image of blacks during the Middle Ages and Renaissance vaguely depicted them as monsters or fabulous monarchs, seventeenth- and eighteenth-century travel writings dismissed the "savage" Africans as intellectually, socially, and politically far inferior to Europeans. Not until the booming years of the slave trade during the Enlightenment was the African—now a slave in the hands of Europeans—born as a literary character. However, as the literary critic Léon-François Hoffman (1973: 96) points out, the creation of this literary figure only reflected a very slow and gradual rise in esteem of the savage African: "barely human, but human nonetheless, one demands for him a minimum of well-being. And the fine optimism of the century hopes that with patience and some good lessons, blacks will one day—in the distant future of course—take their place among the civilized."[2]

The literary critic Roger Mercier (1962b: 197) dates the beginnings of African exoticism in French literature to La Place's translation of *Oroonoko.* The noble African à la Oroonoko made his appearance in a variety of French texts of a highly sentimental nature. The African setting was generally not very authentic and the African protagonists—often described as the ideal of natural man—"bore no physical resemblance to the descriptions made by travelers." Particularly during the last part of the century, the stories were set in the Americas in the context of plantation slavery. They were constructed around two typically recurrent themes. The first was the opposition between the selfishness of the whites and the generosity and nobility of the slaves. The second focused on benevolent mas-

ters who treated their slaves humanely and perhaps even freed
them. This always led to a peaceful and happy ending; all the
while the institution of slavery remained unchallenged (Mercier 1962a).

Europeans were obsessed by the Africans' skin color, their
facial traits, and hair. It symbolized the irreducible difference
that marked blacks, a difference that became the basis of natural, absolute, and essential racial categories (Gates 1985–86:
5–6). All those who wrote about Africans during the eighteenth century addressed the physical aspect of their subjects,
either expressing their utter disgust or trying to make amendments for traits that could seemingly only harbor evil and lowliness. The first noble African character in literary history,
Oroonoko is described in such a way as to minimize his physical difference:

> His face was not of that brown, rusty black which most of that
> nation are, but a perfect ebony, or polish'd jett.... His nose was
> rising and Roman, instead of African and flat. His mouth, the
> finest shap'd that cou'd be seen; far from those great turn'ed
> lips, which are so natural to the rest of the Negroes. The whole
> proportion and air of his face was so noble, and exactly form'd
> that, bating his color, there cou'd be nothing in nature more
> beautiful, agreeable, and handsome. There was no one grace
> wanting, that bears the standard of true beauty: his hair came
> down to his shoulders (Behn [1688] 1995: 62–63).

Contrasting each one of his traits with those commonly found
among Africans, Behn fashions the physical beauty of her
character that was appropriate for his great nobleness. Her
deprecation of the African phenotype highlights Oroonoko's
correspondence to the European standard of beauty. To be convincing in his noble role and to attract the reader's sympathy,
he had to physically distinguish himself from his compatriots.
Due to his extraordinary handsomeness, he could even be for-
given his color.

Skin color was typically believed to reflect a person's moral
character. In his play *Adonis,* J. B. Picquenard (1798: xi) underlines the unique qualities of the black protagonist who inspired his work: "I especially wanted to prove that friendship,
good faith, and gratitude are respected even by the most savage hordes, that black skin can cover a good heart." As in
Oroonoko, the African is shown in an exceptional light that re-
deems his outward appearance. Another such example is Télémaque, the protagonist of Pigault-Lebrun's play *Le blanc et le*

noir (1796: 8). The son of the plantation owner remarks on the similarity between blacks and whites. With the goodwill of whites, black slaves could realize their potential: "Like us they received a heart from nature, and this heart, condemned by fear, only awaits a kind hand that will revive it. Always ready to open his heart to sensitivity, friendship, and gratitude, the good Télémaque proves to the detractors of blacks that virtue exists in all climates and colors."

In his famous passage "De l'esclavage des nègres," Montesquieu ([1748] 1955: 220)—the first French *philosophe* to address the question of slavery—highlights the link between skin color and morality: "Those who I am speaking of are black from the feet to the head. Their nose is so flattened that it is almost impossible to feel sorry for them. One cannot possibly imagine how God in his wisdom could have put a soul, especially a good soul, in such a black body." Considerable debate surrounds Montesquieu's intent in this chapter since not all critics are convinced that he meant to be ironic.[3] Montesquieu's contemporaries, on the other hand, do not question his ironic intent. According to Voltaire ([1756] 1878, 13: 601), Montesquieu "painted Negro slavery in Molière's style [avec le pinceau de Molière]." Bernardin de Saint-Pierre ([1768–70] 1983: 122) deplores the lightness with which slavery was treated: "I am cross that the *philosophes* who fought abuse with so much courage should only have joked about the subject of Negro slavery."

Whether or not Montesquieu's irony was intentional, his passage on black slavery contributed to the spread of ambiguous beliefs regarding the Africans' skin color.[4] Black skin was not only considered aesthetically displeasing, it also made it doubtful that Africans were fully human. Many thinkers wondered if Africans did not belong to a new species. In the article "Nègre" of the *Encyclopédie* (Diderot and d'Alembert [1755] n.d., 11: 1013), the author evokes this possibility: "They do not only distinguish themselves by their color. They also differ from other human beings by all their facial traits, their large and flat noses, their thick lips, and the wool they have instead of hair; they appear to constitute a new species of man." The Africans' irreducible physical differences became the basis for questioning their humanity. The next step was to assume their inferior, animalistic nature.

In a debate between a black protagonist and a priest entitled *L'arrétin moderne*, the Abbé Henri-Joseph Du Laurens ([1763] 1775: 94) ironically portrays racist diatribes made by the church against Africans. He poses the problem in the following terms: "Is there a difference between turkeys and Negroes?" As he concludes that turkeys have no reason, he wonders what the situation is for blacks: "Is this species of two-legged animals included in the class of human beings? Are beings whose physiognomy is as smeared as that of Negroes capable of reasoning?" The subsequent debate between a black protagonist and a priest, in which the former very adroitly disproves all of the latter's claims, serves to illustrate the author's opinion.

Voltaire ([1756] 1878, 12: 357) does not go to the same trouble of proving the Africans' intelligence in his *Essai sur les mœurs*, published a few years earlier. Instead he takes their mental inferiority for granted:

> The inhabitants [of Africa discovered by the Portuguese] were barely above animals.... The race of the Negroes is a human race different from ours.... Their wool does not resemble our hair and one can say that if their intelligence is not of another kind than ours, it is very inferior. They are not capable of much attention, they devise very little, and they do not seem to be made for the advantages and abuses of our philosophy.

Voltaire creates a linear connection between the Africans' physical and racial difference and their inability to reason and therefore prove their full human capacity. During the Enlightenment, as noted by Henry Louis Gates Jr. (1985–86: 8), reason became the basis for evaluating a person's humanity. Lack thereof in any given culture was considered a clear sign that it was questionable if that group belonged to the same human race as Europeans.

The close connection made between the Africans' physical appearance and their intellectual inferiority, relegating them to a subhuman position, became evident after midcentury even in fashionable Parisian circles. Women of high society at one point replaced their fashionable domestic parrots, dogs, and cats with black boys. In the article "Petits nègres" of *Tableau de Paris,* Louis-Sébastien Mercier (1783: 177–178) describes this new fashion:

> A young Negro with white teeth, thick lips, satin skin caresses better than a spaniel or an angora. He has therefore obtained preference.... While the black child lives on the knees of these women who feel passionate about his foreign face, his flat nose; while a gentle and caressing hand punishes his rebellions with a light punishment, soon erased by the most intense caresses,

his father groans under the lashes of a merciless master. The father painfully works the sugar the Negro boy drinks in the same cup with his laughing mistress.[5]

The black boy is at the same level as the domestic animals that preceded him. Providing his mistress with intense physical pleasures, he is reduced to the most basic aspect of his being: his body. The temporary taste that women developed for this new commodity physically enslaved black boys in a way that paralleled their fathers' oppression on sugar plantations. Treated as animals, their humanity was denied.

The belief in the Africans' inferiority was largely nourished by the advent of the natural sciences during the eighteenth century (Todorov 1985–86: 372). Based on pseudoscientific theories, the variations between human races were explained, categorized, and integrated into elaborate hierarchies and systems of classification. The opposition between whites and blacks, in particular, was rooted in observable differences such as skin color, physiognomy, and sexual parts, especially in women. Such anatomic markers signaled the nonunity of the races with blacks ranked lower due to their physical deviancies from the white norm.[6]

In his *Histoire naturelle de l'homme*, the French naturalist Buffon ([1749] 1800: 334–37) extensively examines the question of the Africans' blackness and physiognomy. He considers color to be a direct result of climate and thus explains how people in colder climates are white while those living closer to the equator are darker. In Africa, where the climate is the most torrid, the inhabitants are completely black due to their perpetual exposure to the sun. Though color is genetically transmitted, blacks are likely to become completely white after living in a temperate climate for many generations. The primordial role of the environment on outward appearance can be observed within the same nation. Poorer people who are less well fed are generally rather ugly and not very well built, according to Buffon. They degenerate because of their miserable living conditions (340). It is for similar reasons that the Hottentots, whom Buffon considers especially savage, are ugly, dirty, unhealthy, and do not live to be much older than forty. The Africans' physiognomy is a result of the people's traditions. Considering a straight nose to be a deformity, mothers flatten their children's noses. They are also known to pull their eyelids, to lengthen their ears, to thicken their lips, and to flatten their face, all of which explains their unusual features (311–12).

Buffon's explanations of the Africans' physical differences encompass value judgments that take the European model as a norm. As he describes different African groups, individual characteristics are related to the European standard. Ethiopians, for instance, are less black than Nubiens, their facial features are well-defined, their nose is well-made, and their lips are small while Nubians have a flattened nose and big and thick lips (Buffon [1749] 1800: 294). Those Africans who do not purposely change the physiognomy of their children have as beautiful traits as Europeans: their nose is as straight and their lips are as thin (300). The European model of natural physical beauty and color is conditioned by the climate:

> The most temperate climate from the 40th to the 50th degree is also the zone where one can find the most beautiful and well-built human beings. It is in this climate that one can determine the true, natural color of man. It is there that one must take the model or unity to which one must relate all the other nuances of color and beauty (339).

Buffon thus gives a scientific explanation for the European standard in his comparative study of human varieties. Europeans represent the true, original human species that gradually gave rise to different varieties due to climate, nourishment, habits, and illnesses. These divergences from the norm are in constant flux and the human varieties could, with time, become either the same or even more different (Buffon [1792] 1800: 341–42). The inequality between Europeans and Africans is a consequence of these natural changes. Although Africans no longer fit the standard of color, beauty and intelligence, they have the seed of every virtue and can potentially reach the innate superiority of Europeans (307).

Buffon's pseudoscientific study of racial difference and more specifically of racial inequality was typical of the eighteenth century. A number of European scientists, thinkers, and travelers throughout the century attempted to prove the Africans' innate inferiority. They questioned whether they belonged to the same species as Europeans and tried to make evident their animality. The Swedish naturalist Carol Linnaeus, for instance, conceived of the chain of beings in his work, *Systema Naturae* published in 1735. He classified Africans as the lowest rung of human beings just above nonhuman primates, thus underscoring their questionable belonging to the human species. The idea that Africans formed the link between animals and men was quite popular among such eighteenth-century French thinkers as J. D. Robinet and Rousselot de Surgy. Nourishing this belief, Lamiral, a former French official in Senegal, claimed that black women had sexual intercourse with non-human primates (Cohen 1980: 86–89).

The Africans' outward appearance, very displeasing to Europeans, also proved fertile ground for racial prejudice. In vogue in eighteenth-century France, thanks to the work of the Swiss physiognomist Caspar Lavater, the doctrine of physiognomies gave an apparently scientific foundation to the belief that the blacks' physical characteristics, in particular their skin color, symbolized their depravity. Similarly, the aesthetic perception of facial and skull shapes developed by the Dutch painter Peter Camper was widely accepted in France. The blacks' facial angle, thought to be very close to that of apes, was taken as a sign of their animality (Cohen 1980: 90–94).

The rising concern for racial difference throughout the eighteenth century was reflected in the royal decrees drawn up to control slaves in the colonies and in France. While the 1685 *Code Noir*—the first document legalizing slavery in the Americas—contains no racially defined language, by the early eighteenth century royal decrees directly addressed racial issues. The sixty articles of the *Code Noir*, dictating the control of slaves on West Indian plantations, contained no deprecating references to race. In fact, Africans attained the same legal rights as whites once they were manumitted:

> Article 59: We grant emancipated slaves the same rights, privileges, and immunities as those enjoyed by people who are born free. We want the merit of an acquired liberty to have the same effect upon them and upon their possessions as has the happiness of natural liberty upon our other subjects (Sala-Molins 1987: 200).

Their race did not reduce Africans to a permanent state of servitude. At the end of the seventeenth century, a black person was not yet equivalent to a slave. No laws separated racial groups and the rights of a free person were the same for everyone regardless of race. Indeed, mobility between the state of enslavement and freedom were encouraged through miscegenation. In Article 9, free men—who are not explicitly referred to as white men—are encouraged to marry the slave with whom they have been living and had children. Such a Christian marriage automatically emancipated the slave and her children (Sala-Molins 1987: 108).

The beginning of the eighteenth century saw the advent of racially defined legislation aimed at keeping blacks and people of color separate from whites and geographically limited to the colonies. Mixed marriages, for instance, were prohibited in Guadeloupe in 1711. The rapidly increasing number of mulatto offspring might explain the motive for such laws (Sala-Molins 1987: 109).[7] However, the government's main concern was the growing slave population in continental France. It was fashionable at the time for white planters to bring their slaves to France, keeping them at their service during the Atlantic crossing and for the duration of their stay in the home country. As a result, African slaves started to populate France, in particular Paris. In order to limit the expansion of this fringe group, the royal court drew up an edict in 1716 and a declaration in 1738. Both laws allowed slave owners to keep their slaves in France for a limited time only and for the sole purpose of religious education and the apprenticeship of a trade. The slaves' presence in France was to benefit the colonies, not the personal pleasure of the masters. While in 1716 the colonists' noncompliance with the law resulted in the automatic emancipation of the slaves, the king started confiscating and returning them to the colonies in 1738 (Peabody 1996: 15–22, 37–40). The mounting racial concern expressed by the promulgation of these laws is also revealed linguistically. Slaves are no longer called slaves but are further defined by their race; they are referred to as "black slaves" (Archives Départementales de la Martinique 1717). As opposed to the *Code Noir* where slaves and free people were not further qualified as black or white, the king's official language started to racially define slaves by the early eighteenth century.

France's concerns with the racial dimension of the black and free colored population living on French soil gradually increased. Since the 1716 and 1738 laws were never properly enforced and a steady stream of black slaves continued to enter the country, King Louis XVI saw it necessary to enforce a new law in 1777 called *Police des Noirs*. As opposed to the previous two laws that applied to black slaves only, the *Police des Noirs* focused on all nonwhites. Entry into France was prohibited to all blacks and people of color regardless of their status as slaves or as freedmen. Though they could accompany their masters during the Atlantic crossing, they were to be held in prisons at the port until the next ship took them back to the colonies. All those who already had black or colored servants in France were to send them back to the colonies immediately

(Archives Nationales de France, Colonies F1B1, 1777).[8] The number of blacks on French soil had reached the limit of French acceptability and the authorities believed it necessary to stop their influx.[9]

France's increasing concern with the Africans' racial difference might well be attributed to the increasing contacts between the two races. These associations were deemed problematic, especially in continental France. Miscegenation was outlawed in 1778 and whites were prohibited from marrying blacks or people of color (ANF Colonies F1B1, 1778). The mixing of the two races was a disgrace to France and degraded the purity of French blood. Africans had come uncomfortably close to home, thus placing their difference in an entirely new context. While slavery in the colonies did not stir up much concern during the seventeenth century, the identity of these slaves impressed itself upon French society once these Africans mingled with them. The *Code Noir*, with its nonracially defined legislation, had been specifically drawn up for slaves laboring in France's colonies for the commercial benefit of the nation. No provisions had been made for the presence of these slaves in France and the government was clearly not prepared to affront this situation. A magistrate summed up the problem in 1762: "Exclusively destined to cultivate our colonies, [slaves] were introduced out of necessity: this same necessity retains them there and one would have never thought that they would come and drag their chains into the heart of the kingdom" (Des Essarts, Poncet de la Grave, and Dejunquieres 1979: 20).

Through their physical presence on French soil, black slaves "dragged" the problems they were associated with, right before the eyes of the population. Enlightened or not, society was not prepared for this reality check. Abstract philosophical musings and heartfelt pity about the plight of African slaves on West Indian plantations were only possible as long as the slaves remained far away and did not pose a threat. In fact, according to the French social scientist Luc Boltanski (1993: 26–29), the identification with the suffering of others through pity requires the wretched to be at a distance. Once African slaves were too close for comfort, their racial dimension took precedence over all other considerations. Africans had lost their initial exotic appeal and had become an undesirable presence on French soil. The stringent *Police des Noirs* was to be a safeguard for the French population assuring—in the words of a government official—the "total extinction" of the "black species" in France (ANF Colonies F1B1, 1782).

Race and Slavery

According to the American historian Winthrop Jordan (1968: 93–98), it is the Africans' overwhelming difference, their color, and complexion as well as the utter strangeness of their language, gesture, and eating habits that turned them into "savages" in the European's eye. Henry Louis Gates Jr. (1985–86: 5) calls this their "extreme 'otherness.'" Racial theories gave a scientific, therefore seemingly objective, explanation for the displeasure and even outright disgust felt for blacks during the eighteenth century. Justifications of the slave regime readily grew out of the fertile ground of this racialized mentality.

Historians often call into question the belief that racism was the foundation for slavery. In his monumental work, *Capitalism and Slavery*, the Trinidadian social and political scientist Eric Williams (1994: 7–9, 19) claims that it was economic interests not racism that were the driving force behind the phenomenon of African slavery. Africans were only brought to the Caribbean once the enslaved local Indian population had almost entirely succumbed and European indentured servants and convicts did not suffice to maintain the burgeoning plantation economy. The origin of black slavery, according to Williams, lies in the great economic advantages that the inexpensive supply of robust African slaves presented for white plantation owners. It was the cheapness of this new and efficient labor force that allowed colonial economy to take off and reach its peak during the second half of the eighteenth century.

Sharing Williams's perspective, the American historian William B. Cohen (1980: 41) points out, however, that the burden of slavery fell on Africans not on whites. He deems the pre-existence of slavery in Africa to be partly responsible for this. Europeans saw no problem in transporting slaves from one continent to another. On the contrary, they believed that the barbaric Africans would benefit from Christianization and from contact with "civilization." Although this argument may simply have been another a posteriori justification of a very lucrative yet morally dubious undertaking, eighteenth-century narratives were clearly inspired by this reasoning.

White planters were quick to justify slavery in this way. P. J. Laborie (n.d.: 33), a planter from Saint Domingue, did not believe European sensibilities and ideologies to be applicable in the African context: "The Negro does not have your habits, nor your ideas. He is born as a slave. He sees slavery without horror because he is used to it." The planter J. Bellon de Saint-Quentin ([1764] 1972: 61) saw Caribbean slavery as a simple continuation of African slavery, for which Europeans had no responsibility: "by buying the Negroes in Guinea, one does not take freedom away from them. They have already lost it. One doesn't make them slaves; one already finds them such." The question of liberty was not an issue, since it was inherently absent from the Africans' reality. In fact, the French administrator and planter Pierre Victor Malouet (1788: 21) went so far as to accuse Africans of possessing a barbaric social structure that was based on mutual enslavement: "The European merchant did not create servitude on the coast of Africa.... He buys a barbaric society. The members that compose it sell each other, friends, enemies, princes, subjects, fathers, and children according to the will of the strongest."

These rationalizations had little to do with the historic realities prevailing at the time. Cohen (1980: 41) points out the nuances of slavery existing in some West African societies. A form of domestic servitude, this type of enslavement could hardly be compared to the West Indian slave regime. Furthermore, domestic servants were only rarely sold to European slave traders. Even if Europeans found some form of servitude already in place, the avidity with which they bought slaves to satisfy Caribbean demands undeniably impacted the existing African social structure, changing it in the process: slaves had become a desirable and valuable commodity.

The justification of Caribbean slavery based on domestic servitude in Africa was so convincing that planters were not the only ones to make such connections. Even Voltaire ([1756] 1878, 13: 177–78), who presumably wrote about slavery from an objective, philosophical standpoint, sided with this line of reasoning: "We only buy domestic slaves from the Negroes. One reproaches us for this commerce: a people who trade their children are even more condemnable than the buyer; this commerce proves our superiority; the one who gives himself a master is born to have one." This passage illustrates the profoundly ambiguous attitude toward slavery during the Enlightenment. Although the *philosophes* stood for the principle of liberty, a closer scrutiny of their narrative reveals the limited applicability of this maxim. While it was against a citizen's right to be enslaved, those who were already slaves and could lay no claims to citizenship did not benefit from this natural right (Ménil 2000). Since some form of servitude was an element of cultural practices in certain West African societies, Europeans readily appeased the moral qualms the slave trade might have awakened in them. Combined with what Europeans considered a strange physical appearance, the Africans' particular cultural and geographic origin provided fertile ground for endless speculation as to the justifiable link between race and slavery.

The progression from racial difference to enslavement in the French imaginary can be clearly discerned in the court case presented by three Parisian lawyers in the name of the Indian slave Francisque in 1759. Representing Francisque's plea for emancipation from his master, the lawyers partly built their case upon racial justifications. Born in India, they argued, Francisque was born free and had therefore been illegally enslaved. Interestingly, they heavily relied on Francisque's physiognomy, to prove that despite his color this slave in no way resembled Africans, that is, slaves:

> Although the people born on the bank of the Indus and of its tributaries resemble the Negroes from Africa because of their skin color, they at least distinguish themselves from the latter in that they do not have such flattened noses, such thick, protruding lips. Instead of the woolly, frizzy down that covers the head of Africans they have long and beautiful hair similar to that which decorates the head of Europeans.... It is true that [Francisque's] nose is a bit large, his lips are a bit thick; however, aside from his color he resembles Europeans more than many Europeans who would only need to be black to seem African (Joly de Fleury, De la Roue, and Collet 1759: 25).

The lawyers establish an unmistakable link between their client's physiognomy and his right to freedom. By insisting on Francisque's European appearance, they bring him closer to the European norm of beauty. Knowing that the European imaginary identifies dark skin color with evil, barbarity, and subhumaneness, the lawyers construe their client's physical description so that he "resembles Europeans more than many Europeans." Skin color becomes a nonessential physical attribute that a person can be dressed or undressed with and even Europeans might have a Negroid appearance if they have dark skin. The concluding sentence of this defense clearly expresses the assumption that racial attributes, in particular skin color, are linked to slavery: "Even though, because of their ignoble faces, the Negroes from Africa seem more particularly destined for slavery than the blacks from Hindustan, this argument should not be determining here" (Joly de Fleury, De la

Roue; and Collet 1759: 25). Although race was not necessarily a motive for the initial enslavement of Africans, it clearly occupied an important place in eighteenth-century perceptions of West Indian slavery. By tapping into these beliefs, Francisque's lawyers unveiled the essence of an ambiguous racist ideology.

The American historian Sue Peabody (1996: 57–71) believes the originality of this particular case—numerous were the cases of lawyers representing slaves against their masters around midcentury—to lie in its racial foundation. By arguing that Francisque was not African, his lawyers revealed the ways in which racial difference impacted eighteenth-century ideologies of universal liberty. The case underscores the contradictions at the heart of an era confronted with the most lucrative of France's commercial engagements: the African slave trade and plantation slavery. However, while Peabody sees the antislavery movement as an attempted resolution to the dilemma, I would rather argue that these inherent contradictions endured.

A close reading of the *philosophes* and colonial planters reveals the persisting ambiguity surrounding the relationship between race and slavery. Far from trying to resolve the dilemma, the *philosophes* and *encyclopédistes* expressed their ideological struggle with this issue, at times even subscribing to prevailing racist theories. Their narrative often overlapped with arguments voiced by proponents of the slave regime.

In *De l'esprit des lois*, Montesquieu ([1748] 1955: 222–23) exposes his thoughts on climatic determinism as a possible justification of slavery:

> There are countries where the heat enervates the body and so considerably weakens the courage that men can only be led to carry out their difficult duty out of fear of punishment: slavery is less shocking to reason in those places.... However, since all men are born equal it must be said that slavery is against nature although in certain countries it is founded on natural reason.... Natural servitude must therefore be limited to certain countries on this earth.

Two radically opposed ideologies clash together in this passage. On one hand, Montesquieu repeatedly underlines the "natural" reasons that may justify slavery in certain regions of the world due to the excessive heat that makes the inhabitants less productive. His position echoes the pseudoscientific explanations regarding racial variances. On the other hand, nature speaks against slavery altogether since "all men are born

equal" and slavery and equality cannot be reconciled. If "all
men are born equal" and yet slavery may be founded on "natural reason" in "certain countries," does Montesquieu consider
inhabitants of torrid climates to be "men" to the same degree
as Europeans? How can all men be born equal if natural servitude prevails in parts of the world? The French philosopher
Laurent Estève (2002a: 67) wonders whether the natural right
of man stops where climatic necessity takes over. An anthro-
pological incertitude reigns in the zone of excessive climates:
are the inhabitants human or animal? The Enlightenment's
proclaimed universalism seems to be geographically limited to
those living in cool climates. One may legitimately ask if the
universal rights of men are not instead the rights of men from
the north.[10]

Montesquieu ([1748] 1955: 224) struggles with these contradictions and goes on to reconsider his initial viewpoint: "I don't
know if it is the mind or the heart that dictates this point to me.
There is perhaps no climate on earth where one cannot hire free
men. Because the laws were poorly made one found lazy men:
because these men were lazy one enslaved them." Does pity
move Montesquieu to reevaluate climatic determinism? Clearly
though, he does not follow a single, unified line of reasoning.
The arguments regarding slavery are fraught with ambiguity
and Montesquieu does not hesitate to expose his uncertainty.
Nowhere in his work does he recommend the abolition of slavery as one might expect the "father of abolitionism" to do, nor
does he ever unequivocally condemn the institution. Montesquieu's writings appear to be lucid and critical reflections
on a matter that tested the very principles he himself stood for.

As opposed to Montesquieu, Voltaire ([1756] 1878, 12: 380–
81) expresses his belief in racial determinism in *Essai sur les
mœurs* without any hesitation:

> The mucous membrane of Negroes, recognized as being black
> and which causes their color, is obvious proof that there is in
> each human species, as in plants, a principle that differentiates
> them. Nature has subordinated to this principle these different
> degrees of genius, and these national characteristics which one
> rarely sees change. This is why Negroes are the slaves of other
> men.

This passage reflects the scientific reasoning that dominated
the eighteenth century, thus severely limiting the practical implications of universal equality. Voltaire subscribes to the classification of animal and plant species even if it justifies the

enslavement of an entire nation based only on their skin color. This perspective may come as a surprise from the author of *Candide* who is generally remembered for criticizing the Europeans' excessive cruelty in *Candide's* famous passage "the Negro from Suriname." Voltaire's denunciations are clearly not representative of his thought as a whole. This passage in *Essai sur les mœurs* reveals an entirely different dimension of the same thinker. Reducing Voltaire's thoughts on slavery to "the Negro from Suriname," as has generally been done, eliminates the fascinating complexity of a *philosophe* often remembered as a symbol of tolerance, in particular of religious tolerance.

Like Montesquieu's "ironic" indictment of African slavery, "the Negro from Suriname" has left its mark on the realms of the Enlightenment. It is part of a memory that is fueled by chosen excerpts of the *philosophes'* narratives on Africans and slavery. Placing these passages in the context of Montesquieu's hesitations regarding climatic determinism and Voltaire's racial justification of slavery reveals the contradictions at the heart of the Enlightenment. The ideals of universal liberty and equality are unsettled by the remembrance of texts generally forgotten in studies on antislavery thought during the eighteenth century.

The surprising concurrency of pro- and antislavery ideology during the eighteenth century is particularly well exemplified by the *Encyclopédie*. While the *Encyclopédie* was conceived as a collection of reflections on reason, science, and human progress, it at times defended an outright proslavery and racist viewpoint that even inspired colonial planters. A particularly striking example is the article entitled, "Nègres, considérés comme esclaves dans les colonies de l'Amérique" by M. Le Romain ([1755] n.d.). Justifying the institution of slavery on racial grounds, this article was repeatedly cited by colonial planters. For Le Romain (80–83) the need for African laborers was inevitable since Europeans were completely maladjusted to torrid climates. Moreover, he was convinced that Africans benefited in a number of ways from their enslavement by Europeans: "These vigorous black men, used to unrefined food, encounter a mildness in America which considerably improves their animal life over the one they led in their own country. This positive change permits them to withstand work and to multiply abundantly." The author not only deems slavery beneficial, he even maintains that Africans live at a subhuman level at which the state of enslavement does not make a difference. By describing Africans as though they were animals, Le Romain ignores the humanitarian considerations one would expect to find in such a symbolic work of the Enlightenment. Indeed, other articles, in particular those written by the chevalier de Jaucourt ([1755] n.d., 5: 934–39; [1755] n.d., 16: 532–33), denounce slavery from a clearly humanitarian perspective.

The effect of Le Romain's racist position was far-reaching, as colonial planters integrated his argument into their own defense of the slave regime. Half a century later, the white planter S.-J. Ducœurjoly from Saint Domingue (1802: 22) gave a verbatim reproduction of Le Romain's argument in his *Manuel des habitants de Saint Domingue*. The white planter M. R. Hilliard d'Auberteuil's (1776, 1: 132) justification of slavery in 1776 was also unmistakably inspired by Le Romain: "It is from the bosom of ignorance and laziness that [the Negroes] are taken to be put to useful work. The fertility of the country where they are transplanted promises them a relatively mild fate."

A symbol of enlightened ideology, the *Encyclopédie* attests the era's profoundly ambiguous attitude toward Africans and slavery as it also propagates virulent racism. Some thinkers so exclusively focused on the Africans' physical and cultural difference as to exclude them from progressive considerations regarding humanity in general. With Africans in a marginalized, inferior, and even subhuman position, their enslavement was justifiable, even from a philosophical vantage point. The universalism of the Enlightenment did not touch African slaves, which is why the Martinican historian Alain Ménil (2000: 257) referred to it as an "abstract universalism." Even if the *philosophes* and the *encyclopédistes* defended the idea of universal freedom and equality, the practical applications of this maxim were either entirely absent or had limited relevance in the context of African slavery.

The planters' own evaluation of the *philosophes'* writings is quite revealing in regards to this "abstract universalism." Hilliard d'Auberteuil and Moreau de Saint-Méry, the French colonial administrator, lawyer, and deputy for Martinique both commented on the *philosophes'* lack of involvement in the slaves' cause.[11] In 1776, Hilliard d'Auberteuil (1776, 1: 132) pointed out the ineffectiveness of their denunciations: "The *philosophes* ... complain about [Negro slavery] ... do they have the right to blame us for an ill we found in full force? If their writings condemn its birth and progress, their apathy approves ... [it]." The *philosophes'* opposition to slavery did not, according to Hilliard d'Auberteuil, have an impact on the institution itself. On the contrary, their inaction even undermined their credibility. Moreau de Saint-Méry ([1791] 1972: 3) came to a similar conclusion as he mockingly referred to the *philosophes'* denunciations as "speculations." He saw their concern with slavery and the slave trade as limited to "philosophical meditations" and "regrets" that would hardly endanger the institution. If there was anyone during the eighteenth century who was concerned with the *philosophes'* writings about slavery, it was clearly the planters. Proponents of the slave regime, they were understandably worried about the effects that antislavery ideology might have on their livelihood. The *philosophes'* narratives did not, however, seem to trouble them.

It may be difficult, and in the framework of my own study even irrelevant, to establish the motivations for the *philosophes'* ambiguous position. A number of historians have already examined the personal interests that some of the *philosophes,* in particular Voltaire, might have had in the slave trade. Ménil (2000: 258) cites the possibility that Voltaire and Montesquieu, and to some extent even Diderot, might have refrained from directly attacking the all-powerful slave trading establishment in the Caribbean, the *Compagnie des Indes,* in order to protect their pensions. All three might, to a greater or lesser extent, have been linked to trading activity in Nantes and Bordeaux.[12] In his history of antislavery opinion, Edward D. Seeber quotes an incriminating letter allegedly written by Voltaire to a ship owner from Nantes. Seeber (1937: 65) does, however, doubt its authenticity since no satisfying source attests to the letter's existence. Other historical studies on Voltaire's financial activities are not conclusive either.[13] In *Anthropologie et histoire au siècle des lumières,* Duchet (1971: 125–35) provides ample archival proof that the Abbé Raynal and Diderot had direct links with colonial administrators and were therefore considerably influenced by them.

Whatever personal interests the *philosophes* might have had in the slave trade, their ambiguous perspective on slavery stands in stark contrast to the present-day memory of their fervent abolitionism. Violating all human rights, the institution of slavery posed an ideological problem that the *philosophes* and *encyclopédistes* addressed in their reflections. And yet, in the end, it was not so much the need to abolish slavery that moved them to write, as the utter unacceptability of the atrocities committed by a nation of high morals for the simple pleasures of the privileged. It is the fact that the sugar consumed by Europeans was tainted with the blood of African slaves that outraged the *philosophes* and nourished their attacks.

Humanizing the Slave Regime

The humanitarian concerns emerging during the Enlightenment were contrary to a regime legally founded upon the treatment of human beings as objects. Article 44 of the *Code Noir* declared the slaves' judicial status as being that of "movable objects" like animals, furniture, and other movable property (Sala-Molins 1987: 178). Slaves had no rights whatsoever over their own lives. They were subject to capital punishment for repeatedly gathering together by day or by night to celebrate a wedding or a funeral (Article 16), for hitting their master or mistress and causing them to bleed (Article 33), for stealing farm animals (Article 35), or for repeatedly running away from the plantation (Article 38). Slave owners, on the other hand, could be absolved for illegally killing a slave even without the intervention of the king (Sala-Molins 1987: 122–66). As a result of this legislation slaveholders were free to treat their slaves as they pleased and excessively cruel punishments abounded. Quite frequent was mutilation, the rubbing of lemon or salt into wounds, and the use of special metal instruments for torture (Blackburn 1997: 288). In 1774, an interrogated runaway slave from the plantation Dame de l'Isle Adam in Saint Domingue recounted such cruel punishments. He explained that he ran away from the plantation when an animal in his keep died since it was customary for his master Chapulet to punish slaves who were guilty of this crime with death. Asked about the methods used by Chapulet to kill his slaves, he explained: "that Mister Chapulet put some Negroes in a cellar … until they died and … buried others alive, saying that they had made the animals die out of spite" (Archives d'Outre Mer F3 90, 1775). In 1790 the *Société des Amis des Noirs* ([1790c] 1968: 4) denounced one of the most extreme forms of barbarism: the slow burning to death of slaves who were also "torn to pieces with the teeth."[14]

Cruelly punished and overworked, slaves did not live long as plantation laborers and the need for more slaves was constant as shown by the historian Ronald Segal's (1995: 103) numerical evidence. From 1779 to 1788, two-thirds of the slaves in Saint Domingue had died and needed to be replaced. It was arguably more cost-efficient for slaveholders to work their slaves to death and then replace them. Cohen, for instance, points to the success of French colonists who in the late eighteenth century had higher rates of production and a greater sugar yield than their English or Spanish counterparts in the Caribbean.

The French were known for their harsh disciplinary measures especially in Saint Domingue (Cohen 1980: 50).[15]

The cruelty of the slave regime was well-known in France and denunciations of its excesses abounded. Yet, highly criticized as the system might have been, the destruction of slavery was rarely the final aim of these condemnations. As Hoffman (1973: 91) puts it, the institution of slavery was probably less shocking to European sensibilities than were the abuses that accompanied it. This is evidenced by the surprising agreement between the narratives of the *philosophes* and other writers and the proslavery narratives of white planters: all unanimously condemned the barbarity of slavery. Condorcet ([1789] 1968b: 69, 77, 94) considered slavery a crime contrary to man's "natural right." In the same vein, the French colonial administrator and planter Pierre Victor Malouet (1788: 20) declared that "slavery will always be a violation of man's natural right." Although he had written his memoir in defense of slavery, Malouet admitted that slavery was "an unfortunate institution" (5). Slavery, he noted, led to "corruption and abuse" among colonists who followed man's natural tendency to misuse their force when in a position of power (15–16). His attack on planters echoes the *philosophe* Bernardin de Saint-Pierre ([1768–70] 1983: 122) who decried "the greed and cruelty of the most depraved men" in *Voyage à l'île de France*. The theme of the ruthless master also appears in Olympe de Gouges's play *L'esclavage des noirs* ([1786] 1994: 237). The first woman writer to defend the abolitionist cause, De Gouges wanted to bring to the attention of the Parisian public "the cruel and shameful yoke" under which "barbarous masters" had placed black slaves.[16] Both the Abbé Raynal and Hilliard d'Auberteuil, a white planter from Saint Domingue, condemned the excessive death toll among African slaves. In his widely read *Histoire des deux Indes,* Raynal ([1770, 1774, 1780] 1981: 178) provided detailed descriptions of the slaves' deplorable conditions lamenting the "horrible destruction" of millions of these victims due to the way they were governed.[17] Hilliard d'Auberteuil (1776, 2: 63–66) similarly deplored the "barbarous treatments" and "excessive tyranny" leading to an inordinate number of deaths.

The excesses of the regime were not subject to controversy, as even slaveholders agreed to its barbarous nature. Nor did the *philosophes'* denunciations stand out as exceptionally progressive since colonists readily took up the same viewpoint amid an otherwise vehement defense of slavery and the slave trade. Particularly remarkable is the keen awareness on both the pro- and antislavery side that the slaves' humanity was jeopardized by the regime. Buffon ([1749] 1800: 307), for instance, condemned the treatment of slaves like animals: "humanity revolts against such odious treatments." The playwright Pigault-Lebrun (1796: 10) admonished that slaves be treated "humanely." We find the same adjectives expressing humanitarian concerns used by proponents of the slave regime. Hilliard d'Auberteuil (1776, 1: 130, 133, 145) denounced the "inhumane politics" of slavery and called for the "humane treatment" of slaves: "Let us not add to their misery through our harshness, let us listen to the voice of humanity." The white planter S.-J. Ducœurjoly (1802: 52–58) from Saint Domingue similarly admonished fellow planters not to treat slaves too harshly and with too much cruelty: "One must be humane toward one's fellow men. Color must not influence our way of thinking. We must remember that the Negro is a man like us." French colonial administrators also voiced humanitarian concerns. In 1767, for instance, Pierre Poivre, the intendant of Ile de France and Bourbon, recommended that slaveholders be sensitive to the "tender and powerful cry of outraged humanity." He admonished them not to forget that their "unhappy slaves" were "human beings like them" (qtd. in Duchet 1971: 148).

One may argue that planters and administrators became conscious of the slaves' humanity under the influence of the *philosophes*. However, the overriding concern with the inhumanity of the regime even among slaveholders blurs the ultimate motivations behind these sensibilities. Further analysis of the planters' narrative shows that the humane treatment of slaves was fundamental to increasing economic profits. P. J. Laborie (n.d.: 35) clearly explained this link in his defense of the slave regime. One of the greatest problems faced by planters was the high death rate among slaves, in particular among new arrivals from Africa. According to Hilliard d'Auberteuil (1776, 2: 61–62, 70) this problem could only be remedied by treating slaves well and by giving them more care and attention: "It is … essential to … give slaves the means of being as happy as their condition permits." Slaveholders, he maintained, who followed a destructive economy on their plantations were to be punished. Slavery did not have to be abolished in the name of humanitarianism as long as slaves were treated humanely. Malouet (1788: 6) was convinced of this. Since the institution had become unavoidable, its abuses and excesses had to be reduced. Improving the slaves' lot made it unnecessary, however, to emancipate them "in order to be just" (18). While

Malouet readily admitted that slavery was "a bad institution," he was convinced that it was possible to make slaves happy rather than free (143–44). The intendant Poivre defended the same viewpoint. He praised the potential of humanitarianism and its transformative effect on slaves, who, he argued, would "feel free and happy even in the state of servitude" (qtd. in Duchet 1971: 148). To assure the smooth functioning of the regime, humanitarianism was to restore a semblance of freedom, not freedom itself.

The *philosophes'* humanitarianism was not immune to these interests. This was, for instance, the case with the Abbé Raynal ([1770, 1774, 1780] 1981: 178) who called for a reform that would "render the slaves' conditions more bearable." In order for slavery to become a "useful" institution, slaves had to be treated "gently." Economic concerns were not the only motives behind the *philosophes'* humanitarian narrative. Bernardin de Saint-Pierre ([1768–70] 1983: 122), for example, evoked the need to "limit" slavery to the bounds of "human laws." Similarly, in her *Réflexions sur les hommes nègres,* Olympe de Gouges ([1784] 1788: 93) hoped that the "appalling destiny of Negroes" would be changed or at least softened. The question of humanizing the slave regime became a double-edged sword. On one hand, it reflected an increasing sensibility to the fate of African slaves. On the other hand, it was a way of rendering slavery more humanly bearable and thereby also more acceptable. Abolition became less pressing if one thought the slaves were treated well and were perhaps even happy in their condition. Humanitarianism was by no means the first step toward ending slavery.

The *philosophes* had no qualms about criticizing the hypocrisy masking the fashionable concern for human rights during the eighteenth century. In his *Essai sur les mœurs,* Voltaire ([1756] 1878, 12: 416–17) attacks society's moral arrogance in the face of plantation slavery:

> In 1757 one counted approximately … one hundred thousand Negro or mulatto slaves in French Saint Domingue who worked on the sugar, indigo, and cocoa plantations and shortened their lives to flatter our new appetites, to fulfill our new needs which our fathers did not have…. We tell them that they are humans like us … and then we make them work like beasts of burden…. After that we dare speak of human rights!

Voltaire lucidly exposes the contradictions inherent to a society that proclaims its burgeoning social ideals while also profiting from the increasingly lucrative slave trade. In *Candide* ([1759] 1973: 118) he explicitly condemns the disproportion between society's new craving for sugar and the excessive cruelty used to produce this luxury item. After describing the ruthless treatment slaves were subjected to, the black slave from Surinam cries out before his European interlocutors: "It is at this price that you eat sugar in Europe." One finds a similar condemnation of society's superficial humanitarianism in the Abbé Raynal's *Histoire des deux Indes* ([1770, 1774, 1780] 1981: 173):

> For the past century, Europe resounds with the most sublime moral maxims.... Even imaginary calamities make tears swell up in our eyes in the silence of our study and especially in the theater. It is only the fateful destiny of the unhappy Negroes that does not interest us.... The torments of a people whom we owe our delights never go to our heart.

Despite his prejudice against Africans—he believed the Hottentots to be as dirty and stupid as their own animals—Raynal discriminatingly analyzes the limitations of Enlightenment ideology ([1770, 1774, 1780] 1981: 51). Like Voltaire, he denounces the high human cost Europeans were willing to pay to satisfy their whimsical pleasures. By pointing to the racial underpinnings of the European's indifference, Raynal went perhaps even one step further than Voltaire.

Women did not escape the *philosophes'* social criticism. Bernardin de Saint-Pierre ([1768–70] 1983: 122) found those belonging to the higher social milieu to be equally at fault. Their emotional outpouring was purely theatrical and stood in no relationship to real suffering: "Tenderhearted women, you cry at tragedies, and that which serves your pleasures is tainted with the tears and the blood of men." Bernardin de Saint-Pierre's critique echoes the women's fancy for young African boys described by Louis-Sébastien Mercier in *Tableau de Paris* (1783) and by French political writer and lawyer Jacques-Vincent Delacroix in *Peinture des mœurs du siècle* (1777). Fashion powerfully influenced French society. Outward manifestations were not, therefore, conclusive evidence of genuine humanitarianism.

The *philosophes* did not try to reduce the contradictions they were themselves a part of. On the contrary, they openly criticized the ideological failings of their era. The rising concern for the other's humanity, they argued, remained on an idealistic or purely emotional level and was of no consequence in situations of true human suffering such as slavery. Their own writings stopped short of demanding the abolition of slavery in the name of universal freedom and equality. By insisting that slavery become more bearable and humane, they indirectly supported a "softened" version of the regime thus postponing its overthrow.

The Right to Freedom

Despite the conservative approach toward the slave trade and plantation slavery, the prerevolutionary Enlightenment was not without demands for freedom made on behalf of African slaves. Some *philosophes*, in particular the Abbé Raynal and Condorcet, went beyond the typical demands for humaneness and addressed the question of abolition. On a more practical level, an increasing number of Parisian lawyers defended slaves in lawsuits that were filed for freedom from their masters.[18] Both narratives are interesting reflections on the stakes involved in the freedom of African slaves. What motivated these *philosophes* and lawyers to address slave liberty at a time when the idea of abolition evoked horror in the minds of those whose fortunes were linked to the slave trade?

The Abbé Raynal and Condorcet did not limit their condemnation of slavery to the familiar advocation of humanitarian ideals. They considered the humanizing process to be intricately linked to the slaves' rights, in particular their right to freedom. In *Histoire des deux Indes,* Raynal ([1770, 1774, 1780] 1981: 178–79) called for an end to the massive decimation of African slaves due to poor treatment. It was in the slaveholders' best interest to encourage the slaves' desire to live. This could only be achieved if slaves regained their basic rights: "By degrees, one would arrive at this political moderation that consists in reducing the workload, mitigating the punishment, and returning to man a part of his rights in order to more surely obtain from him the tribute of the duty imposed upon him." Again, the interests behind these ameliorations are clearly stated: a slave who is so miserable that he would rather die will not be a useful laborer. However, rather than simply recommend more humaneness, Raynal (190–91) touches upon the delicate subject of the slaves' rights. In a later chapter it becomes clear that he considers freedom to be one of those rights:

[Natural freedom] is, after reason, what distinguishes man.... Without freedom or the ownership of one's body and the possession of one's mind, one is neither husband nor father, nei-

ther parent nor friend. One has no homeland, no fellow citizen,
no God. In the hands of the wicked, instrument of his villainy,
the slave is below the dog ... since man retains the conscience
the dog is lacking.

The *Histoire des deux Indes* is the first work of the Enlightenment
to go beyond the basic question of the slaves' humanity by link-
ing it to the natural right to freedom. While advocating more
humanity did not necessarily challenge the status quo, as evidenced by the participation of colonial planters and administrators in this type of narrative, defending the slaves' right to
freedom opened up new possibilities. The idea of freedom was
contrary to a system entirely based on forced labor. Once the
slaves' natural right to freedom was formulated, the next step
was "to demand the destruction of slavery." Condorcet (1781]
1968a: 90) did so in *Réflexions sur l'esclavage des nègres*.

And yet, the revolutionary aspect of Raynal's and Condorcet's claims is dampened by their conservative approach. Both
initially call into question the slaves' ability to manage their
freedom. In *Histoire des deux Indes,* derogatory remarks show
slaves to be incapable of emancipation: "These stupid men
who would not have been prepared for a change in their state
would be incapable of conducting themselves. Their lives would
consist in habitual idleness or in a web of crimes" (Raynal
[1770, 1774, 1780] 1981: 199–200). Less offensive in his language, Condorcet ([1781] 1968a: 94) is nonetheless as doubtful as Raynal: "Are these men worthy of being entrusted with
their happiness and the care of their families? Are they not in
the unfortunate case of having lost their reason due to the
barbarous treatment they were subjected to?" Although ideologically speaking, slaves had a natural right to freedom, the
practical application of this principle was another story. Neither Raynal nor Condorcet deemed slaves fit for emancipation. Their reticence reveals their refusal to consider slaves as
their equals. Condorcet states as much: "whatever made them
incapable of being men, the legislator owes them not so much
their rights as the assurance of their well-being." The principle
of freedom was lost in the process of applying it to African
slaves. Humanitarianism seemed to suffice for these people
who had become less than human and could therefore not assume the responsibility that came with freedom.

Their skepticism vis-à-vis the slaves informed Raynal's and
Condorcet's projects for ending the slave regime. Although
they did tackle the question of abolition, they only proposed

emancipation after a series of amendments. Inspired by the gradual emancipation plan (Duchet 1971: 153–70) proposed by the baron Bessner, the governor of French Guiana, Raynal ([1770, 1774, 1780] 1981: 199–200) postponed emancipation at least until the next generation, if not later:

> In order to attain this aim, generally considered to be chimerical, one should not, according to the ideas of an enlightened man, remove the chains from those unhappy souls who were born into servitude.... The great benefit of freedom should be reserved to their posterity, and even with some modifications. Until the age of twenty, these children will belong to the master.

The final goal of this project is less humanitarian than economic. Encouraged to have children who would not be born into servitude, "the black population ... would rapidly increase." Freedom is not depicted as a due right but as a tool used to manipulate the slave population.

Condorcet ([1781] 1968a: 99–105) deferred emancipation for seventy years—longer, it should be added, than it eventually took the French government: "We propose not to emancipate Negroes at birth but to give the master the freedom to raise them and use them as slaves, under the condition that they be freed at the age of 35.... Within seventy years there would be no more slaves in the colonies." Both abolitionary projects are introduced by stating their support for the continuation of the slave regime: "one should not remove the chains" and "we propose not to emancipate Negroes at birth." Although these projects do eventually lead to the destruction of slavery, the process is lengthy and the concern is for the masters, not for the slaves. Planters are to be allowed to use their slaves for one generation according to Raynal's plan, and for more than one generation according to Condorcet's plan. Condorcet (105) points out the advantages of such moderation: "This legislation would have none of the inconveniences characterizing abrupt changes since emancipation would be gradual. It would give ... the colonists time to imperceptibly change their method of cultivation." After Raynal's and Condorcet's vehement denunciations of the slaveholders' cruelty, it is surprising that the main focus of their emancipation projects should be upon the allowances made for the planters.

When placing these projects in an eighteenth-century context, however, it becomes clear that the mere idea of emancipation was met with outrage. The audacity of Raynal's and

Condorcet's proposals can be gleaned from the planters' response. While the *philosophes'* denunciations were generally
considered ineffectual, as shown by Hilliard d'Auberteuil's and
Moreau de Saint-Méry's comments, even the most moderate
reference to the potential abolition of slavery was taken very
seriously by colonists. Malouet (1788: 13), for instance, felt
compelled to respond to Condorcet's plea in his *Mémoire sur
l'esclavage des nègres:* "Emancipation is impossible. The pro-
longation of servitude and the slave trade which supplies it is
indispensable until we reconstruct a portion of the social structure upon a new foundation." Malouet's riposte was unequivocal. He further depicted the fatal consequences of abolitionism:
"there is nothing less useful and more dangerous than the violence one wants to do at this moment to the governments, the
colonists, and public opinion on the subject of Negro slavery"
(77). Freedom was an idea that planters did not want anybody
to toy with, even at an abstract level.

On the eve of the French Revolution, the right to freedom
was not universally applicable. Since most *philosophes* did not
challenge this in the context of black slavery, Raynal and Condorcet distinguished themselves for their progressive, if cautious, claims on behalf of slaves. Nonetheless, historical events
would quickly prove that these abolitionary projects were both
impractical and not adapted to colonial reality: only a few
years later, in 1794, slavery would be abruptly abolished under
the mounting pressure of slave revolts sweeping the Caribbean. Those whom Raynal and Condorcet considered incapable of reason and therefore unfit to be emancipated in the
immediate future had to fight for their right to freedom.

The causal link commonly made between Enlightenment
ideology and the abolition of slavery is not born out. Although
eighteenth-century thinkers addressed the issue of slavery and
some went so far as to demand its destruction, their abstract
philosophical musings stand in no relation to the urgency of
the demands made by the slaves themselves. Diderot, writing
under the name of Raynal in *Histoire des deux Indes* ([770, 1774,
1780] 1981: 201), was perhaps the only one to lucidly recognize the practical limitations of eighteenth-century thought in
regards to slavery. After a lengthy explanation of the gradual
emancipation plan, the tone suddenly changes: "What am I
saying? Let us cease to make the people and their masters understand the useless voice of humanity.... Your slaves do not
need your generosity or your advice to break the sacrilegious
yoke that oppresses them. Nature speaks louder than philoso-

phy or interest." This prophetic passage, and even more so the famous description of the black slave who liberates his brothers,[19] evinces the author's deep insight into the relationship between the ideological advances of his time and the realities of slavery and abolition. Even though emancipation logically ensues from humanitarianism, it is not carried out. The voice of humanity is useless on the abstract, philosophical level where it does the oppressed little good. Diderot relinquishes the Enlightenment's ideological claim to paternalistic benevolence. Slaves, he argues, are perfectly capable of freeing themselves. Their natural inclination to freedom does not depend on any outside source and is, in fact, by far more effective than any potential European initiative on their behalf.

While even the plans for abolition retained a decidedly abstract character, a much more practical approach to freedom can be found in the lawsuits for freedom engaged by individual slaves against their masters. A number of Parisian lawyers obtained freedom for slaves residing in France in court cases they fought against individual slave owners around the middle of the eighteenth century.[20] This legal phenomenon was particularly unusual given the increasing sensitivity to the racial question reflected by tightening royal legislation aimed at keeping black slaves and people of color out of France.

The lawyers used a twofold argument to defend their slave clients. In the first place, Louis X had abolished slavery in France on 3 July 1315. Hence, they argued "there are no slaves in France" (Mallet 1738: 4; Pensey and Poncet de la Grave 1770: 15) and "all men who have the good fortune of living in the empire of our kings are free" (Des Essarts, Poncet de la Grave, and Dejunquieres 1776: 17). This argumentation did not attack colonial slavery per se but the enslavement of black slaves on French soil. The *Code Noir,* the exceptional law promulgated by Louis XIV in 1685, permitted slavery for the commercial benefit of France as long as it was limited to France's maritime colonies. Based on the abolition of slavery in France during the fourteenth century and the instauration of black slavery solely in the Americas, the Parisian lawyers advocated their clients' lawful right to freedom as residents of France. Mallet (1738: 4), the lawyer defending the slave Boucaux, thus argued: "It must be concluded that ... outside of the maritime country to which the Edict of 1685 applies, slavery must cease and liberty recovers all its rights.... By leaving the maritime country, [Boucaux] surmounted the obstacle to his freedom and breathed the air of liberty that reigns in this kingdom."

An exceptional aspect of the lawyers' defense was their total disregard for the question of race.[21] Usually omnipresent in
eighteenth-century narratives, even in the writings of the
philosophes, race was not a deciding factor in these court cases.
Within the framework of the legal system, African slaves were
treated on equal terms with other slaves who were traditionally freed when touching French soil. Neither their race nor
their state of servitude in any way limited their right to freedom. As opposed to most eighteenth-century thinkers, the
lawyers followed a consequent line of reasoning. Using the
laws of the kingdom, they paid no heed to institutionalized
prejudice that kept freedom away from black slaves. Even
though the lawyers' efforts were largely motivated by their
own political agendas, their arguments unveiled the practical
potential of France's humanitarian heritage.[22] Within a legal
framework, they confronted France's humanitarian ideals
with the realities of slavery. As opposed to the *philosophes,* the
lawyers aimed for immediate practical results: the emancipation of their clients.

The incongruousness of enslavement by such a "gentle and
human" nation was the second fundamental argument upon
which they built their cases. They denounced the "horrors"
committed by an allegedly humane society: "For the past three
centuries we have filled the immense space that separates the
two tropics with crimes and misfortunes and philosophy, which
like a salutary star rises on our horizon, makes us more enlightened only to makes us more guilty" (Pensey and Poncet de
la Grave 1770: 6). These denunciations supported their larger
mission of freeing their slave clients. In this vein, they focused
their attention on France's humanitarian legacy, making it an
overriding argument in favor of their clients' emancipation:

> All of France is the temple of humanity. Always having pro-
> tected ill-fated kings she especially glorifies herself for liberating
> slaves. As soon as slaves touch this fortunate soil, their chains
> fall off and they become their masters' equals. Everybody is free
> in this kingdom where freedom is seated at the feet of the
> throne and where each and every subject finds the feelings of a
> father in the heart of the king (15).

The lawyers of the slave Roc fought for their client's freedom
by holding up the very idealistic notions France was so proud
of. The clash between these lofty ideals and the horrors of slavery is further dramatized by the lawyers for the slaves Pampy
and Julienne: "Two slaves had the good fortune of reaching

France. They learned that the air one breathes there is that of freedom. Obliterated by the harshest slavery their souls opened themselves to the sweetest hope.... It is humanity itself which presents them before justice" (Des Essarts, Poncet de la Grave, and Dejunquieres 1776: 11). The very principles France stood for were put to trial in these lawsuits. The freedom of these slaves became a stake in the universal freedom trumpeted by the Enlightenment.

The large number of successful lawsuits filed by slaves to obtain freedom between 1730 and 1770 is indicative of the Enlightenment's practical potential. Ideologically speaking, slaves had an undeniable right to freedom. However, on a practical level numerous obstacles kept slaves from attaining their rights. By applying the laws of the kingdom quite literally, the lawyers held France to her professed humanitarianism. Their narrative shows that it was possible, even during the eighteenth century, to disregard the question of race in the name of humanity and thereby to make freedom a reality. Standing out as an exception, this legal phenomenon indirectly reveals the inescapable hurdle of race present in all emancipation proposals. As long as the slaves' race or their state of servitude was thought to conflict with the right to freedom, emancipation was impossible—at least in any immediate future. It was the lawyers' disregard of their clients' race that held the French legal system to its universal laws of freedom, thereby bringing the lawsuits to a favorable outcome.

The realms of the Enlightenment are a complex portrayal of the themes of race, slavery, humanity, and freedom brought into play by diverse narratives without being subordinate to a singular and centralizing representation of enlightened thought. The perspectives of the *philosophes,* playwrights, the royal court, colonists, and lawyers simultaneously overlap and clash with one another around these themes to create multiple layers of ideological battles. Countless forgotten memories are thereby brought to the forefront, creating a contrast with the familiar legacy of reason, justice, and humanitarianism. It becomes evident that the abolition of slavery did not take its root in these mythical notions but resulted from a far more complex interplay of forces. The rise of humanitarian sentiment and the principles of justice and equality so vehemently defended by the *philosophes* were undoubtedly conducive to the first and second abolition of slavery in 1794 and 1848, respectively. However, these ideologies were not representative of the *philosphes'* thought in general nor were they at the origin of abolitionism. By encompassing a wide spectrum of memories, the realms of the Enlightenment leave the door open to diverse interpretations, each of which reveals different facets of the past. Most importantly, they make space for those actors of the past who are generally forgotten: the oppressed. The slaves' part in the construction of their destiny is the focus of chapters 2–4. Chapter 2 brings together diverse historical and literary interpretations of the most mythicized figure of this past: the maroon. The thwarted right to freedom is reappropriated by this symbol of vengeance and freedom thereby turning slaves into agents of their own liberation.

Notes

1. See Hoffman (1973: 96); Gates (1985–86: 407); Sala-Molins (1992: 20); Geggus (1997: 3); Haudrère and Vergès (1998: 12); and Klein (1999: 185).
2. See also Cohen (1980: 21–34).
3. See Sorel (1921: 119); Despin (1977: 102–12); Lafontant (1979); Benrekassa (1987: 164); and Shklar (1987: 96).
4. For detailed discussions of Montesquieu's perceived ambiguity see Fletcher (1933: 414–25); Despin (1977: 102–12); and Whitman (1977: 17–33).
5. See Delacroix (1777: 146) for a similar description of this fashion.
6. See Gilman's (1985–86: 232–35) discussion of European perceptions of the Hottentot women.
7. The lack of white women in the Caribbean led white planters to frequently take slave women as concubines. The offspring of such unions began playing an increasingly important role in the island economy by midcentury.
8. Archives Nationales de France will henceforth be abbreviated as ANF.
9. Cohen (1980: 112) points out the differing sensibilities in France and England during the eighteenth century vis-à-vis the black population: "The possible 5,000 blacks in France were part of a nation of 20 million inhabitants, whereas in England blacks represented 20,000 out of 8 million inhabitants." Though the proportion of blacks in England was ten times larger than in France no legal restraints were placed upon them.
10. The French historian Gauthier (2001: 376) studies the notion that freedom was not a universal right but rather a right belonging only to inhabitants of the northern hemisphere, that is, Europe and the United States. This notion was born in 1795 when the Convention of the Ninth Thermidor overthrew the Constitution of 1793.

11. Born in Martinique in 1750, Moreau de Saint-Méry was a member of a distinguished white Creole family. He served as deputy for Martinique from 1790 to 1793 when he was forced to flee to the United States.

12. Cohen (1980: 137) goes so far as to state that Voltaire owned stock in the *Compagnie des Indes*.

13. See Kozminski (1929: 69–70) and Donvez (1949: 69–71).

14. For more details about the cruelties perpetrated on African slaves in the Caribbean, particularly in Saint Domingue, see Fick (1990: 15–45).

15. On the same subject see also Gautier (1985: 58).

16. Other writers and playwrights similarly focused on the abomination of slavery and the slave trade. See Delacroix (1777: 146–50); L.-S. Mercier (1783); Larivallière (1794: 12–44); and Pigault-Lebrun (1796: 6).

17. According to literary critics and historians, Raynal was not the sole author of this monumental work. Especially the third edition, which is the one I am quoting in my work, was augmented by passages most likely written by Diderot and Pechmeja. This is particularly true in the chapters on colonial slavery. For a detailed analysis of Diderot's and Pechmeja's contributions see the introduction to Bénot's (1981) edition of the *Histoire des deux Indes;* Bénot (1963); and Duchet (1978).

18. Between 1730 and 1759 thirteen slaves obtained freedom in this way while during the 1760s the numbers drastically increased to seventy-one (Peabody 1996: 170).

19. I will analyze the "Black Spartacus" in chapter 2.

20. See Peabody (1996) for an excellent in-depth analysis of the general historical and political movement surrounding these court cases. She examines a number of lawsuits in detail, including the ones I refer to in this chapter.

21. Only in the case of the Indian Francisque, which I referred to earlier in the chapter, did race become an issue.

22. The political motivations behind the lawyers' defense of slaves were linked to their resistance against the authority of Louis XV's regent Philippe, duke of Orléans. As a result of the struggle over fiscal and religious questions between the Parliament of Paris and the regent Orléans, the Parliament of Paris refused to register a number of royal edicts thus leaving a legal loophole for freeing slaves. For more details see Peabody (1996: 18).

❧ CHAPTER 2 ❧

REALMS OF THE MAROON

"The maroon is the only true popular hero of the Caribbean," writes Edouard Glissant in *Le discours antillais* in 1981. A decade later, his compatriots quite literally act on this statement as they begin erecting numerous statues in memory of this emblematic figure of their slave heritage. Symbolizing the slaves' active resistance against oppression spurred by the desire for freedom, maroons occupy an important place in the West Indian imagination today. As Richard D. E. Burton (1997: 23–25) points out, maroons embody the reverse side of assimilation and the possibility of existing outside of the colonial system. Many contemporary Caribbean authors use *marronnage* as a principle theme in their work.[1]

The figure of the maroon is the most mythicized aspect of slave history. While Caribbean, French, and North American historians debate the extent to which maroons contributed to the overthrow of slavery, popular opinion has claimed the maroon as a symbol of the ancestors' resistance against oppression.[2] Even on an island like Martinique, where *marronnage* was a very minor phenomenon, the myth of the maroon is powerfully anchored in the people's imagination (Burton 1997: 26). Regardless of historical facts undermining their revolutionary dimension, the memory of the maroons' opposition to colonial order has lasted across the centuries.

In fact, the importance of resistance and self-liberation is not unique to the contemporary memory of the maroon. Already in the eighteenth century it dominated French literary portrayals of maroons. Maroons fascinated French writers who turned the previously despised barbaric Africans into heroic and noble rebels against injustice (Duchet 1971: 139). One of the most salient characteristics of these literary figures is their violent relationship to their oppressors. Some writers depict this violence in a positive light, considering it the maroons' rightful revenge against the Europeans' outrageous exploitation. Others censure such acts, encouraging instead complete submission to the master. Freedom, according to this perspective, can only be given to slaves who have earned their master's benevolent favors. Both types of portrayals are an indication of the position occupied by maroons in the European imagination. Regardless of the maroons' historical effectiveness, Europeans considered them a real threat to colonial order. The fact that slaves could and often did escape the control of their masters transformed them from mere beasts of burden into human beings. As Frantz Fanon (1991: 67), the Martinican psychiatrist, anticolonial writer, and activist acutely states, "the colonized 'object' becomes human through the very process of self-liberation." Their human dimension turned maroons into a philosophical subject for French thinkers who liked to speculate about aspects of the master-slave relationship in the colonies. Though the resulting literary pieces were mere approximations of historical events on the other side of the Atlantic, they greatly contributed to the ways in which the maroon came to be perceived across the centuries. Myth had a more lasting and profound effect on the people's imagination than did the history of *marronnage*. It is therefore particularly relevant to the memory of the maroon in the present-day Caribbean.

History and Myth

Resistance to slavery was a pervasive phenomenon in the world of Caribbean plantations. It carried over from white indentured servitude predating the first arrival of African slaves in the sixteenth century (Debien 1979: 112). Fugitive slaves and maroons existed since 1503 when the first black slaves brought to Hispaniola from Spain in 1499 began to revolt and were joined by the Indians. Nonetheless, colonial planters rarely refer to the increasing problem posed by fugitive slaves in their writings and appear to have been surprisingly blind to the constant danger of slave revolts (Fouchard 1972: 445–51). Caught off guard by the 1791 rebellions in Saint Domingue, for instance, the planters were bewildered by the extent of organized violence. The planters' apparent naïveté was largely due to the widespread belief that slaves would never muster the courage to revolt as a mass since they were convinced of their inherent inferiority as a race (Debbash 1963: 138). The Haitian Revolution is one of the most blatant historical proofs that colonial planters and French authorities completely misjudged the slaves' quest for freedom.

The phenomena of runaway slaves and maroon bands were the most subversive forms of slave resistance. Some of the most frequent acts of resistance were suicide, arson, poisonings, and gatherings of large groups of slaves from different plantations, generally during the night. Suicides were often committed by new arrivals, in particular by women, who believed they would return to their homeland after death (Gautier 1985: 221–22). Slaves frequently took revenge by poisoning their master and his family, farm animals, as well as fellow slaves on the plantation. Planters dreaded the ravages of arson and poisonings on their properties and the king specifically banned poisoning in December 1746.[3] Slave gatherings were a further concern for colonial authorities as they represented the focal point from which all other forms of resistance, in particular *marronnage* originated. In 1685, Article 16 of the *Code Noir* already prohibited slaves from gathering day or night for whatever reason, including funerals, weddings, and other celebrations (Sala-Molins 1987: 122). During such gatherings slaves might conduct African ceremonies; plan poisonings, arson, or other revolts; or even plan to leave the plantation and found maroon communities. Slaves who were repeatedly convicted of leading such assemblies were generally punished by death (ANF 27 AP 11, 1746).

The example of the African slave Makandal who belonged to a sugar plantation in Saint Domingue during the middle of the eighteenth century shows the close link between these varied forms of resistance. Having had his hand cut off by the sugar mill, Makandal was employed as a cattle guard. He escaped around 1751 and became part of a community of maroons in the mountains. Makandal's great skill in poisoning his enemies brought him fame. He gathered a large crowd of followers and plotted to poison the entire white community of Saint Domingue. However, the rebels were betrayed and Makandal was caught and burned at the stake in 1758 (Segal 1995: 106–7; Bénot 1989: 139–40). Swearing that he would escape the flames by taking the form of a fly, Makandal remained in the imagination of the slaves who believed in his immortality (Moreau de Saint-Méry [1797] 1984: 631). Makandal embodied the planters' worst fears and became a legend among authorities and slaves alike. He was a key element in the formation of the myth surrounding the maroon's power of resistance against colonial oppression.

Two types of *marronnage* were common in the French Caribbean. Fugitive or runaway slaves who only fled from their plantations for a few days and remained close to their master's property, stealing food or exchanging fish, game, and stolen objects against manioc and vegetables were said to engage in *petit marronnage* (Debien 1979: 117–18). This type of *marronnage* did not concern the planters much and runaways had a good chance of being pardoned if they returned within two to four weeks (Debbash 1961: 84). They might return around the time of a big celebration, such as Christmas or New Year's Eve, and enlist the help of a "protector"—the oldest woman in the master's family, the parish priest, or even a neighbor—to plead their cause. Generally they were not denied their pardon and received only mild punishment (Debien 1979: 117–18).

Grand marronnage, on the other hand, was defined as "flight from the plantation with no intention of ever returning" (Debien 1979: 108). Maroons who engaged in this practice usually formed bands in the mountain regions of the islands and established maroon communities that included women as well. Female maroons represented approximately one-fifth of the entire maroon population (Pluchon 1982: 156). Since it was difficult for women to flee from plantations with their children, many women were kidnapped when maroons raided plantations for women, food, farm animals, tools, and arms. Thanks to the presence of these women, maroon communities could perpetuate themselves (Gautier 1985: 232–33). Through pillaging and regular raids on plantations, maroons were able to procure essential food items as well as the necessary tools and arms for survival in the wilderness. However, their precarious living conditions led them to often survive in great physical misery (Debbash 1961: 111–12). Headed by a leader, maroon bands rarely had more than one hundred members. They were present on all islands of the Caribbean. Their devastating effect on the smooth functioning of plantations as well as the magnetic attraction they exerted on future maroons made these bands a prime target for the mounted police, the militia, and even professional troops. Only few bands were eventually captured and punished (Debien 1979: 107–9).

Captured maroons were severely punished. According to Article 38 of the *Code Noir:* "Slaves who have been fugitive for one month ... will have their ears cut off and will be branded with a fleur-de-lis on their shoulder; if they are fugitive again ... they will have their ham cut and will be branded with a fleur-de-lis on the other shoulder; the third time they will be sentenced to die" (Sala-Molins 1987: 166). Despite the severity of these punishments, maroons persisted well into the nineteenth century. In Jamaica and Suriname, full-scale maroon wars forced colonial authorities to negotiate treaties with maroon bands during the eighteenth century. These bands demanded liberty for all their members and the permission to continue living as autonomous and independent communities. In exchange they agreed to hunt down and turn in future maroons in exchange for payment or arms (Debbash 1962: 188). French authorities were almost driven to the same extremity in Saint Domingue when the maroon community of Le Maniel that had survived a century of pursuits could not be dislodged from valuable territory the French wanted to settle. In the end, the maroons of Le Maniel broke the treaty by refusing to relocate to another part of the island. They did, however, keep their promise not to make incursions into the French colony and to return fugitive slaves for a payment of fifty écus each (Debbash 1979: 145–48). It was profoundly humiliating for colonial authorities to be forced to accept the maroons' liberty and autonomy on the margins of the plantation regime.

Disagreement about the causes of *marronnage* has produced inflamed debate among historians. While all historians agree that slaves fled from plantations as a result of poor nourishment, cruelty, exhaustion from work, and fear of capital punishment, they are profoundly divided about the importance that should be given to the slaves' desire for freedom. A number of French as well as Haitian historians known as *l'Ecole haïtienne* agree that it is the slaves' innate desire for freedom that led them to desert the plantations and thus protest against slavery (Fouchard 1972: 165–66).[4] A powerful argument supporting this hypothesis is the historical finding that humane masters were generally plagued with more cases of *marronnage* than were cruel ones (165–66). Poor treatment alone does not seem to solely account for the motivation behind *marronnage*. In his autobiographical *Narrative of the Life of Frederick Douglass an American Slave,* Frederick Douglass ([1845] 1968: 103–4) argues that his desire for freedom was actually spurred by the improvement of his physical conditions:

> I have observed this in my experience of slavery,—that whenever my condition was improved, instead of its increasing my

contentment, it only increased my desire to be free, and set me
to thinking of plans to gain my freedom. I have found that, to
make a contented slave, it is necessary to make a thoughtless
one. It is necessary to darken his moral and mental vision, and,
as far as possible, to annihilate the power of reason. He must be
able to detect no inconsistencies in slavery; he must be made to
feel that slavery is right; and he can be brought to that only
when he ceases to be a man.

The deep-rooted desire for freedom was an integral part of the
slaves' humanity. Only by physically and morally turning
slaves into beasts could this desire be suffocated.

One of the leading French historians on *marronnage* during
the 1960s and still an authority on the question, Yvan Debbash (1961: 10–52) fundamentally calls into question the importance of the slaves' desire for freedom. He believes the
influence of French philanthropic ideals, the fear of capital
punishment, and the desire for improved working conditions
to be the principle cause of *marronnage*. Debbash's claims are
in line with the colonialist perspective that slaves were so in-
nately inferior and uncivilized that they could not possibly
harbor the lofty ideal of liberty. Only Europeans could instill
such sentiments in the barbaric Africans.

Even beyond the debate surrounding the historical causes of
marronnage, the figure of the maroon is profoundly ambiguous. Marginal to the plantation economy, maroons nonetheless maintained a relationship with plantation slaves in order
to secure basic food items and tools for their survival. Their rejection of colonial order was therefore never as complete as
represented through mythicization. In particular, their negotiation of treaties with colonial authorities—particularly in Jamaica and Suriname—undermined the very symbol of liberty
for which they stood. Willing to hunt down and turn in future
fugitives in exchange for the guarantee of freedom and autonomy, established maroon bands ended up aiding the colonial regime rather than contributing to its overthrow (Burton
1997: 33).

Nonetheless, the very idea that slaves could escape the dominion of slaveholders was, and continues to be even today, a
powerful symbol of subversion. The Guadeloupean thinker
Alain Yacou (1984: 92) points to the political, social, economic, and cultural potential of maroon communities:

In Cuba, as in other countries of plantation America, these maroon societies have through their very existence constituted an

important factor of subversion of colonial order by offering a sure refuge and a sanctuary of liberty to fugitive slaves. They constituted a basis for collective military, political, socioeconmic, and cultural resistance to the oppression of the slave regime.

It is this subversive potential that dominates eighteenth-century literary representations of the maroon. Regardless of whether they saw maroons in a positive or negative light, French writers believed maroons considerably impacted the plantation economy.

Violent Revenge

Eighteenth-century thinkers were keenly aware of the violence inherent to the master/slave relationship in the Caribbean. The voices they gave to their literary figures provide invaluable insight into how the memory of such violent rebellion was formed during the Enlightenment. Since there are no known written or oral records left by the maroons in the French Caribbean, these literary figures provide at least partial access to the formation of the myth surrounding the maroon. While these fictional documents cannot by any means claim to provide historical knowledge of maroon communities, they do accurately reveal the French public's reaction to the phenomenon of slave violence. Through their fictive characters, French writers gave a voice to the fears prevailing in continental France. Imaginary maroons largely contributed to the evolving relationship between the French and their projected image of African slaves. They participated in the elaboration of a myth that continues to have a strong hold in France and even more so in the French Caribbean. The numerous statues of maroons erected in Martinique during the past two decades are certainly in part a response to these early literary images.

Violence dominates the following literary portrayals of the maroon: Jean-François Saint-Lambert's *Ziméo* ([1769] 1883), Louis-Sébastien Mercier's *L'an deux mille quatre cent quarante* (1773), Abbé Raynal's *Histoire des deux Indes* ([1770, 1774, 1780] 1981), and French novelist Abbé Prévost's *Le pour et le contre* (1735). The uncompromising revolt against the master that can take the form of total war until the extinction of the oppressor is endemic to the colonial situation. The Tunisian writer Albert Memmi (1985: 143–44) sees no way out of what he calls the "infernal circle" of colonialism than the breaking off of all relations through revolt. According to Fanon (1991: 65–82), a compromise between colonizer and colonized is not possible. The origin of this violent relationship is linked to the subhuman position in which the oppressed are maintained. As the Martinican writer and politician Aimé Césaire (1955: 19) points out, the colonized are turned into objects through the very process of colonization. Bereft of their humanity, they have nothing more to lose and take up arms. This deadly confrontation allows them to reaffirm their humanity, insists Fanon (1991: 67–73). In order to declare their rights, they must declare war (Foucault 1997: 64).

Beyond the basic premise that the master/slave relationship inherently called for rebellion, the literary portrayals of maroons vary considerably in terms of the scope and ultimate goal of their characters' violence. The overriding element of revenge is present in varying degrees. While some literary maroons are intent only upon avenging themselves, others are more concerned with the creation of an autonomous community on the margins of the plantation regime. Some literary portrayals focus on the devastating role of Europeans while others more adequately represent the concerns of the maroons. This analysis is organized from the most negative, violent, and stereotypical portrayal of the maroon who is capable of nothing more than revenge, to the most positive portrayal of the maroon as the founder of freedom, independence, and autonomy from the colonial system.

Saint-Lambert's *Ziméo* (50–53), a short story published in 1769, takes place in Jamaica and is based upon a maroon revolt led by Ziméo, or John. The most interesting aspect of the short story is Ziméo's address to the narrator and to the narrator's friend both of whom are sympathetic to the slaves' cause. After a violent rebellion, before the spectacle of massacred white men, women, and children who have been hung from trees, Ziméo explains the causes for his wrath: "I avenged my race and myself ... do not avert your hearts from the unfortunate Ziméo; do not be horror-stricken by the blood that covers me; it is the blood of the wicked. It is in order to terrify the wicked that I do not limit my vengeance." Ziméo's violence is solely driven by the desire for revenge and by the conviction that he is acting in the name of justice, specifically of divine justice: "Oh, great Orissa, God of blacks and whites! You who made the souls, look at these good men and punish the barbarians who despise us and treat us as we would not even treat our animals." Ziméo acts in the name of God to punish those who deserve it. An instrument of divine justice, Ziméo embodies judgment day for the Europeans rather than liberation for himself and his people. In fact, Ziméo describes the unsatisfying nature of his drive for blood and revenge:

> The Negro, born to love, when forced to hate becomes a tiger and a leopard and I have become that. I am the leader of a people, I am rich, and yet I spend my days grieving. I regret those whom I have lost.... However, after having shed tears, I often feel the need to shed some blood, to hear the screams of the whites having their throats slit. Well, I just satisfied ... this awful need and the blood, the screams still embitter my despair.

His violent acts do not give Ziméo any sense of relief. Even his maroon community does not embody a satisfying alternative to slavery since he is not able to construct a new life for himself, separate from the world of the plantation. As he takes revenge on his former oppressor, Ziméo remains enslaved to the anger the whites instilled in him.

The literary portrayal of Ziméo corresponds more closely to the stereotypical, negative image of the Africans' violent nature than to the idealized myth of the maroon as a founding father of nationhood, so cherished by West Indians today. There is nothing noble and awe-inspiring about this character who asks the narrator to take pity upon him. Freedom, one of the major positive attributes of maroon communities, is entirely absent from Ziméo's narrative. The maroon character's sole purpose in this short story seems to be the divinely inspired punishment of European slaveholders.

Mercier's (1773: 168–70) "avenger of the New World" has a similar role, however, on a much larger scale. In his futuristic novel *L'an deux mille quatre cent quarante,* Mercier envisions the complete reversal of power in the New World. This overthrow is realized under the leadership of a black hero who—under divine guidance—frees the oppressed and wipes out their former tormentors: "I left the square when on my right I noticed a Negro, the head bare, the arm raised, the eye proud, the attitude noble and imposing on a magnificent pedestal. Around him were the fragments of twenty scepters. At his feet one could read the words: 'To the avenger of the New World!'" (168). Remarkable about this fictive black hero is the fact that he is both physically and symbolically raised above the Europeans whose symbols of power he has shattered. Depicted with pride and nobility, characteristics almost never attributed to Africans, he plays a positive role from the start in this brief episode.

However, the surprisingly affirmative portrayal of this black leader is largely divorced from reality since he is part of an idealized world. His surreal bearing is enhanced by the fact that the reader is presented with a statue rather than with a character who is flesh and blood. This hero has the immortality of mythological demigods and his heroic semblance does not correspond to that of common mortals: "Nature finally created this amazing man, this immortal man who was to deliver a world from the most atrocious, the longest, and the most insulting tyranny. His genius, his audacity, his patience, his steadfastness, his virtuous vengeance have been rewarded: he broke the chains of his compatriots" (169). "The avenger of the New World" is much more than a simple hero who rose from the state of servitude to fight for freedom. His immortality gives him a mythical dimension that corresponds well with the myth the maroon leader has become today: everything about him is admirable.

While the myth surrounding the avenger is in keeping with contemporary portrayals of the maroon, the religious overtones are not. Mercier's liberator is likened to a God: "This heroic avenger liberated a world of which he is the God and the other paid him homage and awarded him crowns" (169–170). At this point the avenger completely loses his human qualities as he enters into direct communion with God who has sent him into the world as his servant: "He came like a thunderstorm that spreads out over a criminal city struck by lightening. He was the exterminating angle whom the God of justice gave his sword" (170). The avenger has become an instrument of divine punishment. He does not act on his own accord in pursuit of freedom for himself and his people. As a result, he does not incarnate the ideals the people of the Caribbean project upon their maroon heroes today. As with *Ziméo,* the focus here is on the deserved punishment of Europeans:

> So many slaves oppressed by the most odious slavery seemed to only be waiting for his signal to turn into heroes. The torrent breaking the dike and lightening striking has a less rapid and violent effect. In an instant, they shed the blood of their tyrants. The French, the Spaniards, the English, the Dutch, the Portuguese all fell prey to arms, to poison, and to flames. America's soil avidly drank the blood it had long awaited, and the bones of their ancestors whose throats were cut in a cowardly way seemed to rise and quiver with joy (169).

Vengeance is unrelenting as the wrath of God is unleashed upon the Europeans. Even though the slaves are but instruments in the hands of God, they are again associated with extreme violence. This was generally the case during the eighteenth century. The positive outcome of the episode is limited to the successful punishment of slaveholders and the reestablishment of justice in the Americas. The essential elements of freedom and self-liberation play no role in this divine plot.

In the *Histoire des deux Indes,* Denis Diderot—writing passages of this work in collaboration with the Abbé Raynal ([1770, 1774, 1780] 1981: 201–2)[5]—uses Louis-Sébastien Mercier's description of the African demigod while considerably changing the tone of the slaves' revenge. In the context of elaborate emancipation plans that would gradually free the slaves over a period of one or two generations, Diderot suddenly prophesizes the slaves' self-liberation under the leadership of a great man, called the "Black Spartacus" in the second edition of the *Histoire des deux Indes.* Although the passage is borrowed almost verbatim from Mercier's *L'an deux mille quatre cent quarante,* the focus of the slave revolt is no longer religious. Diderot's black hero symbolizes freedom rather than divine punishment: "Where is he, this great man nature owes its offended, oppressed, and tormented children? Where is he? There is no doubt that he will appear, he will show himself, and he will raise the sacred flag of liberty. This venerable symbol will assemble around him the companions of his misfortune." Diderot turns the statue in Mercier's futuristic novel into a powerful prophecy, especially given the historical context of Saint Domingue. Only ten years later, under the leadership of Toussaint Louverture, the greatest slave rebellion in the Caribbean eventually led to the creation of the first Black Republic in 1804. Diderot's "Black Spartacus" has little in common with Mercier's "avenger." His strength comes from nature rather than from God and in his greatness he never ceases to be mortal. While the "avenger" uses his God-given power to liberate his people, the "Black Spartacus" is responsible for inspiring his companions to fight among themselves for their freedom: "the Negroes are only missing a leader who is courageous enough to lead them to vengeance and carnage." This he will do by raising the flag of liberty as a symbol of their rebellion. And it is strengthened by this ideal, rather than by God that the slaves will take revenge upon their oppressors:

> More impetuous than the torrents, they will leave the indelible traces of their just resentment. The Spaniards, the Portuguese, the English, the French, the Dutch, all their tyrants will fall prey

to arms and flames. The American fields will become intoxicated with transports of delight by the blood they awaited for so
long. The bones of so many wretched piled up for three centuries will quiver with joy.

This passage is almost identical to Mercier's in terms of the very
graphic description of violence. Again, bloody revenge is the
only option for the slaves whose violence feeds into the Europeans' fears. However, while Mercier's rebellion does little more
than symbolize judgment day for the Europeans, Diderot's rebellion ends with philosophical idealism: "The Old World will
join the New World in applause. The name of the hero who will
have reestablished human rights will be blessed and memorials glorifying him will be erected everywhere. The *Code Noir*
will then disappear and the *Code Blanc* will be terrible if the
conquerors only take reprisals!" The slaves' rebellion is placed
in a humanitarian context that reaches beyond the confines
of the Caribbean. It is of fundamental concern to Europe as
well, not just because of the dangerous violence but also because the violation of the slaves' rights has implications for
humanity in general. The "Black Spartacus" is not only a hero
for his companions but also for people everywhere. While
vengeance stands out as one of the principle motivations underlying the slave rebellion, the passage leaves open the possibility for the slaves to go beyond their desire for revenge once
they have vanquished their former oppressors. They will not
necessarily establish a *Code Blanc* that reflects all the barbarity
of the *Code Noir*. This portrays their self-determination. As opposed to Ziméo and also to Mercier's "avenger," the "Black
Spartacus" and his fellow companions are not forcefully governed by an unending thirst for the Europeans' blood. Although Diderot does not describe the creation of a new and
independent community, the slave rebellion is not simply the
"reversal of domination," and passive in its outcome (Foucault
1976: 126). It at least contains the potential of novelty and
change.

The most positive and constructive portrayal of a maroon
leader appears in the first French literary rendition of a slave
rebellion published in 1735 by the Abbé Prévost in *Le pour et
le contre*. According to literary critic Russell Parsons Jameson,
Prévost published the "Harangue (supposée) d'un chef nègre"
in response to the 1734 slave revolt in Jamaica. In his introduction, Prévost explained that he was merely translating a
text published in London by an Englishman who had recently

returned from Jamaica. Given the curiosity awakened in England by this document that may or may not have been the authentic discourse of Moses Bom Saam, the maroon leader of the revolted Jamaican slaves, Prévost wanted to satisfy his French readers with a translation (qtd. in Jameson 1911: 206–7).

In his literary role, the historical figure of the maroon leader Moses Bom Saam, who succeeded Cudjoc in Jamaica, takes on the heroic importance of the maroon, seeker of liberty for all (Duchet 1971: 139). Most remarkable is that the literary figure Moses Bom Saam is already free at the moment he addresses his companion slaves, as his master emancipated him in return for saving his life. Nonetheless, he is drawn to his brothers who are still suffering: "I did not find any pleasure in freedom because I ceased to participate in your misery by becoming free" (qtd. in Jameson 1911: 207). In spite of his freedom, Moses Bom Saam dedicates his life to the liberty of his kin whom he wants to lead into the freedom of *marronnage* in the mountains of Jamaica. Like Moses, the liberator of the Israelites from Egyptian slavery, Moses Bom Saam wants to liberate blacks from the yoke he came to comprehend during his ten years of freedom: "While I was like you, vile and miserable together with my brothers, I did not have enough awareness to reflect on my wretched fate. However, ten years of liberty have given me the ability to judge for myself" (207). Moses Bom Saam's words confirm the notion that slaves became painfully conscious of their yearning for freedom once their misery was alleviated. The black chief explains to his brothers that their rebellion is just and right as God created all men equal. He gives Moses as an example of God's will to end slavery. However, he adds that he and his brothers have been very cowardly to put up with the horrors of slavery and to leave behind descendants who will inherit all this misery. He therefore encourages them to end their suffering now by becoming maroons.

Two of the most notable aspects of Moses Bom Saam's vision are the absence of vengeance and the establishment of autonomous and lawful order. In this regard he differs considerably from Ziméo, the "avenger of the New World," and the "Black Spartacus." Moses Bom Saam does not encourage a bloody rebellion for the sake of vengeance but focuses on the ideal of liberty itself: "Let us think less of avenging our past suffering than of laying the foundation of our freedom and peace." It is through discipline, organization, and hard labor that the leader envisions the possibility of founding a community: "Let us take possession of this vast terrain that we will henceforth share.... Let us cultivate our land ... for ourselves and for posterity. But let us first establish laws which we will cultivate with no less ardor" (Jameson 1911: 211). It is not as outcasts that Moses Bom Saam envisions their *marronnage* but rather as founders of a new lineage, living in freedom but also in social order.

Physical liberty for this hero is a vehicle for attaining the much greater and longer-lasting mental freedom that accompanies those who live with integrity:

> They may despise us; they may think we are weak and miserable. As long as they leave us enough time to establish our new State on a solid foundation, the structure will grow. You will give it a shape that will one day earn respect and admiration. And you can be sure that sooner or later your enemies will embrace you despite your color and that they will find your friendship interesting and comforting (Jameson 1911: 212).

Moses Bom Saams's ideal of liberty goes far beyond the immediate physical conditions of slavery, encompassing the larger issue of human dignity. His heroic example feeds the myth of the maroon in whom Caribbean nations today can identify a past worthy of memory. The originality of this text lies in the creation of a new and autonomous community—even a State— that is separate from colonial order. Moses Bom Saam does not aspire to destroy his oppressors with "arms, flames, and poison," as do the "avenger" and the "Black Spartacus." His goal is not the reversal of power, or to use Foucault's (1976: 126–27) words a "great, radical rupture," but rather the strengthening of "multiple points of resistance" against the whites. He plans to have the maroons strengthen their forces to render themselves fearsome. They will creatively use all the materials and strategies at their disposition to develop and acquire arms for their defense, and they will cultivate their land to become independent from the whites. When they have needs they cannot fulfill otherwise, they will plunder the plantations. In general, however, they will engage in exchanges of merchandise (qtd. in Jameson 1911: 210–11). Moses Bom Saam does not see the blacks' salvation in total destruction but rather in the intelligent use of force to resist the plantation regime and to found an independent community. It is the strategic resistance rather than the use of brute force that distinguishes Moses Bom Saam from the other literary maroons. He is the closest model for the contemporary ideal of the maroon hero, founder of freedom and independence from the colonial regime.

The literary maroons suggest that even during the eighteenth century, French thinkers perceived maroons as the vanguard of the slaves' self-liberation. As Michèle Duchet (1971: 139) argues in *Anthrophologie et histoire au siècle des lumières,* the maroon dominates the literary imagination from 1730 onward: "the Negro is no longer a touching character, he has become a heroic figure who asserts his human dignity through his noble attitude and his refusal of injustice. He is a revolted man who makes his appearance on the historical scene and in the collective consciousness." The contemporary myth surrounding the figure of the maroon is to some extent inherited from the eighteenth century. Literary portrayals reveal the power attributed to maroon leaders. They were perceived as a potentially destructive force against which the colonial regime was powerless. Despite the generalized belief in the slaves' innate inferiority, maroon leaders seemed to escape such stereotypes and stood out as noble, superhuman or even divine individuals. Some portrayals—such as that of Ziméo—fed the Europeans' fears and perpetrated an ambivalent attitude toward Africans. Others represented maroons in a positive light that transformed negative stereotypes. In all cases, violence and revenge appeared to be the inevitable result of the atrocities perpetrated by Europeans for the past three hundred years. Moses Bom Saam is the only literary maroon whose goals reached far beyond mere revenge and who proposed the type of successful maroon community that has become a symbol of the slaves' capacity for self-determination. He most directly contributed to the memory of the maroon as a key figure of slave resistance.

"Civilizing" the Maroon

While some eighteenth-century literary portrayals of maroons contributed to their mythical image as founders of Caribbean nationhood, others systematically transformed maroons into docile, submissive, and "civilized" individuals who became mouthpieces for European values. Slave violence is denounced in these portrayals as entirely counterproductive. Even when slaves have successfully freed themselves or joined maroon bands they are encouraged to go back to their masters to receive their pardons and to wait for them to benevolently emanci-

pate them. Freedom is closely associated with French humanitarianism and as such cannot be self-obtained by beings whose
enslavement has made them vile and degraded. Only through
the transformative contact with enlightened intelligence,
virtue, and humanity is emancipation possible since the debased, savage, and undeveloped African slaves need to first
learn the rudiments of European civilization before they can
be entrusted with the responsibility of freedom.

The following three works are striking examples of the "civilized" maroon: Gabriel Mailhol's *Le philosophe nègre,* a prose
text written in 1764; Olympe de Gouges' *L'esclavage des noirs*
([1786] 1994), performed in 1789; and finally Pigault-Lebrun's
Le blanc et le noir, performed in 1796. Each of these works reflects the sociohistorical context within which it was written.
The passage of Mailhol's text set in the Americas specifically
treats the problem of maroon bands that were of primary concern around the middle of the century. Olympe de Gouges's
play was performed during the French Revolution, and reflects
on the question of liberty and the process of slave emancipation. Finally, the pervasiveness of slave violence in the colonies
after 1789, and the emancipation of slaves in 1793 change the
focus of Pigault-Lebrun's play. The author centers no longer on
liberty itself, but on the possibility of maintaining the economic wealth of the colonies with the black laborers' help.

The earliest of the three texts, *Le philosophe nègre* does not
share the sentimentality of the two plays. Mailhol, the author
of several comedies and whimsical novels, seems to take his
inspiration from Voltaire's *Candide* ([1759] 1973). The protagonist Tintillo, an African prince, experiences numerous adven-
tures during his travels throughout Africa and the rest of the
world. He recounts his life to the narrator, whom he meets in
Germany. The tone is similar to Voltaire's irony, halfway between indignation and joke, as he recounts the wars and su-
perstitions of the blacks as well as the brutality and injustice of
the Europeans (R. Mercier 1962b: 199).

At one point during his travels in the Americas, Tintillo,
having become a slave himself, saves his white master from
the bloody vengeance of a maroon band by making a speech.
Putting himself into the position of the maroons by using the
"we" form to underline the affinity between him and them,
Tintillo initially expresses his comprehension of the maroons'
motives to desert the plantations and to find freedom in the
forest. However, he then goes on to justify their initial enslavement in Africa, claiming that their lives were spared after a

lost battle between African kingdoms, an argument typically used by proslavery advocates. This argument allows him to defend the white colonial viewpoint that censures *marronnage* and slave violence:

> Having become our masters through the sacrifice of a part of their fortune in order not to work themselves, the whites demand that through our labor we bring in a profit. Those of us who have refused to comply with this responsibility have, I believe, become guilty of theft.... Several of us have left homes where they were well nourished, where they had a bed and women. They have come to roam the forests.... Sometimes without food they are forced to become bandits and often murderers (Mailhol 1764: 83).

A mouthpiece for European values, Tintillo stays within the ideological framework of colonialism. He depicts the state of servitude in a positive light, offering all the necessary comforts. *Marronnage*, on the other hand, is a return to chaos and barbarism that can only lead to a miserable death since maroons "end their dismal days shot like wild boars or caught and beaten like assassins" (Mailhol 1764: 81). Their separation from the civilization that reigns on the plantation has brought maroons nothing but misfortune.

Speaking very fondly of his own French master, whom he cherishes like a father, Tintillo encourages the maroons to envision the advantages that a return to their plantations—under the protection of his master—would bring them: "You would probably be satisfied to be pardoned.... And I am certain that you would be delighted to occupy yourself again since it is the fate of men.... In due time you will merit that a good master, satisfied by your services, emancipate you, help you, marry you and maybe even enrich you" (Mailhol 1764: 83). The maroons are encouraged to willingly return to slavery in order to merit their emancipation through obedience, work, and compliance to the colonial regime. Benevolently emancipated, these blacks would not—like maroons—live at the margins of the white man's world. They would become completely integrated into the colonial system to which they would have become perfectly adapted.

Tintillo gives a voice to French colonialist ideology. The colonized were encouraged to become assimilated to the French through meritorious behavior and by learning and adopting the essence of French civilization. Their individual difference was to be reduced as completely as possible. In this regard, the figure of the maroon presented a formidable challenge to the colonial system since maroons escaped from the control of their masters and could potentially represent a subversive force. Successful maroon communities managed to live on the margins of the plantations, unsettling the order of the slave regime through their regular incursions. Though historically speaking maroons often lived in symbiosis with the plantation regime, the very idea that blacks could live independently and autonomously had a profound impact on the European imagination. A text such as that of Mailhol was essential in the process of countering and even destroying this powerful image of the maroon.

As opposed to *Le philosophe nègre,* Olympe De Gouges's play *L'esclavage des noirs* ([1786] 1994) presents a much more progressive portrayal of the relationship between slaves and their masters. In many ways it even revolutionized antislavery writings. De Gouges's outspokenness in favor of people whom she considered deserving of freedom represents a breakthrough at a time when Africans were increasingly linked to evil, savagery, and evolutional inferiority. At the same time, her positive portrayal of black slaves perpetuated a paternalism that made slaves the passive recipients of France's enlightened humanity and justice. While glorifying the abolitionary potential of enlightened thought, De Gouges denied the slaves' own tradition of resistance and revolt.

De Gouges was the first playwright to have the audacity of upholding the cause of a slave who had killed a white man. The power of the play's sociopolitical impact is evidenced by the fact that white colonists successfully opposed its performance. *L'esclavage des noirs,* originally written in 1783 as an "Indian drama" set in the East Indies, was rewritten with black slave protagonists and set in the West Indies only to be performed three times by the *Comédie Française* in December 1789 before it was prohibited by the police tribunal. According to white colonists, the play dangerously focused the attention of the public on the fate of slaves in the colonies. During the turbulent times of the French Revolution, it was in the colonists' best interest to silence compromising support for abolitionism. Beyond the resistance of the colonists, De Gouges was faced with the actors' outright opposition to perform a play they believed would incite slave rebellion in the colonies. As a result of its successful silencing, *L'esclavage des noirs* never became popular. Its apparent failure was generally blamed on the play's excessively melodramatic style and its political nature rather than on the concerted efforts of colonists to prevent the play from reaching a wider audience (Welschinger 1880: 15; R. Mercier 1962a: 186; Carlson 1966: 148; Halpern 1993: 410; Kadish and Massardier-Kenney 1994: 66).

Set on two unspecified islands in the West Indies, *L'esclavage des noirs* is divided into three acts. The first act is set on a deserted island where the two slave protagonists, the educated Zamor and his lover Mirza, are hiding from colonial authorities who are looking for Zamor in order to execute him. Zamor is to be punished for having killed the white intendant of the island in order to save Mirza from the wrath of this jealous man. While Zamor and Mirza are hiding, a ship is wrecked on the island and Zamor saves the young French woman Sophie from drowning. Sophie and her fiancé Valère, who has also escaped the shipwreck, are forever grateful to Zamor for his valorous act. At the end of the first act, the colonial authorities find Zamor and Mirza. Accompanied by Valère and Sophie who will not leave them, they are brought back to the main island. In acts II and III, Valère and Sophie try to convince the colonial authorities to release Zamor. It isn't until the very end of act III that the French governor of the island, M. de Saint-Frémont, discovers that Sophie is his long lost daughter. Moved by this reunion and by his daughter's pleas, he finally decides to exonerate Zamor for his crime.

De Gouges's ([1786] 1994: 247) positive portrayal of slaves enters into a paternalistic dynamic in which slaves emulate the civilization and humanity of their French masters whom they profoundly revere. Educated by the governor of the island, Zamor is a prime example of this relationship, as the slave Coraline points out to her fellow slaves:

> Did Zamor not have his freedom? Did he for that reason want to leave our good master? We will all do the same thing. The masters should give us our freedom; no slave will leave the plantations. Even the most savage among us will imperceptibly become educated, will recognize the laws of humanity and of justice and our superiors will find in our attachment, in our zeal, the reward of their kindness.

Although Zamor's crime has turned him into a rebel, it is circumstances rather than his inner nature that led him to this violent act. Everything about Zamor's demeanor and speech is civilized and submissive to French ideology. When Valère points out the goodness of the French: "If [the governor of this island] is French, he must be human and generous," Zamor quickly responds: "Yes, Sir, he is French and the best of men" (De Gouges [1786] 1994: 242). Other slaves echo Zamor's viewpoint: "How [our governor] is good to us! All the French are the same" (245).

The governor is taken as a model for all French people who, it is maintained throughout the play, are keenly interested in abolishing slavery. Education, civilization and freedom are closely linked together and all emanate from France. Zamor explains to Mirza how slaves will one day receive the gift of freedom from France: "Perhaps our fate will change soon. A gentle and comforting moral doctrine is knocking down the veil of error in Europe. Enlightened men are watching us tenderly: we will owe them the return of this precious liberty" (De Gouges [1786] 1994: 238). A former slave himself, Zamor expresses his deep-set belief in the transformative power of France's enlightened ideology. This paternalistic benevolence is reiterated on two more occasions. Valère explains to the slaves that "the French see slavery with horror" (241) while M. de Saint-Frémont expresses his belief in Europe's engagement to end slavery: "Europe ... is careful to justify [the voice of humanity], and I dare hope that soon there will be no more slaves. O Louis! O beloved Monarch! Why can I not at this moment bring before you the innocence of these outlaws!" (252). Freedom will undoubtedly originate in France and will be bestowed upon the slaves. Born during the Enlightenment, this image of France as liberator has become deeply engrained in the memory of the French and of French West Indians alike. The historical reality of a slavery that was imposed by European nations is completely divorced from the belief in the liberating power of enlightened ideology and humanitarianism.

In keeping with this image, De Gouges severely condemns slave rebellions in the name of freedom. One of Europe's greatest fears in regards to slavery was the danger of uncontrollable slave revolts that could lead to the massive massacres of whites as well as to the destruction of the colonial system. As a result of this constant danger of violent outbreaks, antislavery advocates such as De Gouges encountered considerable resistance to the advancement of their ideas. This no doubt contributed to De Gouges's insistence on the slaves' incapacity to free themselves through rebellion. It is primarily Zamor who voices these views at the beginning and at the end of the play. In the first scene, he shares his thoughts about the utter debasement of slaves with Mirza: "If our eyes were to open, we would find the state to which our [barbarian masters] reduced us horrible and we might shake a yoke which is as cruel as it is humiliating; but is it in our power to change our fate? Degraded by slavery, man has lost all his energy" (De Gouges [1786] 1994: 237–38). Zamor doubts the slaves' capacity to rebel against their cruel masters since slavery has weakened their potential resolve. Toward the very end of the play, just prior to his announced execution, Zamor vehemently advocates nonviolence for the good of the colony. Addressing himself to the slaves he says: "And you, my dear friends, listen to me during my last moment. I leave life, I die innocently; but be careful not to make yourselves guilty by defending me ... never engage in excessive behavior to end slavery; do not break your chains with too much violence; await everything from time and divine justice" (262). By having an educated slave express his refusal of violence, De Gouges argues for the peaceful resolution of injustice in the colonies. Surprisingly, she does not reiterate her belief that the ideals of the Enlightenment will bring change. At this point, she leaves it up to time and divine justice to take things in hand. In the face of death, the optimistic belief in the power of ideals is suspended, only to return again in the last words of the play uttered by the governor:

> My friends, I come to give you my pardon. I wish I could free all slaves, or at least improve their lot! Slaves ... you must know that even free, man must still be submitted to wise and humane laws ... without engaging in reprehensible excesses, hope everything [will come] from an enlightened and benevolent government. Come on, my friends, my children, may a general feast be the happy omen of this gentle liberty (De Gouges [1786] 1994: 265).

Unable to free his slaves—for reasons that are unclear since he has considerable power as governor of the island—M. de Saint-Frémont gives a paternal twist to Zamor's words. In addition, he gives the enlightened French government the benefit of the doubt: freedom will unmistakably originate in France, not in violent rebellion.

By the end of the play, the only thing that is achieved is the exoneration of Zamor for his crime. Even though the need for freedom is talked about at great length, it is eventually only the promise of justice that remains. The slaves have been taught that they must patiently and nonviolently submit themselves to France's just and humane laws and hope to someday benefit from their exemplary behavior. In the mean-

time, their master's generous paternalism includes them in a
grand feast to celebrate this future event while they remain
slaves and their sorry fate prevails.

Ironically, the course of history disproved De Gouges's ideal
portrayal of nonviolent slaves. The outbreak of widespread rebellion in Saint Domingue, two years after the presentation of
L'esclavage des noirs at the *Comédie Française,* prompted De
Gouges's address in the preface of her 1792 publication of the
play: "It is to you, slaves and people of color, that I will speak
now; I may have incontestable rights to blame your ferocity:
cruel and imitating your tyrants, you justify them.... Human
beings were not born for chains and you prove that they are
necessary" (De Gouges [1786] 1994: 233–34). For De Gouges,
as for most abolitionists, violent rebellion was not an option.
The deliberate rejection of the right to self-liberation undermined slaves as makers of their own history; they were reduced to passive, docile, and submissive recipients of French
benevolence. The problem with De Gouges's philanthropic idealism, however, is that it proposed no practical plan for
change. This is a general trend in antislavery writing. While
magnifying the humanitarian potential of the Enlightenment,
De Gouges successfully drew the public's attention to the injustice perpetrated across the Atlantic. Yet, her play ultimately
did little more than further the status quo. With divine intervention, time, and the compassion of enlightened French
thinkers, De Gouges's slave characters—mouthpieces of French
ideals—could only patiently hope one day to be freed or at
least to be treated less cruelly.

The latest and most sentimental of the three literary pieces
is Pigault-Lebrun's *Le blanc et le noir,* performed in 1796 at the
Théâtre de la Cité (R. Mercier 1962a: 193). Similarly to
L'esclavage des noirs it was very badly received and the author
withdrew it after the third performance. Already in his preface,
Pigault-Lebrun expresses his indebtedness to the Abbé Raynal:
"J'ai lu Raynal, et j'ai écrit cet ouvrage" (qtd. in Seeber 1937:
183). However, his sentimentality did not appeal to the public
the way in which Raynal's impassioned monologues did. Set in
a plantation of the Americas, the play depicts the relationship
between the slave protagonist Télémaque and the planter's
son Beauval fils. Disillusioned with his privileged situation
that nonetheless keeps him enslaved, Télémaque plans a slave
revolt and succeeds. Finally, he is moved to spare Beauval père
and agrees to return to the plantation as a free worker.

Similarly to Tintillo and Zamor, Télémaque opposes European civilization and humanitarianism to the lowliness, stupidity, and senseless violence of slaves. They are dependent on the Europeans' goodwill to reach a state of humanity that renders them capable of freedom. It is only through the intervention of Beauval fils that Télémaque is able to overcome his instinctive animalistic qualities and become human:

> Ranked among domestic animals I had acquired their blind submissiveness, their stupid vileness, I vegetated.... An unjust and cruel punishment awakened this dulled soul, a ray of light shed light on my unrecognized and violated rights. I gave in to the need to avenge my blood.... I threw down a barbarian, I grabbed his throat, and I was going to suffocate him. You appeared and snatched this monster from my hands ... surprised by the strong ideas that jostled about in my exalted head, these spirited thoughts common to all men, but that are erased by slavery and misfortune. You became interested in my fate and you were able to soften it.... You taught me to talk and to think, you turned me into a human being, and you acquired a friend (Pigault-Lebrun 1796: 3–4).

Télémaque describes himself as an animal that knows no other way to defend itself than by attacking and killing its aggressor, not unlike the maroons described by Tintillo in *Le philosophe nègre*. Télémaque is not capable of any reflection until Beauval fils teaches him the basic principles of humanity. Although as a slave hero Télémaque is endowed with the potential to rise above his condition, he can only successfully do so with the intervention, guidance, and teaching of a European. Rather than humanize him, his spontaneous and passionate reaction to injustice only serves to further entrench him in his debased state. This passage serves as a commentary on the violent slave rebellions in the colonies. Legitimated by the deep violation of the slaves' rights, these rebellions cannot lead to freedom. Only through the gradual process of civilization can slaves acquire the basic human tools necessary to the state of emancipation. As a result, they are entirely dependent on the goodwill of their masters who alone have the power to civilize and thus humanize them.

The binary opposition between the degraded black slaves and the enlightened and benevolent whites leads to a system of paternalistic emancipation that maintains firm control over the colonized subjects. This system hinders the slaves' creation of an independent identity or community separate from their masters'. Despite Télémaque's successful revolt, the colonist's authority prevails and the newly emancipated slaves become assimilated to their master's plantation. In a desperate effort to save his life from the wrath of the rebels, Beauval père manages to convince Télémaque and his companions to end the rebellion peaceably:

> If you spare my life I will spend the rest of my days assuring your happiness. Let us forget that there were a master and slaves on this plantation. Come my friends, start your fortune by helping me rebuild mine. My son, Télémaque … let us forget our past misfortunes, amid honest wealth and reciprocal trust, founded on esteem, recognition, love, and friendship (Pigault-Lebrun 1796: 92).

Even in the face of death, it is from a paternalistic standpoint that Beauval père addresses the slaves. The slaves may at that moment have the power to kill him, but they do not have the capacity to build anything without his help. He is the key to their future happiness and he must convince them of that in order to save his life. The suggestion that all forget the past and found a new community based on all the sentiments that were formerly impossible between master and slaves is a fundamental aspect of the process of assimilation. The corner stone of postslavery colonial society, the purposeful erasure of the past is present in all narratives aiming at a peaceful understanding between whites and blacks, including narratives by people of color and blacks.[6] It is the building block of the former slaves' assimilation to the French nation during the following two hundred years, leading to the present political status of Martinique, Guadeloupe and Guiana as France's overseas regions. The Martinican historian Myriam Cottias (2000: 96) speaks of the mechanism of forgetting put in place by the Republic on the occasion of the abolition of slavery in 1848: "The social cement and reconciliation" depend on this process. The exchange between Télémaque and his master already point the way to the historical process that turns slave rebels into "civilized," assimilated, and completely submissive children of the French motherland.

Although Télémaque has previously sworn "an implacable, eternal hate that wanted blood and that could not be assuaged by anything" (Pigault-Lebrun 1796: 83) he is willing to erase this past as he makes Beauval père's call for cooperative work his new motto:

Brave companions, let us hurry to prove to our enemies that laziness, banditry, and injustice did not place arms in our hands. Man was born for work. Let us return to the plain; let us fertilize the fields we just ravaged. May the example of Beauval, by enlightening the colonizers about their true interests, finally determine them to consolidate their fortune through justice and humanity (Pigault-Lebrun 1796: 92).

It is the plantation system that wins the battle, as the emancipated slaves choose to continue serving this system, even if it is in the position of so-called friends. Emancipation only succeeds when it is given, and when those who receive their freedom remain attached to their "benevolent" master. Liberation through violence is doomed to failure, as it aims at the overthrow of the colonizer. The colonized subjects cannot change their status; they can only hope for justice and humanity within the confines of a system that will always have the upper hand. Blacks were brought to the colonies to work the land, and the colonial system continues to reinforce the work ethic while humanitarian adjustments are made. Pigault-Lebrun's play primarily depicts the dangers colonists will face if they do not modify their tyrannical relationship with their slaves. Since the prosperity of the French colonies remains the final goal, recommendations are made on how to win the slaves' cooperation as laborers. The plantation system is finally saved and blacks have a chance to become civilized colonial subjects.

The three slave heroes Tintillo, Zamor, and Télémaque embody the vision of the ideal black leader. The positive representation of blacks reflects the general evolution of Africans in the European imagination, and is meant to create interest in the humanity of black slaves. Yet, a closer analysis of these *bons nègres* shows that they actually further the status quo of colonial dominance. The liberty these slaves talk about is conditional, given as a reward for dutiful work and total submission. This freedom is far from the ideal championed by Ziméo, the "avenger of the New World," the "Black Spartacus," and Moses Bom Saam. The revolted maroons aim at freedom through the complete overthrow of the system while the "civilized" maroons are willing to conciliate liberty and dependency upon the white master. The latter perpetuate the belief in the superiority of the benevolent, enlightened European system: freedom is not natural or inherent to slaves, but is a reward given in exchange for hard work. Mental freedom, expressed through autonomous resistance, leads nowhere and actually worsens the conditions of the slaves. They are only capable of violent acts and can only be entrusted with liberty once educated and civilized. Freedom is thus only attainable through the goodwill of the colonizer, not through self-determination.

The divergence between eighteenth-century portrayals of maroons corresponds to the ambiguous image of the revolted slave through the present. Even though during the past decade Martinicans and Guadeloupeans have erected numerous statues honoring the maroon, this positive attitude is a very recent phenomenon. In the West Indian cultural tradition, maroons have generally been attributed negative stereotypes. It isn't until the concerted efforts of intellectuals that the figure of the maroon has been given a positive dimension associated with the historical foundation of a West Indian identity. What little is known about maroons has often been mythicized through the literary imagination of contemporary authors such as Edouard Glissant. What is interesting about the eighteenth-century portrayals is their elaboration of some of the major themes that continue to be at the heart of the debate surrounding the abolition of slavery in 1848. To what extent can maroons be attributed an active role in the historical process leading to emancipation? Did their rebellion against colonial order constitute a major subversive force?

Violence is clearly at the core of all eighteenth-century literary portrayals. While some authors depict violence as the only way out of slavery, others warn against its ineffectiveness. Both viewpoints, however, are primarily a reflection on European beliefs and practices, rather than on the nature of slave rebellion. Those who favor revolt depict Europeans as deserving of violent destruction and killing. They do not believe in the Europeans' capacity to extend the ideals of the Enlightenment to colonial reality. Those who warn against violence, on the other hand, subscribe to the pervasive goodness of European education and civilization. Only assimilation to French values can resolve the slaves' miserable fate. While the former viewpoint is in accordance with the contemporary West Indian ideal of the noble maroon—founding father of Caribbean nationhood—the latter represents the dominant historical belief in France's supremacy during the abolitionary process and during the colonial era. The memory of the maroon that has prevailed until recently was largely born during the eighteenth century with narratives such as these. Assimilation to the French model of civilization was already then hailed as the panacea for colonial problems. The slaves' capacity for self-determination and autonomy was reduced and even entirely disregarded in the process. Chapter 3 offers a counterpoint to this perspective. It reveals the powerful forces surrounding the French Revolution as expressed in the narratives of French thinkers, of colonial planters, and most importantly of slaves.

Notes

1. See Burton (1997) and Ho-Fong-Choy Choucoutou (2000).
2. For the historians' debate see Debbash (1961, 1962, 1979); Fouchard (1972); Manigat (1977); Debien (1979); Geggus (1983); and Fick (1990).
3. "We prohibit ... all slaves from either sex to make or distribute any remedy ... and to undertake the healing of any illness, with the exception of snakebites. Offenders will be subject to corporal punishment and even the death sentence depending on the case" (ANF 27 AP 11, 1746).
4. For a succinct summary of these two perspectives in relationship to the Revolution in Saint Domingue see Burton (1997: 28–38).
5. See chapter 1, footnote 17 for references regarding Diderot's collaboration in the writing of the Abbé Raynal's *Histoire des deux Indes* ([1770, 1774, 1780] 1981).
6. While the two slave letters I analyze in chapter 3 have a rather independent, insubordinate, rebellious, and even aggressive tone, I have found writings by emancipated blacks that convey a political allegiance to France. Amid the turmoil of the Haitian Revolution the principal black leader Toussaint Louverture, and Jean-Baptiste Belley, the black deputy from Saint Domingue under the National Convention, urged their brothers in arms to stop their revolt and submit to France, a nation they described as a generous and sacrificing mother. See archival manuscript and printed sources for references to writings by Louverture and Belley.

CHAPTER 3

REALMS OF FREEDOM

"We the Negroes ... are ready to die for this freedom, for we want to and will obtain it at any price, even with the help of mortars, canons, and rifles" (ANF Colonies F3 29, 1789b). Martinican slaves declared their right to freedom in writing for the first time in August 1789, in a series of letters addressed to colonial administrators. Seeing that their demands went unheeded, they broke out into an insurrection several days later. The relationship between this historic episode and the narratives by the *Société des Amis des Noirs* and colonial planters that preceded and followed it provides unprecedented insight into how the memory of slavery was formed. A test of the Revolution's universalist claims, the colonial question reached its boiling point between 1789 and 1794 (Geggus 1989a: 1291). It is during this period that conflicting interests between slaves, free coloreds, white colonial planters, and French abolitionists clashed together, producing irreversible changes in the French colonies. A number of historians of French slavery deplore the absence of the colonial question in revolutionary historiography.[1] More importantly, the slaves' voices were covered up by more dominant narratives and have thus been lost as a testimony of their rightful share in these historical events.

In 1789, the philosophical condemnation of slavery and the active resistance of slaves in the West Indian sugar plantations converged for the first time. The *Société des Amis des Noirs* engaged in widely publicized written attacks on the institution of slavery and on the slave trade beginning in 1788.[2] At the same time, the August 1789 revolts of Martinican slaves initiated rebellion that went beyond the resistance of maroons, as it was aimed at changing the system in place.[3] Preceding their actions with several letters addressed to colonial authorities, the slaves made specific demands that slavery be ended. Though this particular revolt was unsuccessful, it was of paramount importance as an inspiration for further revolts on other Caribbean islands, in particular in Saint Domingue (Burton 1994: 25; Bénot 1995: 181–82; Geggus 1996: 282–85; 1997: 8). Taking issue with the philanthropic writings from both the metropolis and local insurgencies, white colonial planters decried the dangerous link between philosophical ideals and rebellious actions. For the first time in the history of French Caribbean slavery, philosophical debates were considered to have a historical impact, and slave actions were thought to be inspired by more than a mere desire for revenge.

The convergence of philosophical debate and slave rebellion during the 1789 insurrection in Martinique is an invaluable testimony to the nature of Caribbean history. This history, according to Edouard Glissant (1996: 59), consists of spreading rhizomes rather than of a single root. Like a rhizome, the slave letters and ensuing rebellion branched outward in relation to the narrative of the *Société des Amis des Noirs*. Taking their inspiration from the political pamphlets of the *Amis des Noirs,* the slaves did not, however, merely enact the *Amis des Noirs'* ideals. On the contrary, the slaves' demands for freedom have little in common with the *Amis des Noirs'* philosophical musings on the subject. While colonial white planters brought out the unusual convergence between slaves and abolitionists in their criticism of the insurrection, they failed to recognize the autonomy of the rebels. The slaves, they believed, did not act on their own accord, but followed the lead of the *Amis des Noirs* who instigated them to revolt. As a result of this reading of events, the slave revolt was seen as a mere outgrowth of French abolitionism rather than as an indigenous movement with its own motivation and logic. The slaves' agency was compromised by the planters' hegemonic vision of events that subsumed the revolt within the French abolitionary movement. Glissant (1981: 159) considers such a "univocal conception of History and thus of power" to be one of the most terrifying consequences of colonization. The hegemonic perspective of colonial history does not allow Caribbean nations to understand their past, since it erases their participation in historical events, as was the case with the 1789 slave rebellion in Martinique. The basis for forming a collective memory is jeopardized, as events are remembered from the perspective of those who dominated historic occurrences. The people cannot identify with this imposed story of the past and end up struggling with what Glissant (1981: 130–31) calls their "non-history."

The encounter between the two slave letters, the political pamphlets of the *Société des Amis des Noirs,* and the letters by colonial planters constitutes a realm of memory that stands in opposition to a single abolitionary origin. These new interpretations of the revolutionary period take into account the connections between traditionally dominating and completely marginalized and forgotten voices of the past. The resulting realm of memory thrives on the transformative influence these different testimonies have upon one another.

"They Are Intoxicated with Freedom"

"They are intoxicated with freedom," wrote colonial deputies from France to their compatriots in Saint Domingue on 12 August 1789 ("Correspondance secrète" [1793] 1968: 9). The revolutionary ideals of liberty and equality that abounded around 1789 had far-reaching effects not only on society in France, but also on colonial administration in the French colonies. Profoundly affected by these changes, the planters watched the increasing volume of philanthropic writings by the *Société des Amis des Noirs* in Paris as they worried about the fate of their plantations, entirely upheld by the labor of black slaves. Only two weeks later, a group of slaves from Martinique demanding to be immediately emancipated, realized the planters' fears.

Martinican planters were convinced of the direct link between the writings of the *Société des Amis des Noirs* and the slave rebellion. On 11 September 1789, for instance, a Martinican planter summarized the events as follows: "On August 31, firmly persuaded that they would be supported by the philanthropic Society of Paris, the Negroes dared write three letters to our superiors, one to the governor, the other to the intendant and the third one to the military commander of Saint-Pierre.... These incendiary letters were immediately followed by the revolt of three hundred Negroes from the plantations closest to Saint-Pierre, who claiming to all be free, refused to work" (ANF, DXXV 117, 1789a).[4] The planters' belief that the slaves' actions were directly prompted by the philosophical debates thousands of miles across the Atlantic is fascinating. Slaves were purposely kept analphabetic and in such a degraded state that they were thought of more as animals than as humans. Nonetheless, Martinican planters were convinced that the slaves had read about the political pamphlets of the *Amis des Noirs:* "Interrogated, they [the slaves] responded that they had been urged to revolt upon the counsel of several learned Negroes from the city of Saint-Pierre, that they had assured them that for a while the newspapers coming from France had all been saying that they had distinguished friends in Paris, who had obtained their freedom; that they should have already received it, but that their masters were opposed to it" (ANF DXXV 117, 1789a).

The slaves' "distinguished friends," or the *Société des Amis des Noirs* drew most of its members from Parisian high society. It was rather short-lived, as the leading members—Brissot de Warville, Etienne Clavière, the marquis de Condorcet, and Pétion de Villeneuve—were all killed during the Terror.[5] The principal aim of the *Amis des Noirs,* expressed during its first meeting in February 1788, was to rally support for the abolition of slavery and of the slave trade in view of enlightening the slaves: "Enlighten men and they will better themselves; but experience throughout the centuries tells us: Give men their freedom and they will become necessarily and rapidly enlightened and they will necessarily better themselves" (Société des Amis des Noirs [1788] 1968: 7).

The *Société des Amis des Noirs'* call for freedom was revolutionary at a time when Africans were believed to be so naturally vile as to be incapable of governing themselves in a state of freedom. Even the *philosophes* did not think it wise to free these men who first needed to learn the fundamentals of morality. In their initial address, the *Amis des Noirs* placed black slaves on an equal footing with Europeans, and therefore deserving of the same rights. Setting no limits on this freedom, their statement implicated the abolition of slavery. Colonial planters were in fact wary that the revolutionary ideals of freedom and equality might be extended to their slaves: "[Our wariness] turned into a kind of terror when we saw the Declaration of the Rights of Men establish as the basis of the Constitution absolute equality, the same rights and liberty for all individuals" ("Correspondance secrète" [1793] 1968: 25). A group of planters from Guadeloupe even addressed their concerns directly to the *Assemblée nationale:* "As Frenchmen we accept with transport the new constitution the nation gave itself and we place ourselves under its powerful guard. As planters, compelled by the laws of imperious neces-

sity, we are obliged to make exceptions to some of its principles" ("Cahier adressé à l'Assemblée" 1989: 45).

The *Société des Amis des Noirs* was particularly dangerous as
far as the propagation of the new ideals of liberty was concerned since its members actively rallied for the abolition of
slavery through countless petitions:

> Until then, slavery and the slave trade were only the subject of
> philosophical mediations, of regrets more or less sincerely felt ...
> these speculations did not present any danger to public order....
> At the beginning of 1788 it was no longer the same thing. Since
> there were *Amis des Noirs* among the members of parliament in
> England, suddenly increasing numbers of petitions that had the
> abolition of the slave trade as their objective arrived at this leg-
> islative body.... These periodical writings [of the *Amis des Noirs*]
> were passed on to our colonies; and I remember perfectly well
> that several issues of the *Mercure* that arrived at the Cap
> François during the months of April and May 1788 with details
> and reflections [on the question of abolition], caused much sen-
> sation there (Moreau de Saint-Méry [1791] 1972: 3–4).

Moreau de Saint-Méry, the well-known French colonial administrator, lawyer and deputy for Martinique, highlights the
ways in which the *Amis des Noirs* made the revolutionary ideals
relevant to the colonial situation. The danger of these incendiary writings, as the white planter P. J. Laborie (1798: 38) points
out, is that they cross the ocean and communicate themselves
like a fire, "causing much sensation."

A specific example of the "sensation" caused among the slave
populations of the Caribbean is the 1789 rebellion in Martinique. Inspired, according to planters, by their "distinguished
friends in Paris," the slaves from Saint-Pierre, Martinique, addressed three letters to colonial authorities demanding immediate emancipation and followed up on their threats several
days later by breaking out into an insurrection at the end of
August 1789.[6] Two of the letters that have been found and
published were written on 28 and 29 August 1789, and addressed to the governor of Martinique and to the intendant of
Saint-Pierre, respectively.[7] Even though scholars agree that
these letters are authentic and were most likely written by educated slaves or free blacks, opinions are divided about the
specific identity of their authors. One of the specialists on the
question of literacy among Caribbean slaves, the Haitian historian Jean Fouchard makes extensive use of archival sources

to prove that a few slaves and especially emancipated blacks in the French colonies did know how to read and write already during the eighteenth century. There were two types of literate slaves: those who were literate due to their previous Islamization in Africa and those who became literate through a great deal of perseverance as they somehow managed to thwart the colonial administration's policy of keeping slaves in a state of total ignorance. How they went about acquiring education is a question historians have only been able to speculate about so far. Were they taught by members of the clergy, by philanthropic masters, or perhaps by the white children of the master? Another important question is the extent to which such documents were dictated to a scribe such as an educated emancipated black person or even to a white member of the clergy, since the author was not necessarily literate.

As far as the two letters from Martinique are concerned, one of the primary sources that historians have used to ascertain the identity of the writers is Pierre F. R. Dessalles's *Historique des troubles survenus à la Martinique pendant la Révolution* (1982: 20–21). Written by the magistrate of the *Conseil souverain de la Martinique* between 1794 and 1800, this manuscript remained unpublished until 1982. According to Dessalles, the blacks of the city of Saint-Pierre—who were the primary instigators and authors of the letters—plotted the revolt in cooperation with plantation slaves. They were inspired to revolt by Father Jean-Baptiste, a Capuchin monk who was the blacks' parish priest and who allegedly encouraged them to rebel. As a result of his active involvement in the cause of freedom, he had to take refuge on the island of Dominica even before the slaves' August revolt in order to avoid arrest.[8] This influence may explain the direct references made to the Catholic Church in the two slave letters. Nonetheless, Dessalles establishes no direct link between Father Jean-Baptiste and the slave letters. Rather, he cites another circumstance that supposedly gave the slaves their final push. The new governor of Martinique, Charles de Vioménil—to whom one of the slave letters was addressed—had circulated a letter to all the military commanders of the parish of Saint-Pierre warning against the excessive cruelties committed against slaves. Dessalles (1982: 22–23) claims that the blacks of Saint-Pierre had obtained a copy of this letter and interpreted it as the proclamation of freedom promised earlier by Father Jean-Baptiste. According to this viewpoint, it was their disappointment that led them to write the threatening letters and ultimately to revolt.

In a recent historical analysis of these letters, the historian David P. Geggus (1996: 287) summarizes different perspectives on the authorship of these letters without privileging any particular viewpoint. He does contend, however, that the anti-slavery movement in France had a greater effect on these letters than did the French Revolution, the news of which did not reach Martinique until 15 September of the same year. In fact, Dessalles (1982: 18) states that the *Amis des Noirs'* writings were widely available in the colony and were circulated among the slaves who assembled together to read them aloud. Even though the identity of the authors of the letters and of the instigators of the revolts cannot be ascertained with certainty, eighteenth-century colonial planters popularized the belief that they were written by slaves under the direct inspiration of the *Amis des Noirs*. Considered a mere outgrowth of French abolitionism, the slaves' writings and actions were marginalized and forgotten, contributing to the generalized belief that slavery had so degraded blacks as to render them perfectly incapable of harboring any concrete desire for liberty.

A close reading of the political pamphlets of the *Société des Amis des Noirs* and of the two slave letters reveals that beyond the initial call for freedom, the two narratives bear little if no resemblance. There is already considerable variance between the first claims to freedom. While the *Amis des Noirs* argue that freedom will enlighten men and that the slaves should therefore be emancipated, the slaves consider themselves already enlightened by the amount of suffering they have experienced: "This is no longer a nation blinded by ignorance and trembling before the lightest punishments; its sufferings have enlightened it and determined it to shed its blood to the last drop rather than continue to endure the shameful yoke of slavery, a dreadful yoke, condemned by the laws, by humanity, by nature, by the Divinity, and by our Good King Louis XVI" (ANF Colonies F3 29, 1789b). As opposed to the passive receptors of enlightenment, civilization, and freedom described by the *Amis des Noirs,* the slaves give themselves an active role in the process of liberation. Interestingly, they borrow the typical language of abolitionists, describing themselves as enlightened and condemning slavery as unlawful, inhumane, and unnatural. However, they immediately dispel the myth that they are blinded, ignorant, weak, and fearful, in other words needy of a benefactor such as the *Société des Amis des Noirs*. Instead, they exclaim the force of their determination in the face of adversity. Their reference to themselves as a nation—

reflecting their conscious belonging to African ethnic groups—strengthens the slaves' separateness from French revolutionary discourse (Geggus 1996: 287). It is as Africans that the slaves clamor for freedom, not as members of the French nation. Their language reflects the originality of their demands, which are not outgrowths of a larger abolitionary discourse coming from Europe. The slaves' direct reference to violence—a subject I will discuss at length in the last part of the chapter—is another indication that the slaves are not reproducing the writings of the *Amis des Noirs.* The fear of revolt, resulting in lengthy proposals on avoiding such violence, was always the primary focus of abolitionism. The slaves' willingness to shed their blood to the last drop could hardly be more discordant. Though the slaves share the *Amis des Noirs'* initial "intoxication with freedom," the manner in which they intend to reach this aim is so decidedly different that their revolt can scarcely be seen as a direct outcome of the *Amis des Noirs'* political activism.

"Who Can Contemplate This Spectacle, Without Shuddering in Horror?"

Following their initial cry for freedom, the *Société des Amis des Noirs* ([1789d] 1968: 13) set the tone of their demands in the "Règlements de la Société des Amis des Noirs," published in 1789. Their specific plan of action is exceedingly moderate: "Only a Society of men united through the principles of humanity and justice could gather all the facts ... collect all the plans ... to change the actual system, examine them and submit them to calculations ... finally propose a plan for work, execute it, and maybe even attempt some experiments." Primarily focused on abstract calculations and only vaguely suggesting the possibility of action, this narrative is far from the earlier call for liberty. The sudden moderation has been criticized by various French and American historians.[9] All point to the discrepancy between the *Amis des Noirs'* abolitionary ideals and their very cautious approach toward this objective.

The political philosopher Hannah Arendt's (1967: 113–15) "politics of pity," developed at great length in *Essai sur la Révolution,* provides an invaluable tool for reflecting on the *Société des Amis des Noirs'* contradictory discourse. Drawing on Arendt's work, the French social scientist Luc Boltanski (1993: 15–86) studies the rising role played by pity in political events since the middle of the eighteenth century. Identifying with the suffering of others through the experience of pity was pivotal to the revolutionary struggle and created in people the capacity to lose themselves in the suffering of others. However, the action that is implicit in this identification does not necessarily have to be realized, as the feeling of pity can be maintained through the elaboration of plans for future action, even if these plans are repeatedly postponed. In fact, one of the principal characteristics of the politics of pity is that its loquacity prevails over action—a loquacity that brings the suffering closer to the spectators and provides them with the verbal or visual means of identifying with those who suffer far away.

The *Amis des Noirs'* aim of bringing the question of slavery to the attention of the French public was groundbreaking at a time when Africans were considered barely human and their fate unworthy of a moral dilemma. In order to counter the public's aversion to the uncivilized and barbaric Africans—further bestialized through their enslavement—the *Amis des Noirs* led their readership to lose themselves in the suffering of blacks in the colonies. The misfortune of black slaves had thus far been disregarded for the most part and the *Amis des Noirs* were the first to specifically focus on the human aspect of the slaves' misery, calling for an emotional involvement of the French public in the cause of African slaves.

The *Société des Amis des Noirs'* ([1790a] 1968: 4–7) politics of pity is largely developed through a discursive strategy that brings the plight of the suffering slaves visually closer to the public: "In order to determine you [the *Assemblée nationale*] to [abolish the slave trade], do we have to put before your eyes the picture of this horrible commerce? You would be revolted, if we exposed the circumstances of this atrocious robbery to your sight.... Who can contemplate this spectacle, without shuddering in horror." Visual representation brings the spectacle of suffering into proximity of the audience through the awakened imagination. The readers are led to imagine the spectacle they are called to witness and are told what their emotional reaction should be through descriptive evocations of pity, such as, "you would be revolted" and "shuddering in horror." The readers are further drawn into the discourse as they are repeatedly addressed as "you." The phrase, "if we exposed ... to your sight" brings the readers into a relationship with the writer, who is sharing his knowledge of suffering. The feelings of pity thus take on a personal relevance for the audience.

In the process of drawing the audience—in this case the *Assemblée nationale*—into the abolitionary agenda through emotional identification, the *Amis des Noirs* turn slaves into helpless and passive victims of the middle passage. This approach to abolitionism was typical also of abolitionist propaganda in England from the mid-1780s to the early 1790s. Slaves were presented in such a way as to elicit in the audience a sense of responsibility without revulsion. The middle passage was a perfect subject for such writings since its horrors could be endlessly described, visually represented, and imagined (Wood 2000: 23): "Please follow me [readers], in the rapid sketch I will make for you of a slave ship, of the heaps of victims and of the bad treatment they are subjected to," writes Pétion de Villeneuve ([1790] 1968: 23), inviting his readers to imagine the horrific spectacle onboard a slave ship. The author hopes to convince his audience less through the discursive strategies of his narrative than by touching them through their own imagination.

Frequent citations of eyewitness accounts are key to rendering the descriptions more vivid and thereby more likely to elicit an emotional identification with the victims: "We will give an example here [of the conditions on the slave ships] reported by an eyewitness. It will give you a faint idea of the suffering these wretched, whom we so cruelly tear from their land in order to condemn them to enslavement and perpetual captivity, have to go through" (Société des Amis des Noirs [1789a] 1968: 11–12). Invited to follow the eyewitness account in their imagination, the readers see and visually witness the spectacle of suffering as though they were physically present.

Symbolizing the horrors of the middle passage and of slavery in general, the slave ship became the focus of abolitionary discourse, and across the centuries a site for memory. The famous *Description of a Slave Ship,* a 1789 copper engraving representing the Liverpool slaver the *Brookes* in cross section, front view, and side view, and in a series of overviews of both slave decks, is the most widely reproduced image of the middle passage. It was originally produced by the Plymouth Committee of the Society for the Abolition of the Slave Trade in 1788, and was developed into its most widely disseminated form by the London Committee in 1789. The same year this image was published in England it was also distributed in Paris by Clarkson, becoming a central feature of the *Amis des Noirs'* writings (Wood 2000: 17–18).

More effectively than written descriptions of suffering slaves and even eyewitness accounts, the image of the *Brookes* published in 1789 by the *Société des Amis des Noirs* ([1789a] 1968) brings the plight of the slaves onboard the slave ship closer to the Parisian audience. The drawings and detailed measurements of the manner in which the slaves are packed on the different decks allow readers to see for themselves the inhumane conditions prevailing during the middle passage. They can directly see the slaves and imagine their suffering.

While putting suffering slaves in the spotlight, the *Amis des Noirs* dangerously cast blacks as having been stripped of their African culture through the traumatic experience of the middle passage. Henry Louis Gates Jr.'s (1988: 4) thoughts on the subject bring to light the problematic focus on the middle passage throughout the centuries: "The notion that the Middle Passage was so traumatic that it functioned to create in the African a tabula rasa of consciousness is as odd as it is a fiction, a fiction that has served many economic orders and their attendant ideologies. The full erasure of traces of cultures as splendid, as ancient, and as shared by the slave traveler as the classic cultures of traditional West Africa, would have been extraordinarily difficult." By incessantly emphasizing the Africans' plight during the middle passage without reference to any other aspect of their existence, abolitionists turned them into "cultural absentees ... a blank page for white guilt to inscribe" (Wood 2000: 23). Behind the emotional identification they were trying to elicit from their Parisian audience, the *Amis des Noirs* erased the very subjects they were defending. Reducing the slaves to mere measurements, added to a determined number of other bodies heaped onboard the *Brookes*, abolitionists dehumanized their subjects. It is perhaps more the idea of their miserable condition than their actual experience as captured and transplanted Africans that appealed to abolitionists so much. The engraving of the *Brookes* symbolized the ideal slave for abolitionist propaganda: voiceless, helpless, and permanently victimized. Completely passive, this slave was not potentially violent.

This image of victimized black bodies has become a site of memory representing abolitionist propaganda of the revolutionary period. The notion of freedom is born from the emotional identification with the pitiful black body and the subsequent generous act of liberation. Absent from this site of memory are the slaves themselves as agents of their own destiny. Slaves are given no desire or will, do not act otherwise than in reaction to their physical suffering and are completely voiceless. Absent from this site of memory are the historical episodes of the liberation process during which slaves played an active role. Absent are the rebellions and outright revolutions that forced European nations to abolish slavery. Absent are the few written traces of slave voices.

In 1789, Martinican slaves voiced their desire for freedom, dispelling the myth of their helplessness and victimization generally advanced by abolitionist propaganda. They began and ended the letter addressed to the intendant of Saint-Pierre by proclaiming their own nationhood: "The entire nation of black slaves humbly beseeches your august person ... to take a look of humility at the remarks we are taking the liberty to make"; "We end our reflections by declaring to you that the entire nation of black slaves gathered together forms one single wish, one single desire for independence" (ANF Colonies F3 29, 1789b). The slaves' proud reference to themselves as a nation could hardly be more contrary to their pitiful representation aboard the slaver *Brookes*. It is not pity, but respect they demanded from the intendant of Saint-Pierre, respect for their rights, respect for freedom.

Far from helplessly suffering, Martinican slaves even appropriated European narratives. In particular, they transformed the politics of pity to their own ends: "Gentlemen, we must in fact believe you to be very inhumane since you are not touched with commiseration for the suffering we are enduring. Even the most barbarous nation would dissolve into tears if it knew of our sorrows; we leave it to you to imagine how promptly it would seek to abolish such an odious law; anyway, it is in vain that we appeal to your feelings and humanity, for you have none" (ANF Colonies F3 29, 1789b). Holding their audience personally responsible for the action that needs to be taken, the slaves make an urgent appeal that differs considerably from the *Amis des Noirs'* endless evocations of suffering. By creating tension between the writers' "we" and the readers' "you," the slaves directly confront the colonial administrators with their demands: "we must believe you to be very inhumane"; "I leave it to you to imagine"; and "it is in vain that we appeal to your feelings." Action is not postponed, as it is in the *Amis des Noirs'* discourse. The feelings of pity and the resulting relief of suffering are inextricably linked to immediate abolition. The *Amis des Noirs,* on the other hand, rarely mention their demands for abolition.

The differing ways in which the *Société des Amis des Noirs* and the Martinican slaves employ pity is a result of distance and proximity, a fundamental aspect of the politics of pity. As Boltanski (1993: 29–34) points out, geographic distance allows for the identification with suffering people in another part of the world. The first aim of the politics of pity is to awaken interest in a distant cause through sentimental identification with those who suffer. The *Amis des Noirs* extensively develop this aspect by visually representing suffering slaves. In contrast, by writing to colonial administrators who are confronted daily with the realities of slavery on the plantations, the slaves evoke pity not in order to awaken interest but as a justification for immediate action. In this case the sentiment called for is not so much pity but rather compassion. Arendt (1967: 123) compares the two sentiments, concluding that pity is marked by loquacity due to its methods of persuasion and negotiation aiming at political change. Compassion, on the other hand, lends its voice to suffering itself and demands direct, quick, and immediate action, often through violent means. In their letters, the slaves are clearly not referring to the same type of sentiment as the *Amis des Noirs*. Since their primary concern is freedom, they believe commiseration to call for immediate emancipation. Furthermore, the slaves' accusations of inhumanity are tightly linked to the explosiveness of the colonial situation. The physical closeness of slaves to their colonial audience fundamentally changes the context. The politics of pity cannot develop in the proximity of suffering masses wanting to share the same space and privileges as those who do not suffer, since this contiguity transforms the unhappy masses into dangerous rebels (Arendt 1967: 165). The potential of rebellion inherent to slavery in the Caribbean profoundly divides the narratives of the *Amis des Noirs* and of Martinican slaves. The radically opposing ways in which each group refers to violence reaffirms the originality of the slaves' discourse.

"We Are Ready to Die for Freedom"

While the *Société des Amis des Noirs'* politics of pity is successfully elaborated through visual representation, bringing the spectacle of suffering closer to French readers, the moment of action and relief of suffering is suspended and continually postponed to a distant time in the future: "The moment is not favorable to emancipate the Negroes and to prohibit the slave trade: it would augment the disorder and fears which already torment our existence too much. It would seem infinitely wiser to await a calmer time." French deputy Jean-Louis de Viefville des Essars ([1790] 1968: 3, 40) concludes his "Discours et projet de loi pour l'affranchissement des nègres," in which he elaborates a plan for the abolition of slavery, by postponing the process to an undefined future moment. His initial call for "charitable actions and consolations," even "tender feelings" on behalf of the "miserable slaves" leads to a "waiting period" and to the "consoling idea of this happy time in the not too distant future." The fear of revolt and of the violent loss of plantations led the *Amis des Noirs* to stop short of actually proposing the abolition of slavery and of the slave trade. Economic considerations came to the forefront whenever the question of abolition was brought up. Pétion de Villeneuve ([1790] 1968: 61), for instance, insists that postponing abolition is very beneficial for the colonial system: "I won't conceal that the solutions [regarding slavery and the slave trade] will drag things out.... But these delays, far from being useless or harmful will be very precious. They will give commerce time to prepare for the change without violent or deplorable commotion." There is a glaring contradiction between the endless details about suffering slaves and the willingness of the writers to indefinitely postpone any action that would end these atrocities. However, as Boltanski (1993: 15–86) points out, as long as plans for future action are elaborated, the feeling of pity can be successfully maintained.

Pétion de Villeneuve's ([1790] 1968: 70) rêverie about abolition makes it doubtful that the *Amis des Noirs* were ever seriously striving to abolish slavery: "The day will doubtlessly come, when the African's chains will be broken, when liberty will spread its benefits over the whole earth." The passive voice is used to describe the abolition of slavery, as no agent can yet be pinpointed to this end. While a utopian freedom will spread liberty in the world, human agency is denied, and the future day of freedom appears like a dream. In the meantime, on the road to French civilization, slaves must patiently wait for the colonial system to accept the financial burden of emancipation.

Needless to say, the Martinican slaves were hardly willing to await the unlikely realization of the *Amis des Noirs'* dream. And, it is primarily in this regard that their discourse is opposed to that of their "distinguished friends in Paris." While the *Amis des Noirs* focus on the importance of avoiding violent conflict, Martinican slaves champion the free and willful use of violence as an ultimate tool in the concerted refusal of slavery: "Remember that we the Negroes ... we are ready to die for this freedom, for we want to and will obtain it at any price, even with the help of mortars, canons, and rifles.... If this prejudice is not entirely eradicated before long, there will be torrents of blood, as powerful as our streams flowing in the streets" (ANF Colonies F3 29, 1789a).[10] The slaves' graphic description of imminent bloodshed recasts the ideal of liberty. From a lofty ideal, worthy of enlightened people, freedom is turned into an urgent necessity, the basis of human existence. Emancipation is not something the slaves will patiently wait for, and in this regard they are not following the lead of the *Amis des Noirs*. Since benevolence takes an inordinate amount of time before it will potentially lead to any concrete results, violence remains the only weapon to force the colonizer to take action. According to Frantz Fanon (1991: 67–68), the colonized are keenly aware of the need for "absolute violence" in order to call into question the colonial situation. To change the status quo, they must engage in a "decisive and murderous confrontation" with the colonizer.

Contrary to eighteenth-century representations of African slaves as naturally violent, the Martinican slaves threaten to revert to violence only as a means to an end. Revenge is absent from their narrative as they seek to obtain a right that should already be theirs. Rather than seeking the benevolence of the French, they ask for the restoration of their right to freedom: "We know we are free." This right is God-given and cannot be touched by man: "Did God ever create any man as a slave? The Heavens and the Earth belong to our Lord as well as everything that lives there" (ANF Colonies F3 29, 1789a). The religious inspiration of the letters, probably attributable to Father Jean-Baptiste, does not echo the secular libertarianism of 1789 (Geggus 1996: 287). The *Amis des Noirs* played no role in this aspect of the slaves' demands. On the contrary, relying on God, rather than on enlightened men for their freedom, the blacks distance themselves from the ideals of the Enlightenment:

> God, who sooner or later confounds the arrogant plans of men, this God who is so just knows us deeply, he would know had we ever had any other plan besides patiently enduring the oppression of our persecutors. No longer being able to suffer so many persecutions, this eternal God doubtlessly entrusted Louis XVI the Great Monarch with the responsibility of delivering all the unhappy Christians, oppressed by their unjust fellow men, and you were elected, virtuous Vioménil [governor of Martinique], to announce these good news (ANF Colonies F3 29, 1789b).[11]

The belief that only God could grant them freedom conflicts with the *Amis des Noirs'* eternally postponed plans for abolition, imagined out of heartfelt pity. The slaves' recognition of their

God-given right to freedom casts their demands in a framework that is independent of anyone's pity and benevolence. In
fact, the slaves knew it was hopeless to appeal to the colonizer's "feelings and humanity" (ANF Colonies F3 29, 1789b).

The vehement outburst against abolitionary ideology in the
colonies would soon prove the slaves' concerns to be well-
founded. Under attack from representatives of the planter class
in Paris, who held them responsible for the successive slave revolts in the colonies, the *Amis des Noirs* ([1790a] 1968: 2–4)
stopped short of following through with their projects for abolition. Their disproportionate and even absurd fears—as French
historian Yves Bénot puts it—led them in 1790, in the face of
political adversity, to deny any previous abolitionary goals:
"We do not ask that you [the *Assemblée nationale*] restitute the
political rights, which alone attest to and maintain the dignity
of man, to black Frenchmen; we do not even ask for their freedom.... Immediate emancipation of the blacks would not only
be fatal for the colonies; it would even be a harmful present to
the blacks, who through cupidity have been reduced to a state
of abjection and incompetence." The *Amis des Noirs* completely
adhered to the narrative of anti-abolitionists. Their previous
belief in the transformative power of enlightenment gave way
to a complete disregard for the slaves' humanity.

This turnabout did not escape the watchful eye of the planters who carefully observed the propagation of the revolutionary principles: "In the first place, we are certain that we mustn't
have any fears regarding emancipation; we have just as little
to worry about the suppression of the slave trade.... The *Amis
des Noirs* themselves have changed their mind regarding the
former. M. de Condorcet declared this in public in the journal
of Paris" ("Correspondance secrète" [1793] 1968: 28–29). Ironically, the planters took the revolutionary ideal of "liberté,
égalité, fraternité" more to heart than did the *Amis des Noirs,*
as they believed it to lead to the immediate abolition of slavery and the slave trade in the colonies.

Riveted to news coming from France, however, the planters
failed to interpret local events. Their greatest mistake lay in
their incapacity to recognize the slaves' self-determined will
for emancipation. Contrary to the planters' conviction, Martinican slaves did not depend on the pamphlets of the *Société
des Amis des Noirs* to determine their course of action. Their letters amply prove the originality of demands that did not
merely reproduce French abolitionism. Following their own
agenda, Martinican slaves reverted to violence only a few days

after their initial demands went unheeded by colonial administrators. These actions are a demonstration of the slaves' self-determination. They ultimately knew that they could not rely on anyone's pity to restore their right to freedom. Even though their rebellion was unsuccessful, it contributed to the mounting resistance of slaves throughout the Caribbean and inspired rebellion on other islands. By 1791, the Saint Domingue rebellions had gained such momentum that the French colonial system began vacillating and was forced to take the only action that could save the colonies from total destruction—the abolition of slavery in 1793.

The abolition in 1793 and later in 1848 is generally remembered as an inheritance of the Enlightenment, in particular of the French *philosophes* and of the Revolution. A close reading of eighteenth-century documents, however, brings to light aspects of this past that have been marginalized and forgotten by the dominant discourse. From the outset, colonial planters misread the impact slaves could potentially have on the plantation economy. Disbelieving the slaves' capacity to organize themselves and follow through with specific plans for rebellion, the planters remained blind to local events. Their fears were focused only on revolutionary ideals from France, ideals that would dissipate like smoke as soon as abolition became too great of a political problem.

The slaves' written demands combined with their actions had a profound impact on the "realms of freedom." Asking for the immediate application of abolitionist ideals, the slaves' voices and actions transformed the way in which the *Amis des Noirs* perceived freedom. Held responsible for slave rebellions, the *Amis des Noirs* immediately distanced themselves from their previous claims, refusing to pursue the question of freedom any further. The slaves thus revealed the incoherences of abolitionist narratives that only theoretically strove for emancipation. At the same time, the slaves' actions attracted the attention of colonial planters who immediately turned to French abolitionists as the obvious culprits. Even though it is difficult to determine the extent to which the *Amis des Noirs* actually inspired Martinican slaves, the link perceived by planters allows one to retrospectively reevaluate the role played by slaves in the process of liberation. While the slaves did not act in an ideological vacuum, it is only through their determination that France was finally forced to abolish slavery.

The initiative of the Martinican slaves exemplifies the contentious exchanges between the colonizers and the colonized.

By rising to the awareness of their own black nationhood, demanding the return of a God-given right to liberty, the slaves
began making history. Although, as Glissant (1981: 106) so
poignantly conveys in his theoretical and literary texts, the
history of the French Caribbean is lost, "obliterated in the collective consciousness (memory) through the concerted act of
the colonizer," a return to the primary sources shows that
pieces of history made by the oppressed do remain. Patched
into the larger context of relations between France and the
Caribbean, between enlightened ideologies and principles of
exploitation, the pieces of history born from the slaves' cries
for liberty challenge France's hegemony over the memory of
French Caribbean nations.

Notes

1. See Geggus (1989a: 1291) and Fick (1997: 51).
2. In 1781, the marquis de Condorcet, one of the *Société des Amis des Noirs'* leading members, had already published *Réflexions sur l'esclavage des nègres*—an essay proposing the gradual abolition of slavery over a period of seventy years—under the pseudonym of Joachim Schwartz.
3. For diverging historical studies of the phenomenon of runaway slaves and maroon bands, see Debbash (1961, 1962); Fouchard (1972); and Gautier (1985).
4. For similar archival documents of planters' attacks against the *Société des Amis des Noirs* see ANF Colonies F3 29, folio 211, "Adresse du Comité de Saint-Pierre de la Martinique à l'Assemblée Nationale. Saint-Pierre, 5 octobre 1789" (qtd. in Pouliquen 1989: 55) and ANF DXXV 117, 1789b.
5. For specific information on the members of the *Société des Amis des Noirs,* see Perroud (1916). For general facts on the *Société des Amis des Noirs,* see Resnick (1972). For a printed collection of writings by the *Société des Amis des Noirs,* see Dorigny and Gainot (1998).
6. Saint-Pierre, Martinique, was one of the most important trade and cultural capitals of the French Lesser Antilles until the eruption of the Montagne Pelée in 1902, which completely destroyed the city.
7. These two archival documents have already been published by Elisabeth (1973) and by Pouliquen (1989). Since I directly consulted the letters in the Archives Nationales de France, I am citing them as such in the text.
8. For a description of the blacks of Saint-Pierre and an analysis of their relationship to the blacks on the plantations during the rebellion, see Elisabeth (1973: 38–42).

9. For a historical analysis of the *Société des Amis des Noirs* in the context of French abolitionism see Davis (1975: 41–148); Cohen (1980: 139–40); and Bénot (1989).

10. The powerful image of torrential streams of blood is reminiscent of the images of revenge conjured in L.-S. Mercier, where the black *vengeur du monde* leads the oppressed slaves to the revengeful extermination of European nations: "The French, the Spaniards, the English, the Dutch, the Portuguese all fell victim to swords, poison, and flames. The American soil avidly drank the blood it had been awaiting for a long time" (Mercier 1773: 168–69).

11. Emancipation rumors—consisting in the slaves' belief that a distant government, generally the king, had liberated them but that their masters refused to implement this new law—would make their appearance again during revolts in Tortola, Venezuela, Dominica, Guadeloupe, and Saint Domingue during the following years (Geggus 1996: 288).

CHAPTER 4

REALMS OF ASSIMILATION

Free coloreds from the French Caribbean entertained an altogether different relationship to France and to the revolutionary principles of freedom and equality than did the Martinican slaves. While the slaves—united as a black nationhood—demanded the return of their natural and God-given right to freedom, the free people of color based their demands for equality on their filial relationship to France. Voicing the demands of their social group from the political and social margins of French colonial society, free coloreds appropriated the egalitarian principles of the Revolution to claim their due rights as French citizens. The affirmation of their racial heritage and class status within colonial society became the cornerstone of their combat against racism, violence, and exclusion from the newly born body of free French citizens. On the grounds of their racial kinship with the French and of their considerable wealth as members of the plantation and slaveholding class of the colony, they demanded the right to political representation in the legislative assemblies. Since they were opposed by a powerful lobby of white colonial planters, however, it took several years of petitioning and of violent outbreaks between free coloreds, whites, and slaves before people of color were finally granted equality by the First French Republic. Positioned as powerful economic competitors, they dangerously shook the supremacy of white colonial power. Equality was accorded as a last resort against the unleashed furor of slave revolts sweeping Saint Domingue and other parts of the Caribbean.

Despite the racial discrimination they were subjected to, relegating them to an inferior position similar to that of black

slaves, people of color clearly separated their struggle from the
slaves' quest for liberty. Aspiring to share the political rights of
the white planter class, they were outright in their opposition
to the abolition of slavery, denying any link between their demands and those of the slaves. Their identification with their
white racial heritage and their sense of filiation to the French
led free coloreds to eventually fall victim to yet another kind of
domination through the very achievement of their political
rights. In far more subtle ways, the mother country's generous
liberation of her colored children led to a phenomenon that
Edouard Glissant (1981: 62–66) refers to as "mental alienation." Embracing the ideology of their liberators, who imposed
the erasure of oppression and violence from their collective
memory, free coloreds fully assumed and even promoted the
forgetting of their past. In exchange for the Republic's univer-
salistic ideals of liberty, freedom, and equality, the memory of
their persistent and successful struggle for equality was sup-
pressed. Assimilated by the mother country, people of color
lost their identity as a unique social group rooted in a specifically Caribbean heritage.

Race, Class, and Politics

Free coloreds numbered approximately fourty thousand in the
Caribbean around 1789 (Geggus 1989a: 1296). Their rise to
such a sizable community was tied to the sociological conditions under which the islands were originally settled by French
adventurers. The scarcity of white women and the facility of
interracial marriages and of manumission during the early
period of colonization led to a rapidly increasing number of
enfranchised mulattoes (Foner 1970: 411–12; Bénot 1989: 57).[1]
Manumitted mulatto offspring of rich planters were custom-
arily sent to France to become educated. Upon returning they
would often be entrusted with running their fathers' plantations and would inherit much of their wealth (McCloy 1954:
286; Foner 1970: 425; Quinney 1970: 126). Although in Martinique and Guadeloupe free coloreds always remained a minority, they were a powerful force in Saint Domingue, where
they constituted nearly half of the free population by the time
of the French Revolution.[2] People of color from Saint Domingue
had the greatest demographic and economic strength among
free coloreds in the eighteenth-century Caribbean (Fick 1997:
56). Characterized by their diversity, they included wealthy and

well-educated property and slave owners as well as recently
freed slaves (Geggus 1989a: 1296–97). They owned one-third of
the plantations, one-fourth of the slaves, and one-third of the
real estate (Foner 1970: 425; Fick 1997: 56). It was primarily as
a result of their large numbers, their economically privileged
position in colonial society, and their education that people of
color had the most notable impact upon historical events in
Saint Domingue at the end of the eighteenth century. Representing a considerable part of the total population on the island, they used whatever tools were at their disposition to carve
out the position they felt they deserved in the colonial world.

In spite of their wealth and education, free coloreds were
branded with the "stain of slavery" for six generations as the
white planter M. R. Hilliard d'Auberteuil (1776, 1: 73) from
Saint Domingue pointed out in 1776. Though the *Code Noir*
gave free coloreds the same civil rights as whites, their actual
situation at the end of the eighteenth century did not reflect
this legal privilege.[3] Beginning in midcentury, a rapidly increasing number of restrictions took away the rights and privileges this social group had previously enjoyed. Discriminative
measures relegated people of color to a position of inferiority
in the colonial hierarchy: despite their freedom and wealth they
had few more rights than slaves. In 1758 they were no longer
allowed to wear the sword or the saber; in 1762 this law included firearms and ammunition. They could hold no title of
nobility nor use the same last names as whites. They were not
allowed to work in public service or in a liberal profession such
as that of doctor, pharmacist, surgeon, or lawyer. In 1766 they
were prohibited from wearing the same clothes as whites and
in 1779 they could no longer wear clothes that displayed their
wealth. Their trips to France were rendered increasingly difficult through regulations restricting their departure from the island. By 1778 interracial marriages were outlawed by royal
decree.[4] Despite the progressive loss of their rights, the free coloreds' wealth augmented steadily, especially after 1760, with
the growth of the coffee industry (Debien 1951: 3–6; Foner
1970: 425; Bénot 1989: 60).

Most historians agree that this dramatic increase in discriminatory legislation is not primarily linked to racial prejudice.
Rather, it was the rapidly increasing number of free coloreds
in Saint Domingue, their education and their status as powerful economic competitors that threatened to undermine the
whites' unquestioned supremacy. The precariousness of the
white colonists' position as a small minority heightened their

fears of the oppressed masses. By stamping out the inordinate potential of a social group that rivaled them in too many domains, white planters hoped to reaffirm their total control (Foner 1970: 426–27; Bénot 1989: 60; Pérotin-Dumon 1991: 106; Fick 1997: 55–56).

Suffering from the lack of social equality and the negation of their civil rights, the people of color from Saint Domingue seized the opportunity presented to them by the French Revolution in 1789. They organized politically under the leadership of the quadroon[5] Julien Raimond, son and grandson of rich white property owners (Debien 1951: 7). Raimond had already moved to France in 1784 to plead the case of free coloreds, in particular of quadroons like himself (Cook 1941: 140–41; Mc-Cloy 1954: 288). It was not, however, until the acceleration of political events in 1789 that he joined a group of free coloreds in Paris who had formed the *Société des Colons Américains* (Geggus 1989a: 1298). With the lawyer Joly de Fleury as their spokesperson for a few months and Raimond as their leader, the people of color unsuccessfully pleaded for the support of the *Club Massiac,* a politically influential association of white absentee planters seated in Paris. The latter were far too concerned with maintaining the status quo in the colonies despite the revolutionary turmoil to risk permitting free colored representation (Cook 1941: 139–170; Debien 1953: 156–65). People of color were considered a threat to the colonial hierarchy. Having failed to rally the support of the *Club Massiac,* the free coloreds addressed their claims directly to the National Assembly and finally even enlisted the help of the *Société des Amis des Noirs* to fight for their cause (Geggus 1989a: 1297).

When the Declaration of the Rights of Man and Citizen was voted by the National Assembly on 26 August 1789 there was no longer any doubt as to the legitimacy of the free coloreds' rightful claims to equality. The first article of the declaration is unequivocal: "All men are born and remain free and equal in their rights" (Gauchet 1989:2). When the Estates General were convened in May 1789, white colonists in the Caribbean had quickly organized themselves and sent colonial representatives to Paris.[6] Needless to say, they had prohibited the free coloreds' participation in these elections, which prevented them from obtaining representation in the National Assembly (Bénot 1989: 59). Economically rivaled by people of color, white colonists wanted to assure their own political dominion (61). With free coloreds from Saint Domingue foreseeably outnumbering whites in the near future, it was particularly important to keep their voices from being heard in the National Assembly. White planters hoped to influence the Crown's restrictive mercantile policy and to obtain greater political control of the colony (Fick 1997: 56–57).

The free coloreds' political exclusion from the revolutionary changes taking place in France was in complete contradiction to the Declaration of the Rights of Man: "The aim of all political association is the conservation of man's natural and inalienable rights. These rights are liberty, ownership, safety, and the resistance to oppression.... The law is the expression of the general will. All citizens have the right to participate in its formation either personally or through their representatives" (Gauchet 1989: 2). It did not take long for the people of color in Paris to react to a declaration that seemed to finally propose a solution to their predicament. Only two months later, on 18 October 1789, Joly de Fleury delivered a speech to the National Assembly in the name of all free colored citizens and owners in France's islands and colonies. Denouncing their exclusion by white colonists from all political activities, they made their rightful claims known:

> Instructed by the Declaration of the Rights of Man and Citizen, the people of color became conscious of who they were. They elevated themselves to the dignity you had assigned them; they recognized their rights and used them. They met to compose a register of grievances that contains all their demands. In it they recorded their complaints based on the code you made known to the universe. They put their deputies in charge of delivering these to you. At this moment, they solicit from this august assembly the necessary representation allowing them to make known their rights and especially to defend their interests against the tyrannical claims of the whites (ANF DXXV 110, 1789).

In the eyes of free coloreds, these demands are the logical outgrowth of the Revolution's new principles. If they have been excluded from the National Assembly, it is not because they are naturally inferior and somehow subhuman but because injustice has been done. Trodden on by the tyrannical whites, they "do not ask for a favor." Rather, they demand the return of "rights they have been unjustly deprived of." It is the duty of the National Assembly "to complete its glorious work by ensuring the liberty of French citizens in both hemispheres" (ANF DXXV 110, 1789).

Although the initial demands made in this first address were rather modest—the free coloreds asked to be represented by six deputies, just like the whites—white planters exerted enough political pressure to block the discussion of this issue in the National Assembly (Bénot 1989).[7] Racially stratified for centuries, colonial society was founded on the unquestionable separation between whites, free coloreds, and slaves. Race and slavery went hand in hand to safeguard the foundation upon which the extensive system of exploitation had been built (Geggus 1989a: 1301). The possibility of racial equality would only undermine this basis of control (Fick 1997: 58). Belonging to the same class, free coloreds and whites participated in the same mode of economic production based on the slave regime. Both groups contributed to France's colonial wealth (Bénot 1989: 61). Nonetheless, for the white minority's alleged protection from the black slave majority, people of color were forced into a subordinate caste that was intermediary between whites and slaves (Foner 1970: 420).

In a memoir analyzing the political explosion in Saint Domingue, Raimond (1793a: 5–7) stated that "the prejudice of color is the primary cause behind the upheavals which tore apart the colony of Saint Domingue as well as behind all the successive political crises." This discrimination, Raimond believed, made it impossible for the revolutionary principles of 1789 to take effect in the colonies. He considered the pervasiveness of racial prejudice to be the result of the three-caste system stratifying colonial society:

> The government [Saint Domingue's colonial administration] and arrogant men [wealthy white planters] had succeeded in persuading the majority of colonists that the colonial regime could not be maintained without establishing what they called an intermediary line between whites and slaves. The government had declared that if ever this intermediary line should disappear, the total dissolution and loss of the colonies would be the inevitably result.

According to white colonists, control over the slave population could only be maintained via the subordination of free coloreds for "if one were to ever grant people of color political rights the slaves would revolt" (Raimond 1793a: 26). The colonists' hidden motivations behind their vehement opposition to free colored political representation was unveiled by another person of color from Saint Domingue addressing the National Assembly in 1789 on behalf of his oppressed brothers: "Ambition and cupidity have given birth to the prejudice of color on the islands: under the political pretexts of necessity and security this fatal prejudice has thrown the mulattoes into the greatest calamity" (Américain [1789] 1968: 3). Racism against people of color was primarily motivated by economic rivalry while the need for an intermediary caste was officially defended in the interest of the slave regime—one of France's primary sources of income.[8]

The discriminatory separation between people of color and whites in terms of social and political rights, supposedly to create a protective barrier against slave violence, was not the only strategy that colonial administrators and planters used to thwart the free coloreds' fight for equality. Another way of weakening these competitors was to blur the distinction between their fight for equality and the dreaded question of slave emancipation. White planters considered the granting of political rights the first step toward abolition. The deputy for Martinique, Moreau de Saint-Méry ([1791] 1972: 48) opposed free colored representation on the grounds that it would inspire slaves to seek similar modes of liberation:

> If our slaves come to suspect the existence of a power that can give a ruling on their fate independently of the will of their masters, especially if they gain proof of the mulattoes' successful appeal to this power; if they are convinced that they are no longer absolutely dependent on us; if, finally, they realize that the mulattoes have become equal without our participation, there is no longer any hope for France to conserve her colonies.

Looming over revolutionary France, the specter of the colonies' economic ruin deterred egalitarianism. Deemed the first step toward general emancipation, equality was not an option in the colonial context.[9] This argument was another alibi for the white minority's political dominion as Raimond (1791a: 1) highlighted in a pamphlet on the origins of prejudice:

> White planters, who are the aristocrats and noblemen of the colonies, want to take away these invaluable rights [of active citizens] from free mulattoes whom they hate and want to degrade. In order to achieve this goal they have guilefully confounded the cause of the people of color with that of the slaves. This deliberate confusion has muddled up the true condition of people of color to such an extent that even now most members of the National Assembly still do not have clear notions about the class of free coloreds and property owners.

The confusion between free coloreds and slaves during the early revolutionary period completely obscured the fact that in

terms of economic wealth and education people of color belonged to the same class as whites. In fact, their position as
slaveholders made them vehemently anti-abolitionist. If anything, political equality would make them potential allies
against the black slave masses. By blurring the distinction between free coloreds and slaves, however, white colonists postponed the debate regarding free colored representation, thus
guaranteeing their own political authority. Foreseeing the political influence that such prominent abolitionist deputies as
Lafayette, Mirabeau, and La Rochefoucauld might have on
the colonial question, white planters needed to gain all the
support they could from those who favored the maintenance
of colonial slavery (Geggus 1989a: 1293–94). Moreover, they
felt uneasy about the free coloreds' collaboration with the *Société des Amis des Noirs* since the latter did not hide the fact that
equality was only the first step toward the gradual abolition of
slavery (Bénot 1989: 69). Evoking the economic ruin of the
colonies was the most effective way of lobbying against the
application of egalitarian ideals to nonwhites.

Blocked from political representation in 1789, people of
color petitioned for their rights by developing a political narrative based on the notions of race and class. Turning around
the argument of racial discrimination, they used their white
ancestry to establish their kinship with French citizens and
thus to erase their racial otherness. The free coloreds in Paris
sent a petition to the National Assembly on 2 December 1789
denouncing the deliberate confusion of their demands with
slave emancipation: "Against the beneficent intentions of the
Sovereign, against his paternal considerations, the Citizens of
color have always been confused with the slaves. Forty million
Frenchmen have been confused with the slaves" ("Supplique
des citoyens de couleur" [1789] 1989: 154). By opposing the
terms *Frenchmen* and *slaves,* they clearly distinguished themselves from the black slave masses, emphasizing their white
racial heritage. Frenchness was turned into a racial attribute
that replaced any reference to color. Calling themselves "citizens" and thereby portraying themselves as active political
participants, they further demarcated themselves from the state
of servitude. Rightful members of the newly founded body of
French citizens, they portrayed their unjustified oppression as
an affront against the revolutionary ideals of freedom, equality, and fraternity. Their persecution became an affair that undermined the very foundation of the new constitution.

On 2 February 1792 the council of the free colored army in Saint Domingue wrote a letter to the National Assembly decrying the fact that the Revolution not only completely bypassed them but even worsened their oppression. Similarly to the people of color in Paris, they too grounded their charges on their filial link with the French; a link they felt entitled them to benefit from the new constitution. "French blood circulates in our veins. From the traits, the language, the virtues we practice, can the French ignore us?... this just and powerful nation ... cannot consent to the degradation of part of her children" (ANF DXXV 110, 1792b). The racial bias upon which white planters founded their discriminatory measures was dismantled. By focusing on their white ancestry, free coloreds portrayed themselves as children of the French nation, children whose degradation was entirely unfounded. Through the appropriation of France's filial narrative, they verbally bridged the gap between their perceived racial otherness and the French family they wanted to join. An argument for equality, the question of racial filiation was coherent with the nation's principles.

The free coloreds' claims to equality as racial members of the French nation were complemented by their belonging to the class of property owners. Their important financial contributions to France's glorious overseas possessions reinforced the vital role they played in the French economy. Raimond (1789: 5) pointed this out in a letter addressed to the National Assembly in 1789: "We are free citizens of the colonies, we are owners, taxpayers and moreover very useful, therefore we should be called to the primary assemblies." This social group's financial importance did not warrant their exclusion from the new political assemblies: economically speaking they were on equal footing with white planters.

Defending their class interests, free coloreds drew up a systematic parallel between themselves and white property owners in their 18 October 1789 address to the National Assembly:

> Like [whites], [citizens of color] are citizens, free and French; the March 1685 edict accords them all the corresponding rights [and] privileges....
> Like them, they are owners and taxpayers....
> Like them, they have shed and are ready to shed their blood to defend their homeland (ANF DXXV 110, 1789).

Layer upon layer of similarity made nonwhite property owners appear equal to their white counterparts. Sharing all the characteristics of this class, free coloreds completely erased the racial distinction upon which their oppression was founded. Citizenship symbolized the natural and rightful claim to their political rights while emancipation distinguished them from black slaves. Frenchness became a racial attribute that covered up their African ancestry, while their high economic status placed them firmly in the same social class as whites. Finally, their patriotism eliminated any potential foreignness, completing the free coloreds' allegiance to metropolitan France rather than to the vast majority of Caribbean slaves. With each descriptive sentence, they denounced the whites' deliberate misrepresentations and rectified their own true racial belonging and class before the National Assembly.

The people of color's voluntary identification with the white planter class was not a mere political ploy to further their own cause. It directly reflected their rejection of the slaves' struggle for freedom and their opposition to the abolition of slavery. Free coloreds were traditionally a part of the militia and helped control the slave masses by capturing runaway slaves, fighting maroon communities, and patrolling the island (Foner 1970: 418). Raimond boasted of the free coloreds' vital role in controlling the slave population: "we alone have been able to hold [the slaves] in check" (Cook 1941: 152). During slave revolts, as, for example, during the August 1789 slave uprising in Martinique, free colored militia joined in the suppression of the rebellions (Geggus 1996: 286). Slaveholders themselves, they had little reason to support the slaves' struggle against servitude. François Raimond (1793–1800: 6) pointed this out in a letter to his brother Julien. Accused by white planters of ganging up with the slaves, he commented: "as if I had any other fortune than slaves; certainly, it is not in our interest to be philanthropes." Julien Raimond (1793–1800: 70) defended the same viewpoint in a letter to the free coloreds of Saint Domingue: "Every one admits that it would be impolitic to deal with [the cause of the slaves] at the present moment." In another letter he defended himself from accusations concerning his abolitionary goals: "[they] said that my intentions were to liberate all the slaves ... one could hardly suppose that I would want to ruin my entire family which possesses seven to eight million in property in Saint Domingue" (77).

With very few exceptions, free people of color made no reference to the abolition of slavery in their own petitions for equality.[10] Despite their collaboration with the *Société des Amis des Noirs,* whose original aim was the abolition of slavery and of the slave trade, free coloreds did not share the *Amis des Noirs'* abolitionary goals. Instead, they convinced the latter to make racial equality the first point on their agenda, especially given the unfavorable political climate as far as the colonies were concerned (Cook 1941: 144). The free coloreds' voluntary separation of their cause from that of the slaves was denounced by the slaves themselves. On the occasion of the August 1789 slave uprising in Martinique, crushed with the help of the free colored militia, slaves wrote a letter to colonial officials deploring, among other things, the people of color's rejection of their cause: "We have just learned with extreme despair that rather than take interest in the cause of their mother, brother, and sister slaves, the mulattoes have dared show us to be unworthy of enjoying the happiness procured by peace and liberty" (ANF Colonies F3 29, 1789b). The lack of solidarity between free coloreds and slaves strikingly demonstrates the instability of racial categories in the colonial world. Racial categories were not rigid and were often defined by nonracial factors related to economic and social standing, to education and to political events. Positioned between two racial groups of opposite social standing, people of color manipulated the racial ambivalence of their own social group so as to realize their political interests.

Although the abolition of slavery was in the interest of neither white nor nonwhite property owners, the link that free coloreds tried to establish between their interests and those of whites was a complete failure in the revolutionary context. Refusing to cooperate with the people of color or to implement any of the decrees in their favor proclaimed by the National Assembly, white colonists eventually provoked a civil war in Saint Domingue. Seeing the achievement of their political rights continually sabotaged due to questions of race and slave control, groups of free coloreds began rebelling in Saint Domingue. The mulatto Jeune (Vincent) Ogé led the first such rebellion in 1790 when the decree of 8 March 1790—giving all citizens of the colonies the right to vote in colonial assemblies—was not applied to nonwhites (Debien 1953: 181–98).[11] In the meantime, brutal lynchings of free coloreds had become commonplace in Saint Domingue and progressively increased as the political climate deteriorated (Cook 1941: 148; Debien 1953: 179; Geggus 1989a: 1301). The National Assembly's decree of 15 May 1791 ("Loi relative aux Colonies" [1791] 1968), granting political rights to free coloreds born of free mothers and fathers, caused white planters in Saint Domingue to threaten secession and to bluntly refuse the implementation of the decree (Bénot 1989: 74–75).[12] The conflict between mulattoes and whites was thus further exacerbated. To add to the civil war climate reigning in Saint Domingue, the black masses broke out into the largest slave revolt in the history of the Americas in August 1791 (Geggus 1989a: 1303).[13] It took eight months of warfare between whites, people of color, and slaves before the French legislation finally played its last card and extended full equality to all people of color on 4 April 1792. It was hoped that the appeased rebels would become France's allies and help suppress the massive slave rebellion (James 1989: 110–17; Fick 1997: 60). Based on pragmatic rather than ideological considerations, the Declaration of the Rights of Man had finally been applied to the colonial context. It took two more years of slave rebellions and the threat of losing Saint Domingue, France's most profitable colony, before the government abolished black slavery on 4 February 1794.

Toward Assimilation

The granting of political rights had the desired effect upon the free colored population, as confirmed by their own writings. Across the French Caribbean, people of color reacted to their enfranchisement by expressing their loyalty to the French Republic.[14] Despite their long oppression and the recent brutalities committed against them, the free coloreds from Saint Domingue entirely transformed their narrative vis-à-vis the mother country. Their original demands for an equality they felt should be rightfully theirs was replaced by expressions of overwhelming and subdued gratitude, a new sense of patriotic obligation, and even a feeling of indebtedness.

The decree of 4 April 1792 does not hide the political motivations governing its promulgation:

> The National Assembly considers it in the interest of public safety, in the interest of metropolitan France, and in that of the colonies to take the quickest and most efficient measures to stop the causes of the divisions in the colonies, to repress the revolt of the blacks and to bring back order and peace. Considering that one of the main causes of these troubles is the refusal sustained by free people of color when they asked to enjoy equal political rights ... the National Assembly decrees the following:... Art. II. People of color, mulattoes, and free Negroes, as well as the white colonists will be admitted to vote in all the pri-

mary and electoral assemblies and will be eligible to all seats (ANF DXXV 110, 1792d).

The government's recognition of the free coloreds' potential as a controlling force in the colonies is brought to the forefront. The pragmatic consequences resulting from the refusal of enfranchisement are the most decisive factor in changing the status quo, while the ideological basis for equality is entirely absent. Three years after the Declaration of the Rights of Man, the decree granting people of color equality bears no trace of revolutionary belief. Moreover, there is no acknowledgment whatsoever of the free coloreds' repeated claims based on racial and class considerations. Equality is not portrayed as a natural outgrowth of the free coloreds' kinship with the French and of their class status. Although the people of color's inequality is seen as a cause of turmoil, it is not condemned as an injustice.

Despite the evidence of France's political interests, the free coloreds' reaction to this decree, as well as to the first one proclaimed in 1791 for the benefit of those who were born of free mothers and fathers, was dominated by an immense sense of gratitude. For them it was a sign that they finally officially belonged to the French family. Regarding their political rights as a generous present from the mother country, they thought of themselves as France's children. The filial narrative present in the earlier petitions for equality was further elaborated. Already in 1791, when only a minority of free coloreds were enfranchised, the people of color in Paris strove to convince those suffering under the whites' repressive regime in Saint Domingue that they were becoming integrated into the French family: "Consider everyone as your brother, as a member of the great French family which adopts you" ("Lettre des commissaires" [1791] 1968: 6). And again, on 8 April 1792, a few days after the second decree, Raimond portrayed France as a protective mother in a letter to his brothers in Saint Domingue: "It is for us, brothers and friends, it is to make all her children happy that the French nation will deploy a tremendous and costly force to have her will [regarding equality] carried out" (ANF DXXV 110, 1792c). The image conjured in these remarks is that of forsaken children who have been brought back home. In effect, it appears as though France took pity upon her colored orphans and benevolently decided to adopt them. Equality is not depicted as a right the way it was in the earlier petitions wherein kinship was believed to naturally entail inclusion into the circle of active French citizens. It is the goodwill of the nation, rather than the successful struggle for equality that is brought to the forefront. Particularly noteworthy is the lack of correspondence between the government's political motivations highlighted in the 1792 decree and this filial narrative.

Insisting on the mother country's benevolence, free coloreds voluntarily placed themselves in a submissive position. Already after the first decree, granting partial rights in 1791, those living in Paris wrote back to Saint Domingue urging their brothers to recognize their indebtedness to France: "by recovering your rights, brothers and friends, you will contract great obligations toward the nation which has restored them to you" ("Lettre des commissaires" [1791] 1968: 1). Although only a small minority benefited from this reprieve, the group as a whole had to continue proving its meritoriousness: "Continue to merit the praise that you have received from the friends of justice [the *Amis des Noirs*]" (3). The privileged position of some was contingent upon their complete submission to France and upon their willingness to defend their homeland with their lives: "It is only through such devotion to the French nation that you will show yourselves worthy of its adoption" (3). People of color had become fettered as servants of their nation's needs and interests. Equality appeared to depend on their exemplary behavior.

Even after all were enfranchised in 1792, free coloreds in Paris continued to urge their Caribbean brothers not to take their political equality for granted. On 8 April 1792 Raimond wrote: "I will not remind you what you owe the nation to which we have the great fortune of belonging" (ANF DXXV 110, 1792c). To demonstrate to France that they deserved their new rights, Raimond encouraged them to "practice civic and moral virtues to the highest degree." He further suggested they have the following attitude toward whites: "To all the sacrifices you have already made add the ... [sacrifice] of your fortunes to help those who were your greatest enemies ... your hearts are already burning with the desire to show all the virtues they contain; you need no stimulant for that which is great and generous" (ANF DXXV 110, 1792c).

By using words such as "obligations," "merit," "devotion," "owe," "sacrifice," and "virtues," free coloreds place themselves in a relationship of dependency with France. They portray themselves not as equals, but as servants of the nation. Contrary to their earlier demands in which they put forward their knowledge of what should rightfully be theirs—"we know our rights," and "we are not asking for a favor,"—their postenfranchisement narrative lacks this autonomous vision. Moreover, it contradicts France's avowed need to rally free colored support for the suppression of the uncontrolled slave uprisings. France initially granted equality in exchange for political allegiance, not as a benevolent gesture.

The free coloreds' docility was most likely linked to their awareness that their equality was but a political ploy, rendering their newly acquired political status rather precarious. France could revoke their rights any time if she so decided. Given the brutality that had dominated the relationship between colonial whites and free coloreds in Saint Domingue, upsurges of violence remained a formidable obstacle, making it difficult for the latter to consider those who formerly lynched them as their brothers. Since white planters generally resisted the government's meddling with colonial affairs, threatening secession whenever the status quo was endangered, they were unlikely to change their attitude. By granting people of color political rights and thus encouraging their support of France, the government was trying to tighten its grip on the colonists' autonomist tendencies (Geggus 1989a: 1302). In order for the free coloreds to keep their newly acquired rights, it was imperative that they suppress any vengeful actions directed at their enemies. "Patiently endure the injustices which the former tyranny might commit against you," urged the free coloreds in Paris; "never avenge yourselves by your own means" ("Lettre des commissaires" [1791] 1968: 2).

The pragmatic reality in the colonies did not lend itself very well to political maneuvers staged in Paris, far from the colonial quagmire. As a result, the free coloreds' narrative vis-à-vis their Caribbean brothers was also grossly out of step with their long-standing struggle for their rights. However, if people of color advocated assimilation with the French nation, it was also an indication of their ability to read France's attitude toward the colonized. While the 1792 decree clearly brought out the government's political motivations, the larger narrative of the nation promoted a paternalistic relationship to the colonized. Considering herself a civilizing force as well as the harbinger of universal freedom and equality, France fostered a relationship of dependency between herself and her colonies. Whatever changes took place in the colonial context, they were never thought to result from autonomous action. All initiatives had to come from metropolitan France and from her beneficent influence (Lara 1992, 2: 817–18). As a result of this assimilationist policy, free coloreds could, despite their unique racial, cultural, and historical heritage, believe it possible to become fully integrated into the French family. As the Trinidadian writer V. S. Naipaul (1969: 218) tellingly remarks, "All cannot be white, but all can aspire to Frenchness, and in Frenchness all are equal." This aspiration to Frenchness led to the compromise of the free coloreds' collective memory. Through their subordination to French political and historical thought, they gradually lost the collective consciousness of their own history rooted in the sociogeographic realm of the Caribbean.

Forgetting the Past

The pragmatism underlying France's gradual enfranchisement of free coloreds in 1791 and 1792 was penetratingly brought forward by the Abbé Grégoire, one of the leading figures of the *Société des Amis des Noirs*. It was not only to control the slave population but also in the interest of a commercial partnership that a positive relationship with free coloreds was advantageous for the government. In a letter addressed to the people of color in June 1791, the Abbé Grégoire ([1791] 1968: 11–14) stressed France's vested interests and the nature of her expectations: "In the name of patriotic interest and affection it is toward metropolitan France that you will direct your commercial deals, and ... establish a constant exchange of fortune and fraternal sentiments between France and her colonies." Since fraternity depended on economic profit, free coloreds could never safely presume that equality was fully theirs. To continue demonstrating their complete submission to France, they were obliged to relinquish all forms of rebellion against those who were still brutally attacking them: "those of you who dare conceive the project of vengeance against your persecutors will perish." This self-control, added Grégoire, could be achieved only through a voluntary and profound mental transformation: "Deeply bury and forget all hateful resentment." The erasure of the past was the key to successful integration, making possible the contradiction of artificially building a fraternal relationship upon a basis of mutual hatred.

The people of color in Paris were well aware of the fact that the Frenchness proposed to them could be achieved only if their own racial group was willing to forget the history of its struggles. Already in 1791 they urged their brothers in Saint

Domingue to "forget all resentment" ("Lettre des commissaires" [1791] 1968: 2). Raimond (ANF DXXV 110, 1792c) reiterated these recommendations in 1792: "I repeat it again, brothers and friends, everything must be forgotten, and the hatred which is too manifest must be replaced with sentiments of the most agreeable and close fraternity." Imprisoned for fourteen months in 1793 for allegedly instigating slaves and free coloreds to revolt, he built his defense on the fact that he had always instructed his brothers to aspire to union and fraternity with white colonists by forgetting the past.[15] As proof, Raimond (1793–1800: v–vi) published his complete correspondence prefacing the collection of letters with the following remarks: "[In all the letters] I preached to my brothers total submission to the national decrees.... I recommended the indivisibility between the colonies and the mother country. I never ceased to repeat ... the importance of union and fraternity with the white colonists, to forget all the injustices they have endured ... and to look out for the good of the nation."

Fraternity could not coexist with feelings of anger that were the natural outgrowth of a long and difficult struggle. There was no other way of overcoming this resentment than to mentally eliminate it and with it the entire process of self-liberation. The stepping stone to integration, fraternity became a double-edged sword. On one hand, it seemed the only way to guarantee the maintenance of equality. On the other hand, it led to an erasure of the past that enslaved free coloreds in a historical dependency on France. By wiping out their own past, they were obliged to replace the void with a history that was not theirs and that would never encompass the complex dimensions of their cultural identity.

"Forget the past", "Forget all resentment", "Forget all injustices", "Everything must be forgotten!" Repeated over and again, these words became the motto of the free coloreds' voluntary assimilation to the mother country. From their enfranchisement in 1792 onward, their successful resistance to white oppression in the face of great adversity became a nonevent, unrecognized and even scorned by the mother country. By giving up their rebellious posture and by adopting the colonial discourse as their own, the people of color willingly divorced themselves from their historical struggle for equality, from their mixed-race heritage, and ultimately from their identity. By making the former oppressor's words their own, they foreclosed the possibility of safeguarding their collective memory. The free coloreds' active participation in the systematic erasure of the past ultimately gave France credibility in her claim to egalitarianism, benevolence, and humanism. The people of color preserved no memory to contradict or nuance this hegemonic vision of colonial history.

The willing assimilation of the free people of color to the French nation at the end of the eighteenth century worked as a self-fulfilling prophecy. Throughout the Enlightenment, the narratives of the *philosophes,* of playwrights, of colonial planters, and of the *Société des Amis des Noirs* portrayed blacks as incapable of self-attaining freedom and equality. Only through the generosity of France could those of African descent be taught the principles of civilization and later be entrusted with freedom. Slaves and free people of color were not thought capable of organizing themselves as a group and following through with self-determined plans for rebellion. This is one of the reasons why white planters in Saint Domingue were caught off-guard by the sheer size and strength of the 1791 slave rebellion. Since those of African descent were thought to be unquestioningly inferior to whites, the French considered them dependent on actions originating in France. As a result, events proving the contrary were quickly silenced by colonial administrators. When France was forced to extend equality to the free people of color and to finally even emancipate the slaves, the local events leading to this legislation were buried and replaced by a discourse celebrating French humanism. By participating in this discourse, the free people of color acquiesced to the French version of history, accepting their own passive role.

This image of passivity, inherited from the Enlightenment, has lasted throughout the centuries. Dispossessed of their self-determination, their empowerment as rebels, and their collective memory of self-liberation, free people of color and slaves have become engulfed in French history. Their share of the past has been left by the wayside. It is only in the self-proclaimed Black Republic of Haiti that the people were able to assume their own historical existence and identity separate from France. In Martinique and Guadeloupe, it has taken two centuries for the people to interrogate elements of their daily lives and of their insular environment—"like shells left on the shore when the sea of living memory has receded"—containing hidden treasures of a forgotten past (Nora 1996: 7). Beneath layers and layers of silencing, erasure, and purposeful forgetting, realms of memory are now summoned to narrate the untold story of a people reclaiming their rightful share of the past.

Notes

1. Article 9 of the *Code Noir,* decreed in 1685 under the auspices of Louis XIV, specifies that a white master could manumit his children only if he had previously married his black concubine. Otherwise the offspring were confiscated by the state (Sala-Molins 1987: 108).

2. Bénot gives the following numbers for Saint Domingue (1789): 509,642 slaves; 26,666 people of color; 35,440 whites; for Martinique (1787): 81, 978 slaves, 4,166 people of color, 11,008 whites; and for Guadeloupe (1787): 82,978 slaves; 1,877 people of color; 12,039 whites (Bénot 1989: 60).

3. Article 59 legislates the situation of free coloreds as follows: "We bestow upon free people of color the same rights, privileges, and immunities as those enjoyed by people who are born free; we want the merit of an acquired liberty to have the same effect upon them and upon their possessions as the happiness of natural liberty has upon our other subjects" (Sala-Molins 1987: 200).

4. "Ruling by the King's Council of State ... on April 5, 1778: Whites are prohibited from marrying blacks, mulattoes or people of color, and lawyers are prohibited from wedding them with each other" (ANF Colonies F1 B1, 1775).

5. Quadroon is the term used for those who are one-quarter black. Moreau de Saint-Méry divides the offspring of blacks and whites into 128 categories covering seven generations (Moreau de Saint-Méry [1791] 1972, 1: 85–110).

6. It is important to underline that white colonial representation is entirely separate from the *Club Massiac.* While the former aspired for greater autonomy, the latter preferred the continuing control of France and were against colonial representation in the National Assembly. They knew that such representation would inevitably bring up the dreaded questions of equality and emancipation (Fick 1997: 57).

7. For further analysis of the white planters' concerted efforts to thwart the free coloreds' demands see Debien (1953: 165–98); Quinney (1970: 125–28); Bénot (1989: 70–75); Geggus (1989a: 1301–02); and Fick (1997: 57–60).

8. According to Geggus (1989a: 1291, 1296), colonial commerce was the most dynamic sector of the French economy by the end of the eighteenth century. The slave trade reached its peak between 1789 and 1791.

9. White colonial planters petitioned to be exempted from applying the new constitutions' principles of equality given their exceptional status as slaveholders. See ANF "Cahier adressé à l'Assemblée nationale par les colons de la Guadeloupe, DXXV 120 dossier 940, pièce 9 (qtd. in Pouliquen 1989: 44–46); "Adresse du Comité de Saint-Pierre de la Martinique à l'Assemblée Nationale. Saint-

Pierre, 5 octobre 1789, Colonies F3 29, 1789c (qtd. in Pouliquen 1989: 54–56); "Instructions de la Martinique à ses députés à l'Assemblée nationale du 19 mars 1790," Colonies F3 32, 1790 (qtd. in Pouliquen 1989: 56–69).

10. The only notable exception is that of Ogé who alluded to the end of the slave regime in a speech held before the *Club Massiac* in September 1789. According to Geggus (1989a: 1300), however, he is primarily remembered for excluding slaves from the rebellion he led upon his return to Saint Domingue in 1790.

11. To dissuade further rebellions, Ogé was tortured and broken on the wheel (Geggus 1989a: 1302).

12. According to Fick (1997: 59–60) this decree only affected a very small minority of free coloreds in Saint Domingue, perhaps a few hundred.

13. One aspect of the Saint Domingue conflicts that I do not mention here but that had considerable impact on colonial disorders was the internal fighting between different factions of the white population. For details see James (1989: 27–61).

14. For Guadeloupe see Pérotin-Dumon (1991: 117) and for Martinique see Geggus (1996: 289).

15. The political equality granted free coloreds in April 1792 did not quell the slave uprising in Saint Domingue. Since white planters typically held people of color responsible for fomenting and participating in slave revolts, Raimond was accused and imprisoned as the free coloreds' spokesperson in Paris. He was also charged for bribing members of the *Société des Amis des Noirs*. For more details on this episode see Cook (1941: 156–64).

✤ Chapter 5 ✤

Realms of Memory

The following quote by writer and Nobel Peace Prize Laureate Elie Wiesel points to the very essence of the problem of memory in the French Caribbean today: "The executioner always kills twice, the second time through silence" (qtd. in Chalons 2000: 152). Countless colloquiums organized by the people of Martinique, Guadeloupe and French Guiana on the occasion of the 150th anniversary of the abolitionary decree reveal the same feeling of unease in regards to the way in which France chose to commemorate this event. The Martinican writer Patrick Chamoiseau (2000: 112) laments France's "self-glorification" through the exclusive celebration of the abolitionary moment. The year 1848 became a moment of victory for the French, the victory of humanitarian ideology over a horrific system of human exploitation. However, in the process of remembering the abolition, the government-led celebrations failed to honor the memory of those who were transported across the Atlantic for three centuries, who died laboring for the production of sugar, and who continually rebelled against colonial rule: the slaves.

Chapters 1–4 focus on the slave experience during the eighteenth century, as narratives of the Enlightenment reveal the silencing of compromising attitudes toward slavery, the spread of destructive stereotypes about blacks, and the systematic omission of the slaves' voices. This chapter assesses what has become of memory in the contemporary French Caribbean by letting sites of slavery and memory speak for themselves. Even today, eighteenth-century ruins and restored plantations continue to replicate the selective memory of the colonial era. Any reference to slaves is generally omitted from restorations and descriptions of artifacts dating back to the slave regime. The exposed heritage of Guadeloupe and Martinique is thereby truncated of its slave past. In recent years, Guadeloupeans and Martinicans have begun to take charge of this silenced past by creating sites of memory that celebrate events and heroes of the slave period. Emerging from beneath the ruins, this memory negotiates its relationship to Western portrayals of the past.

The primary source material for the concluding analysis consists in black-and-white photographs of eighteenth-century sites of slavery and contemporary memorials found throughout the islands of Martinique and Guadeloupe. Legends, explanatory panels, brochures, and museum texts complement this visual documentation. The different sites and their accompanying narratives tell stories both of the past and of the present. Some sites reveal the silence about slavery that still governs former plantations. Others embody the people's reactions to this silence as well as their creative reappropriation of their occulted history.

The different sites are linked by three related themes that resurfaced again and again in the colloquiums organized in 1998. The negation of the slaves' humanity—the first theme—is fundamental to the demand that black slavery be recognized as a crime against humanity not only by France but by all nations. In 1998 Christiane Taubira-Delannon (2000), the deputy from French Guiana, proposed a law before the National Assembly that would lead to the recognition of the slave trade and of slavery as crimes against humanity. The National Assembly voted this law into effect in February 1999 and the senate in May 2001. In the construction of a number of memorials, great pains were taken to restitute the slaves' humanity by depicting them not as helpless, passive victims but as individuals who fought for their rights. For the Trinidadian scholar Max Ifill (2000: 68–69), emancipation led to the "transformation of the status of certain humans rather than to the emergence of their mind or the origin of their thought." The sculptures and paintings of slaves as dignified human beings constitute a break with the cultural construction of slavery in European and North American art. Through his superb analysis in *Blind Memory* (2000), British painter and lecturer Marcus Wood shows how blacks are continually stripped of their power whether they are visually represented during the middle passage, as runaways, or as tortured slaves.

The concern with exhibiting the slaves' humanity is evidenced by the large number of *nèg mawon* (maroon) sculptures in Martinique. The portrayal of the maroon with a machete in his hand, breaking his own chains symbolizes the second theme: the diatribe between Enlightenment ideology and the impact of slave rebellions. To what extent was the abolitionary decree a generous donation from France and to what extent did the slaves liberate themselves by forcing authorities to decree the abolition of slavery? While the official French narrative focuses on the impact of the Enlightenment, French Caribbean thinkers consider slave resistance as a historical agent (Rochmann 2000: 7). The Guadeloupean writer Daniel Maximin (2000: 17–18) deplores the silencing of slave revolts that should be fundamental to French history. He believes the abolition of slavery to have resulted from the "dialectic between the resistance of African slaves and the European fight for human rights." Slave resistance is the principal subject of a large number of memorials that purposely disregard the emblematic decree of 1848.

The silencing of slave revolts is part of the larger problem of forgetting—the third theme. In the commemorative context, this question is particularly pervasive. Studying the nineteenth-century process leading to this forgetting, the Martinican historian Myriam Cottias (2000: 97–100) speaks of an "institutionalized obliteration," a "burying" of memory in the name of assimilation. The heritage of this process is particularly visible on former plantations where oftentimes no or little mention is made of slavery and slaves. Many memorials represent a reaction to this lost memory by encouraging the spectator to reconnect with the slave past on either an intellectual or emotional level. A positive outcome of this concern with the silenced past is the stipulation in Article 2 of Taubira-Delannon's law regarding the recognition of slavery as a crime against humanity that the slave trade and slavery be included in the Republic's school curriculum.[1]

Selective Memory

Sites of slavery, such as former plantations, might well be referred to as "sites of forgetting." While eighteenth- and nineteenth-century sugar, indigo, and coffee plantations represent an important aspect of Guadeloupean and Martinican patrimony, their potential as depositories of the islands' cultural and historical wealth is compromised by a one-sided representation of the past. As Cottias (2000: 103) tellingly writes: "the

principal actors of this history, the slaves, are forgotten in favor of an elegant account of the past or of the technicalities of
sugar production." Already forgotten during the eighteenth
century, when the realities of the slave regime clashed with
humanitarian ideologies of the Enlightenment, slaves continue to be absent at the very heart of the islands' heritage: the
plantation itself.

It is the nature of this erasure, accomplished through an
elegant account of the past in the *Musée du Rhum* in Guadeloupe and on the *Habitations La Grivelière* and *Clément* in
Guadeloupe and Martinique respectively, which I examine
here. Photographs, brochures, and descriptive texts on museum panels serve as the basis of my analysis. How could the
principle actors of the past three hundred years be omitted
from these refined stories about daily life on the islands? How
does the narrative formed by nostalgia, awe before technical
brilliance, and euphemistic references to slavery render the
past desirable to visitors while leading them to completely forget the slave labor these places were founded upon?

The *Musée du Rhum* at the *Distillery Reimonenq* in Sainte-
Rose, Guadeloupe, is the most striking example of a fairy-tale
account of the past. In the brochure, the *Guide de vos loisirs*
(Musée du Rhum 2000–2001: 16–17), the potential visitor is
drawn into the enchantment of the past through promises of
a most personal and intimate experience: "Photos turned yel-
low by the impression of time, engravings charged with emo-
tion, tools and relics of the past … everything or almost
everything is shown and told you." The visitor will be introduced to a past that has the personal quality of aged family
photos and of an emotion-filled inheritance. Not everything is
shown, however, as though some things were simply too private
to share with strangers. Ironically, the untold part of the story
is the aspect of the past that should be of the most general and
public concern. None of the photos, engravings, or relics could
have existed without the labor of thousands of African slaves.
This shrouding of disagreeable reminders allows the visitor to
continue on his/her elating journey: "Like a passionate and
unusual trip, the *Musée du Rhum* enables you to relive a fresco
of the sugarcane and rum epic constructed throughout three
hundred long years." The majestic proportions of sugarcane
and rum production are brought alive as pieces of art the visitor is invited to admire. While this marvelous past is presented
as an artwork, it is also historically grounded upon "numerous
and authentic testimonies," allowing history to "snatch up"

the visitor's gaze without letting go. Complementing the technical brilliance of the past, the human testimonials would appear to provide a deeper, more exhaustive understanding of these three hundred years of history. The principal actors during the sugarcane and rum epic are not, however, invited to testify to the historical foundation of the museum's narrative. They are certainly not included in the "profound memory of the West Indian soul," which is "unveiled," ready to be "discovered" by the visitor. If the slaves are not a part of the West Indian soul one may wonder who is. What soul can be depicted in a museum that silences the voices of those whose labor made the sugarcane and rum epic possible in the first place? Silenced during the eighteenth century, when they demanded freedom at any price—as did the Martinican slaves in August 1789, or the free coloreds in their political pamphlets—the voice of slave laborers continues not to be heard in the islands' heritage museums.

References to slaves and slavery are not only omitted in the brochure but also in the *Musée du Rhum* itself. The word slavery is absent from all displays and slaves are referred to as "laborers." Although it is one of the moments when slaves experience the greatest coercive violence, the cutting of sugarcane is described as an idyllic activity: "A colorful and exotic folklore, the cutting of sugarcane is a part of the West Indian soul. A colorful atmosphere, rocked by Creole songs, and punctuated by the movements of the machetes upon the sweetened stems." The sweetness of the cane invades the entire scene turning an exhausting activity, especially under the coercive whip of the overseer, into a moment when the "West Indian soul" can be admired at its best: colorful, exotic, and rhythmic. All of the typical stereotypes applied to the people of the islands, especially in the context of tourism, describe a scene that has historically symbolized the excessive violence of the plantation regime. Any West Indian would find it difficult to identify with this portrayal of his/her soul. As in the brochure, the West Indian soul has a marvelous quality appropriate to a fairy tale, not to the realities of the slave regime (*Musée du Rhum*, n.d.).

These contemporary images are reminiscent of eighteenth-century portrayals of slavery as a beneficial experience for slaves. Colonial planters defended the slave regime by arguing that Africans were saved from barbarism and encountered a far milder fate in the West Indies. Their "work" on the islands did not only benefit the colonial regime; it was even thought useful to counter the Africans' natural laziness. The eighteenth-century representation of slave labor as "useful work" has made its way into the narrative found in the *Musée du Rhum* where slave laborers are euphemistically referred to as a "siz-able workforce" (*Musée du Rhum*, n.d.). Similarly, the fairy-tale quality to the cutting of sugarcane described in the museum echoes Louis-Sébastien Mercier's description of young black boys cajoled on the laps of women in fashionable Parisian cir-cles. Mercier contrasts the "gentle caresses" received by the boys with the "lashes" received by the groaning fathers; the boys drink the sugar worked by their enslaved fathers. There is no place for slavery in the fairy-tale atmosphere of eighteenth-century Parisian high society. Two hundred years later, slave labor is absent again, this time from the visitors' tour of the past in the *Musée du Rhum*.

The brochure's promise of an "Outlook upon three centuries of history, art, and traditions!" is not only misleading but even false. History is absent from a museum focused on the art and tradition of rum making. History is but a frill, decorating the displays with a semblance of authenticity. French metropoli-tan or foreign tourists—the museum's expected clientele—are unlikely to recognize this. The fairy-tale narrative of the mu-seum simply reinforces their preconceived notions of a place full of color, exoticism, and music. Unless they have studied the history of the Caribbean, they are unlikely to question the historical foundation of the museum's narrative.

While the *Musée du Rhum* is the most compelling example of a fairy-tail story that veils the past in the very process of cel-ebrating it, similar narratives can also be found elsewhere. The *Habitation La Grivelière*, in a mountain valley near Vieux-Habitants in Guadeloupe, announces "The history of a pre-served past" on a sign by the entrance (Fig. 1). Sure enough, although the restoration of this eighteenth-century coffee and roucou plantation is entirely focused on the master's house (Fig. 2) and on the buildings and machinery involved in the coffee production, the slave huts are still standing (Fig. 3). Un-fortunately, the latter cannot be visited due to their dilapidated state. However, the guides promise that they will eventually be restored as well. While pointing out the slave huts in the dis-tance, the guides briefly mention the presence of forty-five slaves on this plantation living in the huts that became work-ers' quarters after the abolition of slavery. Nonetheless, this slave past is disregarded in the nostalgic vision of the domain presented on the brochure. Adjectives of marvel describe the plantation not so much as a historical site than as a place of delight. Visitors are promised "unforgettable moments" as they "discover the enchantments of the sumptuous forest domain." They are urged to "take this trip into the past and contemplate the entirely restored master's house as well as the coffee mills," in order to "relive this fabulous page of history." These delights of the plantation's heritage implicate the total neglect of those aspects that are everything but "enchanting" and "fabulous." Again slavery is omitted from the brochure and does not figure as part of the "preserved past" (Habitation La Grivelière n.d.). As opposed to the *Musée du Rhum,* however, where history is transformed by the museum's narrative, *La Grivelière* does offer an authentic outlook upon the past. The exaggerated emphasis upon its marvels, however, obscures the impact that slavery has had upon this "page of history." Were it not for the historical explanations of the guides, the rare testimony to the slaves' existence would go unnoticed yet one more time.

Nostalgia, elicited by the glamour of the master's house (Fig. 4) and park property dominates the brochure about the eighteenth-century *Habitation Clément* in Le François, Martinique. Presented in the form of a letter, the description of the domain overflows with sentimentality and wistful reverie: "Dear Lucie, I am returning from the *Habitation Clément* where I spent an incredible moment. The house, the park, how enchanting!" The author of the letter offers Lucie some sketches that will—better than words—convey the sensations the place called forth in him. The master's house provokes the greatest sentimental outpouring: "I believe, dear Lucie, that like me you will be seduced by the Creole charm of the master's house. Its shingle walls emerging from the vegetation still make me dream!" The living room table is "sumptuous," the flower bouquets are "brilliant," the Creole furniture is "a pleasure for the eyes," the sideboard is "charming," and the master's bedroom "dazzling." The author is so completely seduced that he readily travels back in time: "In the lounge I would have liked to have some tea in your company, you sitting on the medallion sofa and me in the Martinican rocking chair with some sweets at hand on the Pembroque table" (Habitation Clément n.d.). The *Habitation Clément* provides entry into an enchanting dream world. Relics of a grandiose past, the house and its furnishings spark the visitors' fantasy rather than deepen their historical insight into an epoch. Although the property is classified as a historical monument, the brochure divorces the place from its context by celebrating nostalgic reminiscences of colonialism within a historical void. Catering to a delightful experience of the past, the site has carefully removed all potential physical vestiges and verbal reminders of slavery from its memorial heritage.

The brochures about the *Musée du Rhum* and the *Habitations La Grivelière* and *Clément* focus on very selective aspects of the last three hundred years. The enchanting discovery of colonial remains and the awe-inspiring demonstration of technical inheritance are presented to visitors outside of the context of plantation slavery. In fact, the raison d'être of these sites of memory is carefully removed from the narratives describing them. Slaves are not compatible with the nostalgia communicated in the brochures and on the descriptive panels about these places. They are again marginalized from the principle narrative as they were in 1789.

Shortly after Martinican slaves demanded immediate emancipation and led a generalized uprising, Martinican planters attacked the *Société des Amis des Noirs* for igniting these revolts. It was inconceivable for colonists that slaves could initiate an organized rebellion. A similar attitude led planters in Saint Domingue to be unprepared for the rebellion that would sweep the island in 1791, eventually leading to its independence. As a result of the criticism coming from representatives of the planter class in Paris, the *Amis des Noirs* immediately denied any abolitionary plans. The clash between these two interest groups focused the debate on French abolitionary ideology, not on the revolts themselves. As a result, the slaves' voices went unrecorded for posterity, overshadowed by the *Amis des Noirs*.

The selective remembrance of the colonial era displayed in the *Musée du Rhum* and on the *Habitations La Grivelière* and *Clément* is but an outgrowth of eighteenth-century disregard for slaves. From time immemorial black slaves were objectified, reduced to brute laborers without will, desire, or feeling. Maroons—who elicited great fear in the Europeans' imagination—were often depicted as bloodthirsty savages whose only aim was to kill whites. In a sense, it comes as no surprise that these stereotypical attitudes should still underlie eighteenth-century remnants of the slave period. These sites have not yet restituted the slaves' voices as respectable witnesses of the seventeenth, eighteenth, and nineteenth centuries.

Fortunately, the past is not silenced on all sites of slavery. Certain museums, such as the *Ecomusée* in Rivière Pilote, Martinique and the *Musée d'histoire* in Fort-de-France, Martinique include more elaborate exhibits on the subjects of the slave trade and plantation slavery. The most striking example in this regard is the *Maison de la Canne* (Sugarcane House) of the *Conseil Régional* in Trois-Ilets, Martinique. The brochure is already an example of historically conscious language as the museum is immediately placed in its historical context. The *Maison de la Canne* "relates over two centuries of sugar economy, depicting the slave plantations, and from the middle of the 19th century, the factories. Sugarcane has thus left its hegemonic stamp on most aspects of life on the island." (Maison de la Canne n.d.). The museum's exhibits are an example of historical memory at its best. The main actors of this past, the slaves, and after 1848 the factory workers, are placed at the center of the museum's narrative. No nostalgic reminiscences are possible since visitors witness the intertwining of the past with the slave trade and plantation slavery. The technical aspects of sugar and rum production are explained and demonstrated within the context of the lives of those whose labor produced these substances. The *Maison de la Canne* symbolizes the historical potential of sites of slavery turned into repositories of memory.

A Neglected Inheritance

While certain sites of slavery are problematic because they offer a selective memory of the past that contributes to the erasure of slave history, other sites are unavailable to the collective memory of the people. Although they do not transform the past into an elegant narrative dominated by nostalgia, they do not provide much of a narrative at all that might allow people to reconnect with their heritage. Some sites are difficult to find; others are visible but contain no inscriptions explaining their significance. As a result, the potential of these sites as channels of memory is compromised; one might call them "silent sites of memory." Left by the wayside, these "silent sites of memory" have much in common with the silenced memory of the free coloreds' political campaign for equality shortly after the French Revolution. Reminded of France's motivations behind the enfranchisement of their racial group in 1792, free people of color were urged to relinquish all ill-feelings against their former persecutors. The Abbé Grégoire—a leading member of the *Amis des Noirs*—entreated them to "deeply bury and forget" past injustice. Similarly to the free coloreds who buried their political heritage in the name of assimilation, these sites of memory have been literally buried beneath the vegetation, crumbling from neglect, or stripped of their full historical significance.

The small fishing village of Petit-Canal in Guadeloupe has so many sites of slavery that *France-Antilles Magazine Guadeloupe* (Larney 2001: 6–7) entitles an article about this village, "In Petit-Canal, Rendezvous with History." And yet, these historical sites do not make the past any more accessible. The slave prison, for instance, exemplifies the ignorance surrounding these landmarks (Fig. 5). Rebuilt in 1844 after an earthquake destroyed it in 1843, this prison is generally referred to as the "Spanish prison" (Larney 2001: 6–7). Not only were there no Spaniards in Guadeloupe, but the denomination "Spanish prison" conveys the notion that the Spaniards are to be held responsible for the colonization and implantation of slavery in Guadeloupe, not the French. Practically in ruins and gradually destroyed by the roots and branches of an enormous *Figuier-Maudit* (cursed fig tree), the prison does not catch the visitor's eye. In fact, we had to ask people were it was located. No signpost identifies the building or tells its story. Inside, the vegetation has taken over completely (Fig. 6). In an abandoned state, the prison gives little or no hold to the imagination, but a desolate spectacle of a dying past.

The "steps of the slaves," leading from the church down to the small port, are a further misrepresentation of the past. Guadeloupeans generally believe these steps to have been built by slaves, which is why they refer to them as the "steps of the slaves" *(marches des esclaves).* In keeping with this belief, wooden signs, recently affixed alongside the steps, display the names of the different African ethnic groups enslaved during the slave trade, including among others the *Ibos,* the *Ouolofs,* and the *Yoruba* (Fig. 7). However, historical sources date these steps as a postslavery construction. Although the tradition still holds that the fourty-nine steps were built at the moment of emancipation by the plantations and by the municipality, practical reasons are a more likely origin of this construction. Since the commercial activity of the town was displaced from the low-lying port to the upper town, steps were needed to provide easy access to the new developing area (Larney 2001a: 6; n.d.: 86). Although the "steps of the slaves" do provide a connection to the past—if a mythical one—the confusion surrounding their historical significance is problematic in several respects. In the first place, the site offers no explanation as to what it proposes to remember about slavery and the slave trade. What are the names of the African ethnic groups supposed to symbolize? At most, they indicate to the uninformed visitor that the place is meant to recall something about the slave trade. Second, the random attribution of an origin to this construction discredits the historical foundation of the slave past. Slavery becomes a fanciful embellishment that gives any ordinary site an exotic appeal. Of course, one may also argue that the popularization of slavery, even at the expense of historical veracity, renders slavery more alive and meaningful to the people. Even if the steps were built after 1848 for no other purpose than to make the higher lying parts of the town more accessible, the myth surrounding their construction allows the inhabitants of Petit-Canal to identify with their slave heritage on their own terms. Edouard Glissant's call for a prophetic vision of the past is really not much different from the people's appropriation of their steps. In the end, what really matters is that slavery not be erased from collective memory.

The last site of slavery in Petit-Canal—a more overt site of memory—is the monument to the Unknown Slave built in 1994 at the bottom of the "steps of the slaves." The monument consists of a large drum with a burning flame raised up on a cement base (Fig. 8). Again, no inscription explains the meaning of this stele and the uninformed visitor is simply left to imagine that the drum symbolizes the African heritage brought to the Caribbean through the slave trade. Those who know that this monument is dedicated to the unknown slave might make a parallel to the tombstone of the Unknown Soldier below the *Arc de triomphe* in Paris because of the burning flame present in both memorials. Such a parallel with a European monument weakens the African symbolism possibly linked to slave resistance. The Unknown Soldier is associated with the *Arc de triomphe* built by Napoleon, who was responsible for reinstating slavery in 1802. The lack of explanation weakens the impact of the Unknown Slave as a site of memory. One finds oneself missing a contextual framework that would substantiate the scanty connotations of the drum and the flame.

Although Petit-Canal offers historic landmarks and sites of memory, the absence of signposts, legends, or explanations renders these constructions relatively cryptic for all but the most informed. They do not signify much to the casual visitor who is not specifically looking for such sites. Even for those who know about their existence, their historical relevance is muddled. Earlier I referred to these sites as "silent sites of memory," for they do not speak to the viewer's imagination. So funda-

mental to the historical consciousness of Pierre Nora's realms
of memory, the imaginary process is stunted (Kritzman 1996:
X). The past is there, before the viewer, but does not have a direct bearing on the historical consciousness he/she brings to
the scene.

The numerous ruins of windmills found throughout the
countryside of Grande-Terre, one of the main islands of the
Guadeloupean archipelago, are another example of "silent
sites of memory" (Fig. 9). These imposing landmarks once symbolized the sugar economy and are present on most illustrations
of seventeenth- to nineteenth-century sugar plantations. Today
they are totally abandoned, without signposts or explanatory
panels. Like the slave prison, they bear testimony to a dying
past that is of nobody's concern. Sites of slavery par excellence,
windmills do not elicit the same interest as plantations. One
may speculate whether or not this is tied to the fact that windmills are too intimately associated with slave labor since they
were only used during the period of plantation slavery. After
the abolition of slavery, far less labor-intensive factories replaced windmills for sugar production. Whatever reasons may
have led to their neglect, the potential memory these sites
embody has so far been lost. Even in 1998 nobody deemed it
worthwhile to reinstate windmills as symbolic landmarks of
the island's heritage.

The comparative neglect of constructions that recall the
slave past can clearly be seen on the seventeenth-century
Habitation Anse Latouche in Martinique. While signs guide the
visitor through the ruins of the living quarters, the distillery,
the aqueduct, the dam, and the production areas of indigo
and manioc, no signs point the way to the slave quarters and
in fact there is no path leading there. Elaborate flowerbeds
decorate the hillside and were it not for the penciled-in reference to the slave quarters on the visitor's map, one would not
even notice the crumbling walls disappearing into the lush
vegetation at the top of the hill (Fig. 10).

The marginalization of the slave heritage stands in sharp
contrast to the embellishment of the white Creole colonial
lifestyle and property. Although slaves and masters can hardly
be dissociated in historical accounts of the past, this is systematically the case with seventeenth- to nineteenth-century
vestiges. The aspects of the past that are unblemished by slavery give rise to wistful reverie while the unmistakable symbols
of the slave heritage are abandoned. As a result, the slaves'

impact on the islands' historical and cultural processes is marginalized and forgotten.

The *philosophes'* writings about slavery are also selectively remembered today. The 1998 commemoration, for instance, focused exclusively on the *philosophes'* criticism of the slave regime. Journal articles and exhibitions cited Voltaire's condemnations through the mouth of Candide, Montesquieu's alleged ironic indictment, and the Abbé Raynal's fiery portrayal of the "Black Spartacus," among others. Excerpts expressing a far more nuanced, at times even racist or proslavery viewpoint were carefully omitted. The *philosophes'* silence as far as the blacks' natural rights are concerned is not discussed either (Estève 2002b: 20). Having sunk into oblivion, the contradictions inherent to their writings have not tarnished the *philosophes'* reputation as abolitionists.

Since the late 1990s and most notably since 1998, Guadeloupeans and Martinicans have addressed the omission of their heritage from their islands' memory. Through their personal vision and understanding, they have sought to bring to their compatriots' attention aspects of the past that can no longer be ignored. Some memorials are artistically influenced while others are primarily historical markers. Some focus on events, others on heroes. Others again use the Caribbean land- and seascape as their primary inspiration. All tell fascinating stories of the past that reveal the vivid spark of memory still alive in the imagination of French West Indians today.

"The Sea is History"

Where are your monuments, your battles, martyrs?
Where is your tribal memory? Sirs,
in that gray vault. The sea. The sea
has locked them up. The sea is history (Walcott 1992: 364).

In the first stanza of his poem "The Sea is History," St. Lucian poet Derek Walcott beautifully conjures up the singular quality of Caribbean history. Though it is not defined by historical markers typically recognized by Europeans, the Caribbean is rich in traces of its past. Inscribed into the land- and especially seascape, Caribbean history is almost palpable, ready to spill out into the consciousness of the people at any time. West Indians have recently begun appreciating the uniqueness of

their physical environment and have turned to nature to bring
them in touch with their failing memory. As opposed to man-
made vestiges of slavery that fail to communicate the rich inheritance of slave ancestors, nature is a faithful witness of the
past. Particularly compelling in this regard is the *Mémorial de
l'Anse Caffard,* erected before the ocean in 1998 to commemorate the shipwreck of a slave ship. The group of fifteen statues
draws its power from the serenity of the ocean stretching before
the memorial. The stele in memory of the *nèg mawon* erected
in 1998 atop Guadeloupe's mountain range is similarly capti-
vating as the forested mountains trigger the imaginary recon-
struction of the maroons' lives amid a natural haven. Finally,
the slave cemetery in Capesterre Belle-Eau, Guadeloupe, has a
solemn quality about it with the simple earth tombs marked by
conches hidden in the forest on a cliff overhanging the ocean.

These three "topographical realms of memory" (Nora 1996:
18–19)—the ocean, the forest and the earth—fill a unique role.
They are physically "rooted" in the islands' past. As opposed to
the spectacle of the white planters' glorious history contained
in vestiges and restored plantations, these realms are "places of
refuge, sanctuaries of instinctive devotion and hushed pilgrim-
ages, where the living heart of memory still beats." Repositories
of memory, these sites escape the burial of the slave past beneath layers of history. By bringing to consciousness the collective memory of the people, they allow the spectator to experience the past in his/her imagination. Contrary to the nostalgia
elicited on plantations, this remembrance is of an immaterial
nature, attaching itself to a collective experience rather than
to physical vestiges. The natural environment surrounding
these sites enables the spectator to enter into communion with
three centuries of collective suffering and resistance.

The erection of the *Mémorial de l'Anse Caffard* on the southern
tip of Martinique was initiated by the city of Diamant in 1998.
Sculpted by Laurent Valère, the fifteen cement statues are two
and a half meters high, and each weighs four tons. They are
arranged in a triangle on a cliff overhanging the ocean to symbolize the triangular trade between Europe, Africa, and the
Americas (Figs. 11–14). The white color of the statues is the traditional color of sepulture in the Caribbean. It draws attention
to the funerary dimension of the site, which beyond the shipwreck of a slave ship on 8 April 1830 leading to the death of
nearly three hundred enchained slaves also commemorates
all the unknown victims of the slave trade. It is for this reason
that the statues face the Gulf of Guinea at a 110 degree angle.

The memorial's motto, "Memory and Fraternity"—inscribed on the first statue—highlights its primary purpose: to remember the victims of the slave trade in a spirit of fraternity between human beings.

The *Mémorial de l'Anse Caffard* is perhaps one of the most remarkable memorials erected in memory of slavery and the slave trade during the past ten years in the French West Indies. The communication between the fifteen, giant, white statues and the vast expanse of water below the cliff creates a reverential quality about the memorial that is quite uncanny. Slightly bowed, their posture is solemn and reflective as though they were in prayer before the collective grave of their brothers (Fig. 13). The ocean surrounding the islands "is history." The imposing white sculptures powerfully convey the message of this past by taking the spectators back in time in their imagination, guiding them in their vision of the middle passage.

The persuasiveness of the memorial lies not only in the communion between the sculptures and the geographic surroundings, but also in the detailed historical description of the site provided on panels in both French and English. As opposed to most memorials that present only minimal or no information about the artwork, these explanatory panels provide a detailed account of the shipwreck commemorated here, historical facts about the slave trade accompanied by illustrations, as well as the background and meaning of the memorial itself.

One illustration on the panels is particularly significant. It is the famous copper engraving, *Description of a Slave Ship,* commissioned by the London Society for the Abolition of the Slave Trade in April 1789 (Fig. 15). In *Blind Memory,* Wood (2000: 36) wonders if this image, used over and over again across the centuries has not in a sense become a monument to the middle passage. This heritage, however, is not unproblematic. It is based on an image popularized by abolitionists who portrayed slaves as totally passive and helpless victims (19). The "cultural void" created around the slave in this Western visualization of the middle passage was obtained by focusing on the economically efficient packing of the slave cargo. The striking contrast between the black bodies and the white spaces accentuates the stillness of the slaves, completely subdued by Western commercial venture (29).

It is interesting to examine some of these arguments in the context of the *Mémorial de l'Anse Caffard.* The *Description of the Slave Ship* along with the other illustrations and maps on the panels alongside the statues firmly root the memorial in the Western tradition of visually representing slavery and the slave trade. Notable in this regard is also the image of the slave man and woman embracing each other with opened chains in their hands (Fig. 16). This scene is taken from the famous painting by Auguste-François Biard entitled *L'abolition de l'esclavage dans les colonies françaises en 1848* (The abolition of slavery in the French colonies in 1848) painted in 1849. Similarly to the *Description of the Slave Ship*, this painting has come to symbolize slavery in the Western, and more specifically, in the French imagination. It is used in many textbooks and on the covers of novels (Delas 2001: 271). The emancipated slaves are depicted as joyful beneficiaries of France's generosity. No longer helpless victims, they nonetheless remain passive recipients of Western humanitarianism.

What is striking about the memorial is the contrast between the Western narrative found on the panels and the non-Western atmosphere exuded by the scene of the fifteen statues. Their imposing stature gives everything but an impression of passivity. Facing the vast body of water in the direction of the Gulf of Guinea, the statues embody the memory of the West Indians' ancestors: their origin, their violent uprooting, and the middle passage ending for many in the ocean's "gray vault." Although the memory is tragic, nothing about the scene evokes the pity commonly elicited by Western representations of slavery and the slave trade. On the contrary, the dignified bearing of the statues portrays them as strong symbols of the past, facing squarely the vicissitudes of slavery (Fig. 14). And yet, the explanatory panels alongside the memorial reproduce Western narratives of helpless, victimized, passive and dependent slaves. While the statues are respectfully bowed before the memory of the middle passage, the black bodies of the *Description of a Slave Ship* have lost all individuality, all will, and all capacity to remember. The fifteen statues willfully remember the past, physically rooted as they are in the land- and seascape of the island. The slaves on the panels, on the other hand, do not elicit memory as much as horror before the inhumanity of the trade and relief at its abolition: they tap into a store of emotions present in European audiences of the late eighteenth and early nineteenth centuries.

On the eve of the French Revolution, the *Société des Amis des Noirs* already used this emotional leverage to impress upon their audience the inhumanity of the slave trade, publicizing among others, the famous *Description of a Slave Ship*. In contrast, Martinican slaves wrote to colonial authorities in August

1789 to directly and unwaveringly request the return of their God-given right to freedom. They were willing to die for their freedom, breaking out into a generalized revolt shortly after their threats. In the face of this colonial turmoil, the *Amis des Noirs* immediately rescinded their pleas, abandoning the cause of the slaves and free people of color altogether. The pity solicited in the imagination of the public had little effect on the course of events in the colonies.

It is therefore surprising that the creators of the *Mémorial de l'Anse Caffard* should have accompanied the powerful presence of the fifteen statues with relatively ineffectual Western imagery. Perpetrating colonial dominance already during the eighteenth and nineteenth centuries, it is difficult to imagine what these images might add to a Caribbean-based site of memory. Notwithstanding, the *Description of a Slave Ship* and Biard's *L'abolition de l'esclavage* are far from negligible in the context of the *Mémorial de l'Anse Caffard*. Visitors are witness to a heritage, which—at the beginning of the twenty-first century—is inextricably linked to Europe and to the French colonial regime. While the people from Martinique and Guadeloupe are faced with the challenge of recuperating their history from the ruins and omissions of the past three hundred years, their memory has also been profoundly impacted by Western thought. The contrast between Western and non-Western influences at the memorial is an insightful rendition of this double heritage.

The stele in memory of the *nèg mawon* on the Col des Mamelles in Guadeloupe commands the same respectful gaze as the statues at Anse Caffard: it also draws its inspiration from the natural surroundings. The stele consists in a large rock set upon a cement slab. A plaque with the inscription *Ba nèg mawon* (For the maroons) is affixed to the rock signed *Tras' Memoires 98* (Fig. 17). *Tras' memoires* means either "the path of memory" or "traces of memory" in Creole. It is a project of the *Association Tout-Monde,* which includes among its members the Martinican writers Edouard Glissant, Patrick Chamoiseau, and Raphaël Confiant and is directed by the Guadeloupean politician and writer Gérard Delver; its goal is to identify important sites of memory. Every year, the members of this association convene at the stele on the Col des Deux Mamelles to commemorate the forest as a site of resistance through *marronnage.* The simplicity of the memorial allows visitors to focus on the most salient characteristic of this site of memory: the lush mountain ranges extending in every direction. The serenity of the spot is very suggestive of the protection the forest pro-

vided maroons. For Glissant (1981: 159), the forest was a haven
allowing the maroon to seek refuge from those pursuing him/
her by becoming completely one with the vegetation:

> He imagined his pursuers, dogs and hunters, in the distant
> woods where they had gotten lost. He had followed the trace of
> the ravines when the others were looking for him on all the
> ridges. From below he sometimes felt like the hunter and it
> made him laugh. He had opened up a track from hiding place
> to hiding place and was turning in circles: it was the only way
> to escape from the others; to be constantly on the move. He had
> become indistinct from the branches and the mud, from the
> earth and the stumps among which one might have taken him
> for a *figuier-maudit* (cursed fig tree).

Glissant's maroon is literally rooted in the island; he becomes
one with his surroundings. It is through this identification between the maroon and nature that visitors can vividly imagine
the past as they survey the surroundings beyond the inscription *Ba nèg mawon*. Again it is nature's evocative power that
turns this particular site into a realm of memory. As opposed
to the *Mémorial de l'Anse Caffard,* however, this site provides no
historical information. No panel or legend explains the meaning behind the erection of the stele. Although the figure of the
maroon has become an integral part of the West Indian imaginary, information on maroon communities and on their role
in resistance movements would considerably enhance the
potential of the site as a vehicle of historical understanding.
When I interviewed Delver in June 2001, he mentioned that
the *Association Tout-Monde* planned to expand the memorial.[2]

The Guadeloupean slave cemetery in Capesterre Belle-Eau
is an example of how the earth itself can become a repository
of memory. Although two signposts on the side of the road indicate the existence of this cemetery (Fig. 18), it is very difficult
to find, hidden in the underbrush of the forest on a cliff overhanging the ocean. A cement slab with the name of the town
and the inscription "To the Memory of Our Slave Ancestors
Honor and Respect" signed by the municipality and dated 1994
signals the beginning of the cemetery (Fig. 19). Conches of
lambi arranged in circles mark approximately twenty graves.
A few graves are also decorated with crosses and palm leaves
(Fig. 20). Although again there are no historical explanations,
the site itself is very suggestive and solemn, allowing the visitor's imagination to envision the past. The authenticity of this

and other slave cemeteries in Guadeloupe is contested by historians. Alain Yacou, for instance, believes that slave cemeteries
are a pure invention, a myth. Archaeological searches have
not yet been able to provide conclusive evidence leading to the
positive identification of many of the presumed slave cemeteries. Nonetheless, archaeologists believe in the hypothesis
that they are African slave cemeteries (Courteaud, Delpuech,
and Romon 1999: 277–90). The cemetery at Capesterre Belle-
Eau has not yet been excavated. As far as the question of memory is concerned, however, it is irrelevant whether or not slave
cemeteries are authentic. Realms of memory, according to
Nora (1996: 19), do not need to refer to a specific reality. This
is what allows them to escape from history. What is important
about the slave cemetery at Capesterre Belle-Eau is that it symbolizes honor and respect for slave ancestors. It has become a
place of devotion where the people can reconnect with their
slave heritage. In this regard the slave cemetery is very much
like the memorials to the maroons and to the drowned slaves:
it turns nature into a sacred place where the memory of the
past has been preserved. The sea, the forest, and the earth are
history because they are the only witnesses of a past that was
not deemed worthy of official historical accounts.

The Maroon as Liberator

Maroons are the most complete and vivid embodiment of popular memory in the Caribbean today. Having left imaginary
traces in the forested mountain regions of the islands, maroons
are very much tied to the Caribbean landscape, as can be
noted with the stele on the Col des Mamelles in Guadeloupe.
However, the ephemeral quality of these traces has turned the
figure of the maroon into a myth both in the literary and popular imagination. The Guyanese critic Lydie Ho-Fong-Choy
Choucoutou (2000: 20–23) considers literary representations
of the maroon to be a way of reappropriating history by turning blacks into agents of their destiny. The figure of the literary
maroon thus denounces the "decorative role" often attributed
to blacks who are considered unsuited for freedom. Haunting
the West Indians' imagination (Burton 1997: 10), the maroon
dismantles Western representations of the slave as a passive
victim who will tend to run away rather than fight the oppressor (Wood 2000: 97, 113, 218).

In the context of the celebrations surrounding the anniversary of the abolition of slavery, Martinican historians underline
the fundamental role played by slave revolts in the historical
process.[3] The iconography of the maroon, particularly dominating in Martinique, provides invaluable insight into the
people's reappropriation of their rightful share. During the
past decade, French Caribbean artists have brought slave resistance as a major historical agent into center stage (Rochmann
2000: 7). Their sculptures typically focus on the independent
will of the maroon, determined to fight for freedom with his own
physical strength and through violent means. This portrayal
of violence echoes the literary maroons of the eighteenth century. Jean-François Saint-Lambert, Louis-Sébastien Mercier,
and Denis Diderot imagined maroons whose raison d'être was
to avenge their compatriots. Characterized by the same violence as these eighteenth-century figures, the Martinican maroon statues in Diamant, Saint Esprit, and Fort-de-France,
nonetheless distinguish themselves by their focus on freedom.
Violence is a means to an end symbolized by broken chains.
Furthermore, the *lambi* shell and drum, symbols of their Afro-
American heritage, root these maroons in their own tradition.
They are not—like their eighteenth-century counterparts—ab-
sorbed by the infliction of judgment day upon Europeans.

Sculpted in 1998 by Hector Charpentier, the statue of the
maroon in the city of Diamant embodies strength, pride, and
dignity (Fig. 21). The physical and mental weight of the maroon is directed toward the fist that has just broken the chains
of slavery. The act of self-liberation lends an air of assurance
and nobility to his facial expression. He holds his head high,
intently gazing into the distance over his fist as though focusing and concentrating his energies. Though assuredly ready to
fight for his freedom, his muscular body is graced with a dignified posture that ennobles his physical and mental power.

This maroon statue is strikingly similar to L.-S. Mercier's
"avenger of the New World" with his "noble and imposing" attitude. However, while the fragments of twenty scepters at the
feet of Mercier's black hero directly associate the statue with
Europe, the maroon in Diamant draws the source of his energy
from the *lambi* shell in his right hand and from the drum lying
between his feet. Not only does this symbolism root his actions
in a decidedly non-European tradition, it also makes him part
of a larger community with whom he communicates through
the *lambi* shell and the drum. Rather than violently opposing

himself to Europe, this maroon relates himself to his Caribbean compatriots.

While the maroon in Diamant resembles his eighteenth-century counterpart in L.-S. Mercier's novel, he stands in opposition to more traditional Western representations of slaves as passive recipients of European benevolence. This is particularly striking on the seal of the London Society for the Abolition of the Slave Trade. Made by Josiah Wedgwood in 1788, the seal represents a kneeling, enchained slave pleading: "Am I not a man and a brother?" The submissiveness of the man on the seal portrays his dependency on the Europeans' pity. On the contrary, the maroon of Diamant depends on none other than himself and his maroon community to attain freedom; he literally and figuratively stands up to his inherent rights.

The maroons' struggle for freedom is often symbolized by violence. The sculpture by Coco René Corail in the neighborhood of Trénelle in Fort-de-France illustrates this facet of rebellion very poignantly. Sculpted out of wrought iron, the maroon holds what appears to be a dead or dying child in his left arm while raising a machete up above his head in his right hand in an attacking gesture: he is ready to avenge his child's death (Fig. 22). The violence rendered by this artwork is reminiscent of the wrath expressed by literary maroons of the eighteenth century, in particular by Saint-Lambert's Ziméo. Having massacred white men, women, and children during a rebellion, Ziméo is faced with his relentless desire for blood. He feels perpetually unsatisfied and is unable to alleviate his deep grief for those he has lost. While the maroon in Trénelle appears to be similarly motivated by revenge, the words inscribed on a plaque below the sculpture offer a more constructive motive: "Square of 22 May 1848. Martinican remember!" The violence symbolized by the attacking figure is in the name of freedom. On 22 May 1848 a generalized slave rebellion forced Claude Rostoland, the governor of Martinique, to decree the abolition of slavery on 23 May before the arrival of the official decree from France. Martinicans are admonished to remember the slave-led rebellion that brought about their own local abolition, independently of events in France. By simultaneously embodying violence and freedom, the sculpture escapes the dichotomy facing Ziméo. Unlike Ziméo, the attacking figure does not merely oppose himself to whites; he is engaged in a constructive fight that frees him from bondage.

The effectiveness of the sculpture as a representation of slavery in the popular imagination was born out by an unusual incident. Fixed to a stone wall, the sculpture is located in the middle of a working-class neighborhood surrounded by public sector housing. At one time it was supposed to be lent to the city of Fort-de-France. However, afraid that the sculpture would not be returned, the youths of the neighborhood attached it with pikes thereby managing to keep it in place.[4] The youths' desire to protect the sculpture shows the extent to which they were able to identify with its message. Making the past come alive, the maroon of Trénelle imprints itself on the youth's present reality, thus creating a meaningful link between the slave past and contemporary Martinican society.

The memorial to the maroon in Saint Esprit sculpted and painted by Michel Glondu in February 2000 combines elements of the maroons of Diamant and Trénelle with traditional Western representations of slavery, not unlike those found at Anse Caffard. Sculpted out of wrought iron, a maroon brandishes his machete high up in the air in an exalted gesture with broken chains hanging from his wrists (Figs. 23 and 24). He is standing on a drum with a *lambi* shell attached to its side. The drum is on top of a cone shaped structure that is decorated with objects of torture, masks of skeleton faces, bones, and blood. On the large square cement base below the sculpture are four paintings of the slave trade and plantation slavery in the Caribbean.

The theme of self-liberation, interpreted as well by the sculptor of the Diamant memorial, is again symbolized here by the machete, the drum, and the *lambi* shell. The raised machete embodies the violent aspect of self-liberation present in the sculpture of Trénelle, though the Saint Esprit maroon holds up his machete in an exalted gesture rather than in the attacking thrust of the Trénelle figure. What makes the memorial in Saint Esprit so arresting is the defiance of the self-liberated slave vis-à-vis the Western style paintings of dying and tortured slaves on the base. The middle passage, inspired by J. M. W. Turner's 1840 painting, *Slavers Throwing Overboard the Dead and Dying, Typhoon Coming On,* depicts drowning slaves who have just been thrown overboard a slave ship and are eaten by sharks (Fig. 25). Although Glondu's painting does not share the artistic qualities of Turner's, the allusion to this well-known and controversial English painting is striking.[5] The scenes of tortured slaves are similarly inspired by Western representations of slavery, in particular by William Blakes's 1798 copper engraving, *A Negro hung alive by the Ribs to a Gallows* from John Stedman's *Narrative of a Five Years' Expedition Against the Revolted Negroes of Suriname* (Fig. 26). The message of these scenes is, however, transformed by the representation at the center of the painting of maroons dancing around a fire in a thick forest. The joyfulness expressed by these characters responds to the rejoicing sculpture above. Exuberant in the face of death, the maroons symbolize the inevitable coexistence of slavery and self-liberation, and of torture and autonomy. The imprint of Western images on the memory of slavery is challenged by expressions of freedom attained independently of colonial power.

The confrontation between self-liberation and European authority over the slaves' fate contrasts sharply with eighteenth-century portrayals of "civilized" maroons by Gabriel Mailhol, Olympe De Gouges, and Pigault-Lebrun. Tintillo, Zamor, and Télémaque become heroes not because of their rebellion, but because they willingly submit to the master's control after their brief escapades. Voicing European values, they insist on the impossibility of self-liberation. Not only does rebellion lead to savagery, it is not compatible with freedom. Only when it is benevolently extended by the white master can liberty lead to a happy and civilized existence. The Saint Esprit maroon provokes this European belief with his jubilant stance. He defies the Europeans' tyranny as well as their representations of blacks as helpless and submissive victims. His machete triumphantly raised, the maroon proclaims his freedom not only from slavery but also from European thought: he owes his freedom to nobody but himself.

The Emergence of a Caribbean Identity

Maroons are not the only symbol people from the French Caribbean have used to give a material reality to their memory of the past. Martinicans disfigured the statue of Josephine de Beauharnais, wife of Napoleon, to turn a mere colonial representation into a site of memory. This overt attack on colonialism refuses to let French history cover up the local histories of slave descendents. Similarly, Guadeloupeans celebrate the heroes of their 1802 revolution against the reinstatement of slavery by Napoleon.[6] Countless statues, paintings, and memorials of Louis Delgrès, Ignace, and Mulâtresse Solitude remind the Guadeloupean population of their ancestors' violent opposition to French hegemony. Embedded in these memorials is not only the desire to recollect the past, but also a rejection of mainstream history.

In September 1991 somebody decapitated the statue of Joséphine de Beauharnais in La Savanne, the central park of Fort-de-France. The person smeared the statue with red paint to give it a bloody appearance and wrote the following Creole words across the different faces of the cement base: *Rèspé ba Matinik* (Respect for Martinique) and *Rèspé ba 22 mé* (Respect for 22 May.) (Figs. 27 and 28). The culprit has never been found but people imagine that he/she was a member of the independence movement. Although the head of the statue has been redone, nobody has dared replace it on the bust since it would be a profoundly political act with potentially dangerous consequences. The possibility of moving the statue to another location has also been evoked.

The statue of Joséphine is a threefold symbol of colonialism, slavery, and alienation. A member of a white Martinican planter family, Joséphine represents four hundred years of white colonial hegemony. Moreover, as the wife of Napoleon Bonaparte, she is closely associated with the reestablishment of slavery in 1802, which she is partly responsible for. Finally, the glorification of French history despite its devastating effects on the lives of African slaves is a sign of the alienation that has befallen parts of the Martinican population. One might liken it to the erection of statues of Adolf Hitler in Poland, France or Germany. The disparity between all that Joséphine embodies and the population's slave heritage is irreconcilable. The political act of decapitating the statue was a violent way of physically destroying these symbols. However, beyond the violence of the severed head and the blood, a constructive message is conveyed by the graffiti. By calling for the respect of Martinique and of the slave insurrection on 22 May 1848, the author of this act asks the people to become conscious of their own local histories. The slave population successfully fought for the promulgation of the abolitionary decree, thus taking an active part in the history of their island: this memory must be honored today. The passive acceptance of an overt symbol of colonialism and slavery, on the other hand, has to be vehemently rejected by a people who know their heritage.

In Guadeloupe, efforts to make the general population aware of their own history have focused on Delgrès, Ignace, and Mulâtresse Solitude. Each of these figures played a leading role in the attack against Napoleon's troops, which came to re-establish slavery under the orders of the general Antoine Riche-panse. Mulâtresse Solitude is remembered for her tireless fight. Although she was pregnant she never ceased to abandon the cause of freedom until her capture and hanging. Ignace was one of the leading figures of the Revolution. He died in combat on 25 May 1802. The military leader Delgrès has become the principal symbol of the antislavery revolution because of the extraordinary mass suicide he participated in with several hundred of his companions once it was clear they had lost the war and slavery would be reestablished in Guadeloupe. Del-grès lived the revolutionaries' rallying cry until the very end: *Vivre libres ou mourir!* (To live in freedom or to die!).

Statues were erected in memory of each one of these emblematic figures on the Boulevard des Héros in Pointe-à-Pitre, Guadeloupe, in 1998, 1999, and 2001 (Figs. 29–32). Particularly noteworthy about Mulâtresse Solitude and Ignace is their proud and insubordinate stance. The statue of Delgrès, consisting in disconnected body parts, symbolizes the suicidal explosion. This memorial bears an uncanny resemblance with Diderot's description of the "Black Spartacus" in the Abbé Raynal's *Histoire des deux Indes* ([1770, 1774, 1780] 1981: 201–202): the leader of the slaves "will assemble around him the companions of his misfortune." Parallel to this image, the statue of Delgrès in Pointe-à-Pitre is surrounded by eight statues of his companions (Fig. 32). The conclusion of Diderot's prophecy seems to further describe the memorial: "The Old World will join the New World in applause. The name of the hero who will have reestablished the human rights will be blessed and memorials glorifying him will be erected everywhere." Incidentally, Delgrès is pensively looking at a book lying before him entitled *1789—Human Rights*. The eighteenth-century literary figure and the 2001 memorial have a similar ideological thrust: freedom is a basic human right the enslaved will fight for until the very end. The prophetic "Black Spartacus," imagined by Diderot three decades before Delgrès's fight against the French troops—and incidentally only a few years before Toussaint Louverture's leadership of the Haitian Revolution—communicates an idealism that is absent from the dismembered Delgrès. While the "Black Spartacus" raises the sacred flag of liberty, Delgrès and his companions are faced with defeat.

And yet, the powerful message conveyed by the memorial—and in fact all three memorials—honors the memory of these heroes. They symbolize the slaves' desire and capacity to resist

European domination. Two hundred years later, these memorials are erected in the name of resistance. Besides providing a brief biography of the heroes and explaining the purpose of these memorials, the plaques below the statues accentuate this message: *Gwadloupéyen sonjé Milatres Solitid (Ignace/Delgres) en mé 1802* (Guadeloupeans remember Mulâtresse Solitude [Ignace/Delgrès] in May 1802). Erected on the anniversary date of the abolition of slavery, the statues do not memorialize the 1848 French abolitionary decree. On the contrary, they are contrapuntal to the overpowering narrative of the French abolitionist movement led by Victor Schœlcher. The plaque on the statue of Ignace hones in on the Caribbean focus of the memorials: "Honor and Respect to all the Negro maroons, to all Guadeloupean freedom fighters who preferred death in Baimbridge, on the heights of Matouba and everywhere else to the humiliation of a return to slavery." Through these statues, Guadeloupeans lay claim to their memory of the past. Refusing to let Mulâtresse Solitude, Ignace, and Delgrès be overshadowed by celebrated French abolitionists, Guadeloupeans narrate a history that embodies their own unique social and geographic reality.

Painted in May 1998 by Guadeloupean high school artists, the mural in front of Baimbridge High School in the neighborhood of Les Abymes, Pointe-à-Pitre, is perhaps the most accomplished expression of popular memory to be found in Guadeloupe. Ignace and Delgrès are principal figures on the mural along with images from Africa, from the middle passage, from the Declaration of the Rights of Man, and from the abolition of slavery among others (Figs. 33–34). Guadeloupean youths have made these historical images their own, turning them into realms of memory for their generation. With the following words painted on the mural, a high school student, Valérie Mylène poetically impels the past into her present-day reality:

> Born from the blood shed by our enslaved fathers.
> Today you exist.
> I want you and I experience you.
> I cry out your name.
> Liberty.

The past has come to life under the stroke of these young people. Similarly to the sculptors of the *Mémorial de l'Anse Caffard* and of the maroon in Saint Esprit, they have depicted symbols of their Caribbean heritage alongside Western visualizations of slavery and liberation. Ignace and Delgrès are painted right next to the *Description of a Slave Ship* and the famous scene from Biard's *L'abolition de l'esclavage*, in which the recently emancipated man and woman embrace one another with chains still hanging from their wrists (Fig. 33). The juxtaposition of Caribbean and Western images symbolizes the West Indians' double heritage: uniquely tied to the geography and history of their islands, they also have to continually negotiate their relationship to France, both historically and in the present. With one out of four persons born in the French Caribbean residing in France today, the acknowledgment of this double heritage has become paramount.[7] Amid the bustling city life of Pointe-à-Pitre, the mural of Baimbridge High School is reckoning with past, present, and future. It is rooting an experience in the collective consciousness of the people thereby turning the past into an identity-forging process for the future: "We are coming out of the shadow, we had no rights, and we had no glory; that is precisely why we are speaking up and starting to tell our history" (Foucault 1997: 62).

Notes

1. "The textbooks and research programs in history and in the social sciences will give to the slave trade and to slavery the importance they deserve" ("Proposition de loi" 2000).
2. When I visited the site in January 2005 it had not yet been expanded.
3. See Rochmann (2000: 5–14) and Delas (2001: 266–67).
4. The author was told this story by an artist living in that part of Fort-de-France.
5. For more information on Turner's painting see Wood's (2000: 41–68) excellent analysis.
6. Under English control at the time, Martinique never experienced the first abolition of slavery in 1794. As a result, the reinstatement of slavery by Napoleon in 1802 had no direct impact on this island.
7. According to the *Institut National de la statistique et des études économiques* (INSEE), the number of natives from France's *départements d'outre mer* (Guadeloupe, Martinique, French Guiana, and Reunion) has been multiplied by fifteen during the past fifty years. These numbers are based on the 1999 census. The study led by the INSEE focused on persons born in the *départements d'outre mer* and residing in France. It did not take into account individu-

als originating from the *départements d'outre mer,* including those born in the *départements d'outre mer* as well as their children regardless of their place of birth (Marie and Qualité 2002).

BEYOND SLAVERY

Guadeloupean and Martinican artists have been reclaiming the Caribbean past. They have enfranchised themselves from the symbolically charged heritage of the Enlightenment and of the nineteenth-century abolitionist movement. Refusing to subscribe to the cultural construction of victimization, they communicate dignity, strength, and determination through their artwork. While the memorials are often accompanied by Western representations of slavery, their message emerges from a combination of Caribbean and European heritages. They narrate stories of the past that fill the void left by the silence of history.

This artwork envisions the present and the future through the past. While facing the collective grave of their ancestors in the "gray vault," or the symbols of torture and death, the statues exude a celebratory quality that goes beyond the tragic memory evoked. The memory has engendered strength; death and torture have been overcome; the chains of servitude have been broken; and liberty has been born. The symbolic thrust is into the present and future as expressed by Valérie Mylène: "today you exist / I want you and I experience you." While the poet knows that her liberty was "born from the blood shed by our enslaved fathers," she jubilates because she is free today. Informed by the knowledge of the past, she looks toward the future now.

The slave past must be told, the silences voiced, and the incoherences analyzed. There is an important place for exploring the correlation between the Enlightenment, the slave regime, and emancipation. Understanding the impact of the maroon both as a historical and mythical figure is primordial. Fascinating are the crisscrossings of ideologies and revolts during the age of revolutions. The transformation of this memory through the process of assimilation sheds light on the French Caribbeans' troubled relationship to the past. And finally, contemporary artistic renderings of the slaves' silenced engagement for freedom claim a rightful share of the past. Nonetheless, it is crucial to go beyond the slave era once it has been appropriately brought to light and rendered conscious in the people's imagination.

In her thought-provoking novel *La Belle Créole,* the Guadeloupean writer Maryse Condé (2001) depicts the dangerous obsession with the slave past. The protagonist Dieudonné was exonerated for killing his white mistress. His defense lawyer Maître Serbulon successfully built his case on the premise that Dieudonné was reenacting the age-old rebellion of the defenseless slave against the cruel white mistress. He killed her to liberate himself (44). Operating under the assumption that the country had only recently emerged from slavery—no less than a hundred fifty years ago—(40), Serbulon made a collective drama out of a trivial event (164). The people, he believed, still identified themselves as descendants of slaves (48) and shared a generalized hatred of the békés (white Creole planters) (138). While Serbulon convinced the jury, his "absurd theories" misrepresented his client's experience (227). Dieudonné felt that "he had no truth; he was nothing but a carnival figure, dressed in rags, travestied by his compatriots' fantasies" (52). He was not the revolted slave people saw in him, but a grieving lover who had acted in self-defense and deeply mourned the loss of his love (227).

Dieudonné refused to see himself as a victim of society. He did not feel that he belonged to the oppressed classes: "Oppressed by whom? Oppressed by what?" He had simply been unlucky, born into a bad cradle. It was a question of fate (Condé 2001: 75). He had certainly never considered himself oppressed by Loraine, his white mistress. On the contrary, she was everything for him; she was his life; he was enslaved by his love for her. Dieudonné was not the only one to disbelieve Serbulon's theories. Both Loraine and his father Milo scoffed at the lingering presence of slavery. As far as Loraine was concerned only idiots thought that slavery was still alive today (179). Milo considered the talk of slavery foolishness nobody believed in anymore; he remained unconvinced by Serbulon's case (193). Dieudonné became entrapped in the superimposition of the slave past on his present reality. Ironically, his juridical liberation fettered him. Having officially been turned into a victim of slavery, he could no longer project himself into the future—a future of which Loraine was forever absent. Ultimately, Dieudonné was only able to imagine his freedom through suicide.

La Belle Créole shows what is at stake in the mythicization of slavery. The past has a limited applicability when it comes to explaining the ills of the present. Not all tribulations that befall the people from Guadeloupe and Martinique find their origin in the master/slave dichotomy. In fact, the excessive focus on the slave past leads to yet another kind of artificial enslavement. Victimized by the past, the people cannot overcome their dependency on the West and on Western portrayals of history. Trying to understand the sociohistorical phenomena leading to their present-day reality, the artists described in chapter 5 model a creative reappropriation of the past. These "prophetic visions of the past"—to use Edouard Glissant's terms one more time—spread outward like rhizomes creating a dense mesh of interpretations. The exclusive projection of society's ailments upon the slave past, on the other hand, might be likened to the unique root, seeking a singular origin to explain the failings of contemporary society. Such a narrow perspective disregards the broad spectrum of experiences comprising the French Caribbean heritage. It simply reenacts the one-sided portrayal of slave victims by the Western historical and artistic tradition.

It is in an effort to avoid this pitfall, to avoid victimizing slaves yet one more time that I studied the memory of slavery against the backdrop of embroiled eighteenth-century voices. It was not my aim to establish the origin of French Caribbean slavery and emancipation. I did not wish to write a diatribe against proponents of the slave regime or a eulogy for its opponents. By confronting dominant narratives with the silence of the past, remembered sources with forgotten documents, and triumphant memories with hidden shadows, I sought to capture memories of the past beyond commonly held beliefs about slavery and emancipation. This endeavor is finally punctuated by the creative voices of contemporary Guadeloupean and Martinican artists and writers. Their imaginative appropriation of the past opens a door to the future.

Postscript

Since I initially completed this book in the fall of 2003 the debate surrounding the memory of slavery in France has far from subsided. Quite on the contrary, France's slave past has become a burning question not only for the descendants of slaves, but also for the French government and for the French public at large. Most notable in this regard is the *Comité pour la mémoire de l'esclavage* (Committee for the memory of slavery) appointed by the French government in accordance with the statutory order of 5 January 2004, which applies the law of 10 May 2001 qualifying slavery and the slave trade as crimes against humanity. In its first rapport handed over to the Prime Minister on 12 April 2005, the committee details the inadequate official treatment of slavery by the government as a major historical event, and as an integral part of the school curriculum. The committee makes a series of specific propositions to remedy these deficiencies including the choice of 10 May as an official date of national commemoration, the extensive incorporation of all aspects of slavery and the slave trade into the school curriculum, and the creation of research and cultural centers which integrate these hitherto marginalized issues into the national memory. The tardy acceptance by President Jacques Chirac on 30 January 2006 of the committee's proposal, and his pronouncement of 10 May as a national day commemorating the abolition of slavery, comes in the midst of fierce debate over the memory of the French colonial past. The nation at large has begun calling into question the inadequate memory of French colonization, thereby placing this marginalized past in the center of legal, political and cultural battles.

Los Angeles, February 7, 2006

APPENDIX

Figure 1: Welcome sign of the *Habitation La Grivelière* near Vieux-Habitants, Guadeloupe

Figure 2: Restored eighteenth-century house of the master on the *Habitation La Grivelière*

Figure 3: Dilapidated eighteenth-century slave huts on the *Habitation La Grivelière*

Figure 4: Restored house of the master on the eighteenth-century *Habitation Clément* near Le François, Martinique

Figure 5: Ruins of the slave prison in the small fishing village of Petit-Canal, Guadeloupe

Figure 6: Vegetation has completely taken over the inside of the slave prison in Petit-Canal

Figure 7: "Steps of the slaves" in Petit-Canal

Figure 8: Monument to the Unknown Slave built in 1994 in Petit-Canal

Figure 9: Windmill in ruins in the Guadeloupean countryside

Figure 10: Crumbling walls of the slave quarters on the seventeenth-century *Habitation Anse Latouche*, Martinique

Figure 11: *Mémorial de l'Anse Caffard* erected in 1998 on the southern tip of Martinique near Diamant

Figure 12: Group of statues at the *Mémorial de l'Anse Caffard* facing the Caribbean Sea

Figure 13: The statues are slightly bowed as though in prayer before the collective grave of their brothers

Figure 14: Statues at the *Mémorial de l'Anse Caffard*

Figure 15: *Description of a Slave Ship* on a panel describing the memorial at the *Mémorial de l'Anse Caffard*

Figure 16: Scene from Biard's painting *L'abolition de l'esclavage* on another panel at the *Mémorial de l'Anse Caffard*

Figure 17: Stele in memory of the *nèg mawon* on the Col des Mamelles, Guadeloupe

Figure 18: Signpost in the bushes by the roadside indicating the slave cemetery in Capesterre Belle-Eau, Guadeloupe

Figure 19: Cement slab at the entrance of the slave cemetery in Capesterre Belle-Eau

Figure 20: Graves marked with conches of *lambi* in the slave cemetery in Capesterre Belle-Eau

Figure 21: Statue of a maroon in Diamant, Martinique, sculpted in 1998

Figure 22: Sculpture of maroon holding a dying child in Fort-de-France, Martinique

Figure 23:
Memorial to
the maroon in
Saint Esprit,
Martinique,
sculpted in
2000

Figure 24: Memorial to the
maroon in Saint Esprit

Figure 25: Painting of the middle passage on the base of the memorial to the maroon in Saint Esprit

Figure 26: Painting of tortured slaves on the base of the memorial to the maroon in Saint Esprit

Figure 27: Decapitated statue of Joséphine de Beauharnais in La Savanne, the central park of Fort-de-France, Martinique

Figure 28: Creole denunciations written across the cement base of the statue of Joséphine

Figure 29: Statue of Ignace erected on 27 May 27 1998 on the Boule-vard des Héros in Pointe-à-Pitre, Guadeloupe

Figure 30: Statue of Mulâtresse Solitude erected on 27 May 1999 on the Boule-vard des Héros

Figure 31: Statue of
Louis Delgrès erected
on 27 May 2001 on
the Boulevard des
Héros

Figure 32: Delgrès
surrounded by his
companions

Figure 33: Ignace and Delgrès next to the *Description of a Slave Ship* and the embracing slaves from Biard's *L'abolition de l'esclavage* on the mural painted in May 1998 in front of Baimbridge High School, Pointe-à-Pitre

Figure 34: Captured, enchained Africans walking to slave ships on the West African coast next to the first four articles of the Declaration of the Rights of Man painted on the mural

~ BIBLIOGRAPHY ~

I. Archival Manuscript Sources

Archives Départementales de la Martinique. 1717. "Conseil souverain de la Martinique." B2, 118, 3 mai.

Archives Nationales de France (Paris)

27 AP 11. 1746. Papiers de François de Neuchâteau. Dossier 3. Procès instruit en la cour au sujet des assemblées nocturnes de nègres tenues au quartier de la Marmelade; Extrait de la déclaration du roi concernant les crimes qui se commettent par les vénéficiers et poisons. 30 décembre.

DXXV 110. Papiers de l'abbé Ouvière.

1789. Dossier 876, pièce 14. Adresse à l'Assemblée nationale des citoyens libres de couleur. 18 octobre.

1790. Dossier 876, pièce 11. De Joly, Lettre au sujet des hommes de couleur. 7 février.

1791a. Dossier 867, pièce 2. Citoyens de couleur à messieurs les membres de l'Assemblée nationale à Paris. Saint-Marc ce 16 septembre.

1791b. Dossier 869, pièce 3. Bauvais et al, adresse des citoyens de couleur à messieurs les commissaires civils envoyés à Saint Domingue. 6 décembre.

1791c. Dossier 871, pièce 1. Lettre de Raimond, mulâtre, Paris, le 4 mars.

1792a. Dossier 867, pièce 3. Les membres du conseil d'administration des citoyens de couleur, campés à St. Marc à messieurs les membres de l'Assemblée nationale à Paris. Saint Marc, 15 décembre.

1792b. Dossier 867, pièce 7. Le conseil de l'armée des citoyens de couleur réunis et campés à Saint Marc le 2 février 1792 à messieurs les membres de l'Assemblée nationale à Paris.

1792c. Dossier 873, pièce 4. Copie de la lettre écrite par monsieur Raymond, aux citoyens de couleur de Saint Domingue, le 8 avril.

1792d. Dossier 876, pièce 9. Décret de l'Assemblée nationale, concernant les hommes de couleur, rendu dans la séance du 24 mars 1792, l'an 4ème de la liberté.

n.d. Dossier 877, pièce 11. Pinchinat et al., copie d'une lettre des chefs des gens de couleur de la Croix-des Louquets, à ceux du quartier de l'Artibonite.

D XXV 117

1789a. Dossier 914, pièce 3. Lettre d'un habitant de Saint-Pierre, Martinique. Le 11 septembre.

1789b. Dossier 915, pièce 3 bis. Lettre d'un habitant de la Martinique à tous les amis des noirs ou négromanes de France. Remis au comité le 1er décembre.

DXXV 118. 1793. Dossier 924, pièce 21. Les hommes libres (ci-devant dits de couleur) de la Martinique à la Convention nationale. Mars-juillet.

DXXV 120, dossier 940, pièce 9. Cahier adressé à l'Assemblée nationale par les colons de la Guadeloupe.

Colonies F1B 1. Police des Noirs.

1777. Folio 2. Déclaration du roi pour la police des noirs, Versailles le 9 août.

1778. Folio 10. Arrêt du Conseil d'Etat du roi concernant les mariages des noirs, mulâtres ou autres gens de couleur, 5 avril.

1782. Folio 56. Résumé d'opinion sur ce qui concerne la police des noirs par Devaivre, Paris le 17 mai.

Colonies F3 29. Collection Moreau de Saint-Méry.

1789a. Folio 83. Esclaves de la Martinique, copie d'une lettre adressée à monsieur de Molerat. Saint-Pierre le 28 août.

1789b. Folio 84. Esclaves de la Martinique, copie d'une lettre adressée au général Viomesnil. Saint-Pierre le 29 août.

1789c. Folio 211. Adresse du comité de Saint-Pierre de la Martinique à l'Assemblée nationale. Saint-Pierre le 5 octobre.

Colonies F3 32. Collection Moreau de Saint-Méry. 1790. Folios 304–321. Instructions de la Martinique à ses députés à l'Assemblée nationale du 19 mars.

Archives d'Outre Mer (Aix-en-Provence)

APC 42. 1790. Papiers d'Agout. Sur Saint-Domingue.

F3 90. 1775. Collection Moreau de Saint-Méry. Folio 160. Interrogatoire d'un nègre de l'habitation de la dame de l'Isle Adam, du 25 janvier.

Bibliothèque Nationale de France (Paris)

ms. FR-12102, Correspondance de Toussaint Louverture avec Laveaux.

II. Printed Sources

Adelaïde-Merlande, Jacques. 1992. *La Caraïbe et la Guyane au temps de la Révolution et de l'Empire (1789–1804)*. Paris: Karthala.

"Adresse du Comité de Saint-Pierre de la Martinique à l'Assemblé nationale. Saint Pierre, 5 octobre 1789." 1989. In *Doléances des*

peuples coloniaux à l'Assemblée nationale constituante 1789–1790,
comp. Monique Pouliquen, 54–55. Paris: Archives Nationales de France.

Américain, J. M. C., Sang-mêlé. [1789] 1968. "Précis des gémisse-mens des sang mêlés dans les colonies françaises." In *La Révolution française et l'abolition de l'esclavage.* Vol. 11. Paris: EDHIS.

Anderson, Benedict. 1991. *Imagined Communities: Reflections on the Origin and Spread of Nationalism.* London and New York: Verso.

Antoine, Régis. 1978. *Les écrivains français et les Antilles: Des premiers pères blancs aux surréalistes noirs.* Paris: Maisonneuve et Larose.

———. 1992. *La littérature franco-antillaise: Haïti, Guadeloupe et Martinique.* Paris: Karthala.

Archives Départementales de la Guadeloupe. 1998. *1848—Une Aube de Liberté: L'abolition de l'esclavage à la Guadeloupe.* Catalogue de l'exposition réalisée par la direction des Archives Départementales de la Guadeloupe, 27 avril—28 juin 1998. Gourbeyre, Guadeloupe.

Arendt, Hannah. 1967. *Essai sur la révolution.* Paris: Gallimard.

———. 1969. *On Violence.* New York: Harcourt.

Avalle. 1799. *Ouvrage du citoyen Avalle sur l'importance des colonies françaises aux Antilles.* Paris: Goujon fils.

Bangou, Henri. 1989. *La révolution et l'esclavage à la Guadeloupe, 1789–1802: Epopée noire et génocide.* Paris: Messidor, Editions Sociales.

Bantman, Béatrice. 1998a. "Sur les traces du commerce triangu-laire: Martinique, terre de castes." *Libération* 25–26 April.

———. 1998b. "Abolition de l'esclavage: L'anniversaire ambigu." *Libération* 25–26 April.

Baudry-Des Lozières, L.-N. 1802. *Les Egarements du negrophilisme.* Paris: Migneret.

Bédarida, Catherine. 1998. "Esclavage: Les Antilles se confrontent au devoir de mémoire." *Le Monde* 31 May.

Behn, Aphra. [1688] 1995. *Oroonoko, or the Royal Slave.* Vol. 3. Columbus: Ohio State University Press.

Bélénus, René. 1998. "René Bélénus: 'Un non-événement en Guade-loupe.'" *France-Antilles: Supplément-Edition* (Guadeloupe) 25 May.

Belley, Jean-Baptiste. n.d. *Le bout d'oreille des colons ou les systèmes de l'Hôtel de Massiac, mis au jour par Gouli. Belley, député noir de Saint-Domingue, à ses collègues.* Paris: Imprimerie de Pain.

———. 1790. *Belley, de Saint-Domingue représentant du peuple, à ses collègues. 6 fructidor l'an 2e.* Paris: Imprimerie de Pain.

———. 1793. *Lettre de Belley, député à la Convention nationale, à ses frères. New York, 14 décembre 1793.* Paris: Imprimerie Nationale.

Belley, Mills, Dufay. 1793. *Lettre écrite de New-York par les députés de Saint-Domingue, à leurs commettans. Imprimée par ordre de la Convention nationale. 14 décembre 1793.* Paris: Imprimerie Nationale.

Bellon de Saint-Quentin, J. [1764] 1972. *Dissertation sur la traite et le commerce des nègres.* Paris: Hachette.

Benjamin, Walter. 1969. "Theses on the Philosophy of History." In *Illuminations*. New York: Schocken.

Bénot, Yves. 1963. "Diderot, Pechmeja, Raynal et l'anticolonialisme." *Europe* 41: 137–53.

———. 1970. *Diderot, de l'athéisme à l'anticolonialisme*. Paris: Maspero.

———. 1991. "Traces de l'*Histoire des deux Indes* chez les anti-esclavagistes sous la Révolution." *Studies on Voltaire and the Eighteenth Century* 286: 141–54.

———. 1993. "Comment la Convention a-t-elle voté l'abolition de l'esclavage en l'an II?" *Annales historiques de la Révolution française* 293–94: 349–62.

———. 1995. "La chaîne des insurrections d'esclaves aux Caraïbes de 1789 à 1791." In *Les abolitions de l'esclavage de L.F. Sonthonax à V. Schœlcher, 1793–1794–1848*, ed. Marcel Dorigny, 179–86. Paris: Presses Universitaires de Vincennes.

Benrekassa, Georges. 1987. *Montesquieu: La liberté et l'histoire*. Paris: Librairie Générale Française.

Bernardin de Saint-Pierre. [1768–70] 1983. *Voyage à l'île de France, Un officier du roi à l'île Maurice, 1768–1770*. Paris: La Découverte/ Maspero.

Besson, Maurice. 1928. "La police des noirs sous Louis XVI en France." *Revue de l'histoire des colonies françaises* 21: 433–46.

Bhabba, Homi. 1990. *Nation and Narration*. London: Routledge.

———. 1994. *The Location of Culture*. London: Routledge.

Blackburn, Robin. 1988. *The Overthrow of Colonial Slavery: 1776–1848*. London: Verso.

———. 1997. *The Making of New World Slavery: From the Baroque to the Modern 1492–1800*. London: Verso.

Bolland, Nigel O. 1994. "Current Caribbean Research Five Centuries after Columbus." *Latin American Research Review* 29: 202–19.

Boltanski, Luc. 1993. *La souffrance à distance: Morale humanitaire, médias et politique*. Paris: Métailié.

Bonniol, Jean-Luc. 1990. "La couleur des hommes, principe d'organisation sociale: Le cas antillais". *Ethnologie française* 20: 410–18.

———. 1992. *La couleur comme maléfice. Une illustration créole de la généalogie des blancs et des noirs*. Paris: Albin Michel.

Brissot de Warville, Jacques-Pierre. [1789] 1968. "Mémoire sur les noirs de l'Amérique septentrionale." In *La Révolution française et l'abolition de l'esclavage*. Vol. 7. Paris: EDHIS.

———. [1791] 1968. "Discours sur un projet de décret relatif à la révolte des noirs." In *La Révolution française et l'abolition de l'esclavage*. Vol. 8. Paris: EDHIS.

———. [1791] 1968. "Réplique à la première et dernière lettre de Louis-Marthe Gouy, défenseur de la traite des noirs et de l'esclavage." In *La Révolution française et l'abolition de l'esclavage*. Vol. 8. Paris: EDHIS.

———. [1792] 1968. "Discours sur la nécessité de maintenir le décret rendu le 15 mai 1792, en faveur des hommes de couleur libres, prononcé le 12 septembre 1791." In *La Révolution française et l'abolition de l'esclavage*. Vol. 8. Paris: EDHIS.

Buffon. [1749] 1800. "Variétés dans l'espèce humaine." In *Histoire naturelle de l'homme*, 249–342. Paris.

Burton, Richard D. E. 1994. *La Famille coloniale. La Martinique et la mère-patrie. 1789–1992*. Paris: L'Harmattan.

——. 1997. *Le roman marron: Etudes sur la littérature martiniquaise contemporaine*. Paris: L'Harmattan.

Cabanis, André and Michel L. Martin. 1989. "La question économique et l'abolition de l'esclavage dans le discours révolutionnaire, 1791–94." In *De la Révolution française aux révolutions créoles et nègres*, eds. Michel L. Martin and Alain Yacou, 69–80. Paris: Editions Caribéennes.

Cahen, Léon. 1906. "La Société des Amis des Noirs et Condorcet." *La Révolution française* 50: 481–511.

——. 1970. *Condorcet et la Révolution française*. Genève: Slatkine.

"Cahier adressé à l'Assemblée nationale par les colons de la Guadeloupe." 1989. In *Doléances des peuples coloniaux à l'Assemblée nationale constituante 1789–1790*, comp. Monique Pouliquen, 44–46. Paris: Archives Nationales de France.

Carlson, Marvin. 1966. *The Theatre of the French Revolution*. Ithaca: Cornell University Press.

Carpentier, Alejo. 1990. *El siglo de la luces*. Barcelona: Seix Barral.

Castro Henriques, Isabel and Louis Sala-Molins. 2002. *Déraison, esclavage et droit: Les fondements idéologiques et juridiques de la traite négrière et de l'esclavage*. Paris: Editions UNESCO.

Césaire, Aimé. 1955. *Discours sur le colonialisme*. Paris: Présence Africaine.

——. 1998. "Le discours du centenaire." *Le Monde*. Cahier spécial abolition de l'esclavage 24 April.

Chalons, Serge. 2000. "150 ans après l'esclavage, la blessure." In *De l'esclavage aux réparations*, eds. Serge Chalons et al., 117–19. Paris: Karthala.

Chamoiseau, Patrick. 1998a. "Fils d'esclaves, soyez fiers." *Le Nouvel Observateur* 19–25 February.

——. 1998b. "La mémoire obscure de l'esclavage." *Le Figaro* 24 April.

——. 1998c. "Recréer la créolité." *Le Monde des Livres* 24 April.

——. 2000. "De la mémoire obscure à la mémoire consciente." In *De l'esclavage aux réparations*, eds. Serge Chalons et al., 109–15. Paris: Karthala.

Chamoiseau, Patrick, Raphaël Confiant, and Jean Bernabe. 1989. *Eloge de la créolité*. Paris: Gallimard.

Champion, Jean-Marcel. 1995. "30 floréal an X: Le rétablissement de l'esclavage par Bonaparte." In *Les abolitions de l'esclavage de L.F. Sonthonax à V. Schœlcher, 1793–1794–1848*, ed. Marcel Dorigny, 265–71. Paris: Presses Universitaires de Vincennes.

Chapelle, David. 1998. "Patrick Chamoiseau: 'Une catharsis collective nécessaire.'" *France-Antilles: Supplément-Edition* (Guadeloupe) 25 May.

Charlevoix, Pierre-François Xavier de. 1730–31. *Histoire de l'Ile espagnole de Saint-Domingue.* 2 vols. Paris: J. Guérin.

Chauleau, Liliane. n.d. "La ville de Saint-Pierre sous la Révolution française." *La période révolutionnaire aux Antilles: Images et résonances.* Actes du Colloque International Pluridisciplinaire, Nov. 1986, Fort-de France, Point-à-Pitre, eds. Roger Toumson and Charles Porset, 115–35. Schoelcher: GRELCA.

Clavière, Etienne. [1791] 1968. "Adresse de la Société des Amis des Noirs, à l'Assemblée Nationale, à toutes les Villes de Commerce, à toutes les Manufactures, aux Colonies, à toutes les Société des Amis de la Constitution." In *La Révolution Française et l'abolition de l'esclavage.* Vol. 9. Paris: EDHIS.

Cohen, William B. 1980. *The French Encounter with Africans: White Response to Blacks, 1530–1880.* Bloomington: Indiana University Press.

Cojean, Annick. 1998a. "En Guadeloupe, des voix demandent à la France de reconnaître son passé esclavagiste." *Le Monde* 26–27 April.

———. 1998b. "En Martinique, la commémoration de l'abolition est d'abord celle de la révolte des esclaves." *Le Monde* 26–27 April.

———. 1998c. "L'"héritage" de l'esclavage aux Antilles." *Le Monde* 24 April: Cahier spécial abolition de l'esclavage.

Colombani, Jean-Marie. 1998. "La dette de l'esclavage." *Le Monde* 26–27 April.

Comité pour la mémoire de l'esclavage. 2005. *Mémoires de la traite négrière, de l'esclavage et de leucs abolitions.* Paris: La Découverte.

Condé, Maryse. 2001. *La Belle Créole.* Paris: Mercure de France.

Condorcet. [1781] 1968a. *Réflexions sur l'esclavage des nègres, par monsieur Schwartz, pasteur du Saint Evangile à Bienne.* In *Œuvres.* Vol. 7. Stuttgart-Bad Cannstatt: Friedrich Frommann Verlag.

———. [1789] 1968b. *Au Corps électoral contre l'esclavage des noirs.* In *Œuvres.* Vol. 9. Stuttgart-Bad Cannstatt: Friedrich Frommann Verlag.

Cook, Mercer. 1936. "Jean-Jacques Rousseau and the Negro." *Journal of Negro History* 21: 294–303.

———. 1941. "Julien Raimond." *Journal of Negro History* 26: 139–170.

"Correspondance secrète des Colons députés à l'Assemblée Constituante, servant à faire connaître l'esprit des colons en général, sur la Révolution." [1793] 1968. In *La Révolution française et l'abolition de l'esclavage.* Vol. 8. Paris: EDHIS.

Cottias, Myriam. 1998. "La politique de l'oubli." *France-Antilles: Supplément-Edition* (Guadeloupe) 25 May.

———. 2000. "Le triomphe de l'oubli ou la mémoire tronquée." In *De l'esclavage aux réparations,* eds. Serge Chalons et al., 95–103. Paris: Karthala.

Courtaud, Patrice, André Delpuech, and Thomas Romon. 1999. "Archaeological Investigations at Colonial Cemeteries on Guadeloupe: African Slave Burial Sites or Not?" In *African Sites Archaeology in the Caribbean,* ed. Jay B. Haviser, 277–90. Princeton: Markus Wiener Publishers.

Courtine, Jean-Jacques. 1981. "Analyse du discours politique." *Langages* 62 (June): 9–128.

Craton, Michael. 1982. *Testing the Chains.* Ithaca: Cornell University.

Curtin, Philip. 1969. *The Atlantic Slave Trade.* Madison: University of Wisconsin Press.

Daget, Serge. 1973. "Les mots esclave, nègre, noir, et les jugements de valeur sur la traite négrière dans la littérature abolitionniste française de 1770 à 1845." *Revue française d'histoire d'outre-mer* 60: 511–48.

——— ed. 1988. *De la traite à l'esclavage.* Actes du Colloque international sur la traite des noirs, Nantes 1985. Nantes: Centre de Recherche sur l'Histoire du Monde Atlantique.

Davis, David Brion. 1966. *The Problem of Slavery in Western Culture.* Ithaca: Cornell University Press.

———. 1975. *The Problem of Slavery in the Age of Revolution 1770–1823.* Ithaca: Cornell University Press.

Debbash, Yvan. 1961. "Le marronage: Essai sur la désertion de l'esclavage antillais." *Année Sociologique* 3rd ser: 1–112.

———. 1962. "Le marronage: Essai sur la désertion de l'esclavage antillais." *Année Sociologique* 3rd ser: 117–95.

———. 1963. "Le Crime d'empoisonnement aux îles pendant la période esclavagiste." *Revue française d'histoire d'outre-mer* 50: 137–88.

———. 1979. "Le Maniel: Further Notes." *Maroon Societies: Rebel Slave Communities in the Americas,* ed. Richard Price, 143–48. Baltimore: Johns Hopkins.

Debien, Gabriel. 1951. *Gens de couleur et colons de Saint-Domingue devant la constituante (1789–mars 1790).* Montréal: Revue d'Histoire de l'Amérique Française.

———. 1953. *Les colons de Saint-Domingue et la Révolution: Essai sur le Club Massiac (août 1789–août 1792).* Paris: Armand Colin.

———. 1979. "Marronage in the French Caribbean." In *Maroon Societies: Rebel Slave Communities in the Americas,* ed. Richard Price, 107–34. Baltimore: Johns Hopkins.

"Décret de la Convention nationale, du 16 jour de pluviôse, an second de la République française, une et indivisible, qui abolit l'esclavage des nègres dans les colonies." [1794] 1968. In *La Révolution française et l'abolition de l'esclavage.* Vol. 12. Paris: EDHIS.

"Décret de la Convention Nationale, du 27 juillet 1793, l'an second de la république Française, qui supprime les primes pour la traite des esclaves." [1793] 1968. In *La Révolution Française et l'abolition de l'esclavage.* Vol. 12. Paris: EDHIS.

De Gouges, Olympe. [1784] 1788. *Réflexions sur les hommes nègres.* In
     Œuvres. Vol. 3. Paris.
———. [1786] 1994. *L'esclavage des noirs.* In *Translating Slavery: Gen-
     der and Race in French Women's Writings, 1783–1823,* eds. Doris
     Kadish and F. Massardier-Kenney, 229–70. Kent, Ohio: Kent State
     University Press.
———. [1790] 1968. *Réponse au champion américain.* In *La Révolution
     française et l'abolition de l'esclavage.* Vol. 4. Paris: EDHIS.
Delacroix, Jacques-Vincent. 1777. *Peinture des mœurs du siècle.* Paris:
     Jejay.
Delas, Daniel. 2001. "Commémorer/Manipuler—A propos du cent-
     cinquantième anniversaire de l'abolition de l'esclavage (1998)."
     In *Esclavage: libérations, abolitions, commémorations,* eds. Christiane
     Chaulet-Achour and Romual-Blaise Fonkoua, 263–81. Paris: Edi-
     tions Séguir.
Delesalle, Simone and Lucette Valensi. 1972. "Le mot 'nègre' dans
     les dictionnaires français de l'ancine régime: Histoire et léxi-
     cographie." *Langue française* 15 (September): 86.
—. 1977. "Nègre/Negro: Recherches dans les dictionnaires français
     et anglais au XVIIe siècle." *L'idée de race dans la pensée politique
     française contemporaine,* eds. Pierre Guiral and Emile Temime,
     158–62. Paris.
Deleuze, Gilles and Félix Guattari. 1989. *Mille plateaux.* Paris: Edi-
     tions de Minuit.
Derrida, Jacques. 1996. *Le monolinguisme de l'autre.* Paris: Galilée.
Descourtilz, Michel Etienne. 1809. *Voyages d'un naturaliste.* Paris:
     Dufart père.
Des Essarts (avocat), Poncet de la Grave (avocat et procureur du roi),
     and Dejunquieres (procureur). 1979. "Mémoire pour Gabriel
     Pampy, nègre originaire de Saint-Domingue; et Amynte Julienne,
     Négresse originaire de Congo, contre le sieur Mendès, Juif." In *Un
     négociant juif et deux esclaves nègres à Paris: Aspects du racisme au
     siècle des lumières,* comp. Pierre Pluchon, 10–24. Port-au-Prince:
     Institut français d'Haïti.
Despin, Jean-Pierre. 1977. "Montesquieu était-il esclavagiste?" *Pen-
     sée* 193: 102–12.
Dessalles, Pierre F.R. 1982. *Historique des troubles survenus à la Mar-
     tinique pendant la Révolution. 1794–1800.* Ed. Henri de Fremont.
     Fort-de-France: Société d'Histoire de la Martinique.
Dicale, Bertrand. 1998a. "La mémoire obscure de l'esclavage." *Le
     Figaro* 24 April.
———. 1998b. "Aimé Césaire ou l'orgueil réinventé." *Le Figaro*
     25–26 April.
Diderot, Denis. [1772] 1875. *Fragments échappés du portefeuille d'un
     philosophe.* In *Œuvres complètes.* Vol. 6: 450–57. Paris: Garnier.
Diderot and d'Alembert. [1755] n.d. *Encyclopédie (ou dictionnaire
     raisonné des sciences, des arts et des métiers).* Vols. 2, 5, 8, 11, 16.
     Paris: Pergamon Press.

Donvez, Jacques. 1949. *De Quoi vivait Voltaire?* Paris: Editions des Deux-Rives.

Dorigny, Marcel, ed. 1995. "Mirabeau et la Société des Amis des Noirs: Quelles voies pour l'abolition de l'esclavage?" *Les abolitions de l'esclavage de L. F. Sonthonax à V. Schœlcher, 1793–1794–1848.* Actes du Colloque international tenu à l'Université de Paris VIII les 3, 4, et 5 février 1994, 153–64. Paris: Presses Universitaires de Vincennes.

Dorigny, Marcel and Bernard Gainot. 1998. *La Société des Amis des Noirs 1788–1799: Contribution à l'histoire de l'abolition de l'esclavage.* Paris: Editions UNESCO.

Douglass, Frederick. [1845] 1968. *Narrative of the Life of Frederick Douglass an American Slave.* New York: Signet.

Duchet, Michèle. 1965. "Esclavage et humanisme en 1787: Réflexions sur les moyens de rendre meilleur l'état des nègres ou des affranchis de nos colonies." *Annales historiques de la Révolution française* 37: 350–51.

———. 1969. "Esclavage et préjugé de couleur." In *Racisme et société*, eds. Patrice de Comarmond and Claude Duchet, 121–32. Paris: Maspero.

———. 1971. *Anthropologie et histoire au siècle des lumières. Buffon, Voltaire, Helvétius, Diderot.* Paris: Maspero.

———. 1978. *Diderot et l'Histoire des deux Indes ou l'écriture fragmentaire.* Paris: Nizet.

Ducœurjoly, S.-J. 1802. *Manuel des habitants de Saint-Domingue.* Paris: Lenoir.

Du Laurens, Henri-Joseph. [1763] 1775. *L'arrétin moderne.* Rome.

Durand, Carine. 2001. "Mémoires et oublis des resistances esclaves au Brésil. Vers une réinterprétation théâtralisée des processus de domination." *Cahiers des anneaux de la mémoire* 3: 303–26.

Du Tertre, J.-B. 1667–71. *Histoire générale des Antilles habitées par les Français.* Paris.

Ehrard, Jean. 1995. "L'esclavage devant la conscience morale des lumières françaises: Indifférences, gêne, révolte. In *Les abolitions de l'esclavage de L.F. Sonthonax à V. Schœlcher (1793, 1794, 1848).* Paris: Presses Universitaires de Vincennes et Editions UNESCO.

Elizabeth, Léo. 1973. "Saint-Pierre, août 1789." *Compte rendu des travaux du colloque de Saint-Pierre, 14, 15, 16 décembre 1973*, 35–43. Centre Universitaire Antilles-Guyane.

———. 1993. "La République dans les Iles du Vent: Décembre 1792– avril 1794." *Annales historiques de la Révolution française* 293–94: 373–408.

Estève, Laurent. 2002a. "La théorie des climats ou l'encodage d'une servitude naturelle." In *Déraison, esclavage et droit: Les fondements ideologiques et juridiques de la traite négrière et de l'esclavage*, eds. Isabel Castro Henriques and Louis Sala-Molins, 59–68. Paris: Editions UNESCO.

———. 2002b. *Montesquieu, Rousseau, Diderot: Du genre humain au bois d'ébène: Les silences du droit naturel.* Paris: Editions UNESCO.

"Extraits des registres des délibérations de l'assemblée générale colo-
    niale de la Guadeloupe. 13 mars 1790." In *Doléances des peuples
    coloniaux à l'Assemblée nationale constituante 1789–1790*, comp.
    Monique Pouliquen, 43. Paris: Archives Nationales de France.
Fanon, Frantz. 1952. *Peau noire, masques blancs*. Paris: Seuil.
———. 1991. *Les damnés de la terre*. Paris: Gallimard.
Feugères, A. 1922. *Un précurseur de la Révolution, l'abbé Raynal, 1719–
    1796*. Angoulême, France: Editions Ouvrières.
Fick, Carolyn E. 1990. *The Making of Haiti: The Saint Domingue Revo-
    lution from Below*. Knoxville: University of Tennessee Press.
———. 1997. "The French Revolution in Saint Domingue: A Tri-
    umph or a Failure?" In *A Turbulent Time: The French Revolution and
    the Greater Caribbean*, eds. David B. Gaspar and David P. Geggus,
    51–75. Bloomington and Indianapolis: Indiana University Press.
Fischer, Sibylle. 2004. *Modernity Disavowed: Haiti and the Cultures of
    Slavery in the Age of Revolution*. Durham, North Carolina and Lon-
    don: Duke University Press.
Fletcher, F. T. H. 1933. "Montesquieu's Influence on Anti-Slavery
    Opinion in England." *Journal of Negro History* 18: 414–25.
Foner, Laura. 1970. "The Free People of Color in Louisiana and
    Saint Domingue." *Journal of Social History* 3: 406–30.
Foucault, Michel. 1969. *L'archéologie du savoir*. Paris: Gallimard.
———. 1976. "Film and Popular Memory." *Radical Philosophy* 11:
    24–29.
———. 1977. "Revolutionary Action." In *Language, Counter-Memory,
    Practice*. Ithaca: Cornell University Press.
———. 1980. "Lecture One: 7 January 1976." In *Power/Knowledge:
    Selected Interviews and Other Writings, 1972–1977*, 78–92. New
    York: Pantheon Books.
———. 1997. *"Il faut défendre la société": Cours au Collège de France.
    (1975–1976)*. Paris: Gallimard, Seuil.
Fouchard, Jean. 1953. *Les Marrons du Syllabaire*. Port-au-Prince,
    Haïti: Deschamps.
———. 1972. *Les Marrons de la liberté*. Paris: Editions de l'Ecole.
Gaspar, David B. and David P. Geggus, eds. 1997. *A Turbulent Time:
    The French Revolution and the Greater Caribbean*. Bloomington and
    Indianapolis: Indiana University Press.
Gates, Henry Louis Jr., ed. 1985–86. *"Race," Writing, and Difference*.
    Chicago and London: University of Chicago Press.
———. 1988. *The Signifying Monkey: A Theory of African-American Lit-
    erary Criticism*. London: Oxford University Press.
Gauchet, Marcel. 1989. *La révolution des droits de l'homme*. Paris:
    Gallimard.
Gautier, Arlette. 1985. *Les sœurs de solitude: La condition féminine
    dans l'esclavage aux Antilles du XVIIe au XIXe siècle*. Paris: Editions
    Caribéennes.
Gauthier, Florence. 2001. "La Révolution française et le problème
    colonial. Droits de l'homme universels ou droits de l'homme du
    nord?" *Cahiers des anneaux de la mémoire* 3: 363–80.

Gayot de Pitaval, François. 1747. "Liberté réclamée par un nègre, contre son maître qui l'a amené en France." In *Causes célèbres et intéressantes, avec les jugements qui les ont décidées.* Vol. 13. Paris.

Geggus, David P. 1983. *Slave Resistance Studies and the Saint Domingue Slave Revolt. Some Preliminary Considerations.* Miami: Latin American and Caribbean Center, Florida International University.

———. 1989a. "Racial Equality, Slavery, and Colonial Secession during the Constituent Assembly." *American Historical Review* 94: 1290–1308.

———. 1989b. "The French and Haitian Revolutions, and Resistance to Slavery in the Americas. An Overview." *Revue française d'histoire d'outre-mer* 76: 107–24.

———. 1996. "The Slaves and Free Coloreds of Martinique during the Age of the French and Haitian Revolutions." In *The Lesser Antilles in the Age of European Expansion,* eds. Robert L. Paquette and Stanley L. Engerman, 280–301. Gainesville: University Press of Florida.

———. 1997. "Slavery, War, and Revolution in the Greater Caribbean, 1789–1815." In *A Turbulent Time: The French Revolution and the Greater Caribbean,* eds. David B. Gaspar and David P. Geggus, 1–50. Bloomington and Indianapolis: Indiana University Press.

Genovese, Eugene D. 1979. *From Rebellion to Revolution: Afro-American Slave Revolts in the Making of the Modern World.* Baton Rouge: Louisiana State University Press.

Gilman, Sander L. 1985–86. "Black Bodies, White Bodies." In *"Race," Writing, and Difference,* ed. Henry Louis Gates Jr., 223–61. Chicago: University of Chicago Press.

Girod-Chantrans. 1785. *Voyage d'un Suisse dans différentes colonies d'Amérique.* Neuchâtel, Switzerland.

Gisler, Antoine. 1965. *L'Esclavage aux Antilles françaises (XVIIe–XIXe siècle): Contribution au problème de l'esclavage.* Fribourg, Switzerland: Editions Universitaires Fribourg.

Glissant, Edouard. 1981. *Le discours antillais.* Paris: Seuil.

———. 1996. *Introduction à une poétique du divers.* Paris: Gallimard.

———. [1964] 1997. *Le quatrième siècle.* Paris: Gallimard.

Grégoire, Abbé. [1789] 1968. "Mémoire en faveur des gens de couleur ou sang-mêlés de St. Domingue, et des autres îles françaises de l'Amérique." In *La Revolution française et l'abolition de l'esclavage.* Vol. 1. Paris: EDHIS.

———. [1790] 1968. "Lettre aux philanthropes sur les malheurs, les droits et les réclamations des gens de couleur de Saint-Domingue et les autres îles françaises de l'Amérique." In *La Révolution Française et l'abolition de l'esclavage.* Vol. 4. Paris: EDHIS.

———. [1791] 1968. "Lettre aux citoyens de couleur et nègres libres de Saint-Domingue et des autres îles françaises de l'Amérique." In *La Révolution Française et l'abolition de l'esclavage.* Vol. 4. Paris: EDHIS.

———. 1808. *De la littérature des nègres.* Paris: Maradan.

Habitation Clément. n.d. Brochure published by the Habitation Clément, Monument Historique, Le François, Martinique.

Habitation La Grivelière. n.d. Brochure published by the Habitation La Grivelière, Maison du Café, Vallé de Grand-Rivière, Vieux-Habitants, Guadeloupe.

Halbwachs, Maurice. 1992. *On Collective Memory.* Chicago: University of Chicago Press.

Halpern, Jean-Claude. 1993. "L'esclavage sur la scène révolutionnaire." *Annales Historiques de La Révolution Française* 293–294: 409–20.

Haudrère, Philippe and Françoise Vergès. 1998. *De l'esclave au citoyen.* Paris: Gallimard.

Hausser, Michel. 1986. *Essai sur la poétique de la négritude.* Paris: Editions Silex.

Hilliard d'Auberteuil, M. R. 1776. *Considérations sur l'état présent de la colonie française de Saint-Domingue: Ouvrage politique et législatif.* 2 vols. Paris.

Hoffman, Léon-François. 1973. *Le nègre romantique: Personnage littéraire et obsession collective.* Paris: Payot.

Ho-Fong-Choy Choucoutou, Lydie. 2000. "Littérature et esclavage." In *De l'esclavage aux réparations,* eds. Serge Chalons et al., 13–31. Paris: Karthala.

Ifill, Max. 2000. "Le rôle de l'esclavage dans la société caribéenne." In *De l'esclavage aux réparations,* eds. Serge Chalons et al., 65–69. Paris: Karthala.

"Instructions de la Martinique à ses députés à l'Assemblée nationale du 19 mars 1790." In *Doléances des peuples coloniaux à l'Assemblée nationale constituante 1789–1790,* comp. Monique Pouliquen, 56–69. Paris: Archives Nationales de France.

Ivernel, Martin, ed. 1998. *Histoire/Géographie-4e, nouveau programme.* Paris: Hatier.

James, C.L.R. 1989. *The Black Jacobins: Toussaint L'Ouverture and the San Domingo Revolution.* New York: Vintage Books.

Jameson, Russell Parsons. 1911. *Montesquieu et l'esclavage, étude sur les origines de l'opinion anti-esclavagiste en France au XVIIIe siècle.* New York: Lenox Hill Publisher.

Jaucourt, de. [1755] n.d. "Esclavage." In *Encyclopédie.* Vol. 5: 934–39. Paris: Pergamon Press.

———. [1755] n.d. "Traite des nègre (Commerce d'Afrique)." In *Encyclopédie.* Vol. 16: 532–33. Paris: Pergamon Press.

Joffrin, Laurent. 1998. "Crime contre l'humanité." *Libération* 25–26 April.

Joly de Fleury (avocat général), De la Roue (avocat), and Collet (procureur). 1759. *Mémoire signifié pour le nommé Francisque, Indien de nation ... contre le sieur Allain-François-Ignace Brignon, se disant écuyer, appelant.* Paris.

Jordan, Winthrop. 1968. *White over Black: American Attitudes toward the Negro, 1550–1812.* Chapel Hill: University of North Carolina Press.

Jurt, Joseph. 1991. "Sozialkritik und literarische Vermittlung: Die Slavereidebatte in der französischen Literatur des 18. Jahrhunderts." *Literaturwissenschaftliches Jahrbuch der Görres-Gesellschaft* 32: 97–110.

Kadish, Doris Y. 1995. "The Black Terror: Women's Responses to Slave Revolts in Haiti." *French Review* 68: 668–80.

Kadish, Doris and F. Massardier-Kenney, eds. 1994. *Translating Slavery: Gender and Race in French Women's Writing, 1783–1823.* Kent, Ohio: Kent State University Press.

Klein, Bernard and Gérard Hugonie, eds. 1998. *Histoire/Géographie-4e, nouveau programme.* Paris: Bordas.

Klein, Herbert S. 1999. *The Atlantic Slave Trade.* Cambridge: Cambridge University Press.

Kozminski, Léon. 1929. *Voltaire financier.* Paris: Presses Universitaires de France.

Kritzman, Lawrence D. 1996. "Forward." In *Realms of Memory. Vol. 1, Conflicts and Divisions,* trans. Arthur Goldhammer. New York: Columbia University Press.

Kundera, Milan. 1980. "Afterword: A Talk with the Author by Philip Roth." In *The Book of Laughter and Forgetting.* New York: Penguin.

Labat, J.-B. [1724] 1972. *Nouveau voyage aux îles de l'Amérique.* 4 vols. Fort-de-France, Martinique: Editions des Horizons Caraïbes.

Laborie, P.J. 1798. *The Coffe Planter of Saint Domingue.* London: Cadel.

———. n.d. *Réflexions sommaires addressés à la France et à la colonie de Saint Domingue.* Paris: Imprimerie de Chardon.

Lafontant, Julien J. 1979. *Montesquieu et le problème de l'esclavage dans "L'esprit des lois."* Quebec: Editions Naaman.

Lambin, Jean-Michel, ed. 1996. *Histoire-Seconde.* Paris: Hachette.

Landi, Elisabeth. 1998. "La construction d'un événement historique." *France-Antilles: Supplément-Edition* (Guadeloupe) 25 May.

Lara, Oruno D. 1998a. "Histoire et abolition." *France-Antilles: Supplément-Edition* (Guadeloupe) 25 May.

———. 1998b. "Les réflexions d'un historien guadeloupéen." *France-Antilles* (Guadeloupe) 13 May.

———. 1992. *Caraïbes en construction: Espace, colonisation, résistance.* 2 vols. Paris: Editions du CERCAM.

Larchevesque-Thibaud, G. J. B. [1796] 1968. "Lettre d'un colon de Saint-Domingue à un de ses amis." In *La Révolution Française et l'abolition de l'esclavage.* Vol. 11. Paris: EDHIS.

Larivallière. 1794. *Les Africains, ou le triomphe de l'humanité. Comédie en un acte et en prose.* Paris: Meurant.

Larney, Cécilia. 2001. "A Petit-Canal, rendez-vous avec l'histoire." *France-Antilles Magazine Guadeloupe.* 16–22 June: 6–7.

———. n.d. "Petit-Canal." In *Voyage culturel en Guadeloupe: Le guide première édition,* ed. Office du tourisme de la Guadeloupe, 86–87.

Leclerc, Gérard. 1972. "Les Lumières, préanthropologie et précolonialisme." *Anthropologie et colonialisme.* Paris: Fayard.

Leiris, Michel. 1974. *Contacts de civilisations en Martinique et en Guadeloupe.* Paris: Gallimard et Presses de l'UNESCO.

Le Moyne des Essarts, N.-T. 1775–89. *Causes célèbres, curieuses et intéressantes de toutes les Cours sovereigns du royaume avec les jugements qui les ont décidées.* Vol. 36: 80–83. Paris.

Le Romain, M. [1755] n.d. "Nègres, considérés comme esclaves dans les colonies de l'Amérique." In *Encyclopédie.* Vol. 8: 80–83. Paris: Pergamon Press.

"Lettre des commissaires des citoyens de couleur en France, à leurs frères et commettans dans les îles françaises." [1791] 1968. In *La Révolution française et l'abolition de l'esclavage.* Vol. 11. Paris: EDHIS.

"L'hommage au neg mawon." 1997. *France-Antilles* (Guadeloupe) 11 May.

"L'humanisme est aussi une politique." 1998. *Le Figaro* 24 April.

Linnaeus, Carol. [1735] 1964. *Systema Naturae.* Nieuwkoop: B. de Graaf.

"Lionel Jospin lance un appel à la vigilance." 1998. *Le Figaro* 27 April.

"Loi portant que tout homme est libre en France, et que quelle que soit sa couleur, il y jouit de tous les droits de citoyen, s'il a les qualités prescrites par la constitution. Donnée à Paris, le 16 octobre 1791." [1791] 1968. In *La Révolution française et l'abolition de l'esclavage.* Vol. 12. Paris: EDHIS.

"Loi relative aux colonies, avec l'exposition des motifs qui en ont déterminé les dispositions. Donnée à Paris le 1. juin 1791." [1791] 1968. In *La Révolution française et l'abolition de l'esclavage.* Vol. 12. Paris: EDHIS.

Louverture, Toussaint. 1853. *Mémoires du général Toussaint Louverture écrits par lui-même, pouvant servir à l'histoire de sa vie.* Paris: Pagnerre.

———. n.d. *Extrait du rapport adressé au directoire exécutif par Toussaint Louverture … conférences entre Sonthonax et Toussaint Louverture (18 fructidor an V).* Cap-Français, Haïti: Imprimerie Roux.

———. 1855. *Lettre inédite, qu'on pourrait appeler testament politique. (24 germinal an VII).* Paris.

———. n.d.a. *Constitution française des colonies de Saint Domingue (19 floréal an IX).* Paris: Veuve Leroux.

———. n.d.b. *A tous les bons français, aux vrais et sincères amis de la liberté.* Cap-Français, Haïti: Imprimerie Roux.

———. "Réfutations de quelques assertions d'un discours prononcé au corps législatif le 10 prairial an V, par Viénot Vaublanc." [An 5] 1968. In *La Révolution française et l'abolition de l'esclavage.* Vol. 11. Paris: EDHIS.

Mailhol, Gabriel. 1764. *Le Philosophe nègre et les secrets des Grecs.* Londres.

Maingueneau, Dominique. 1991. *L'analyse du discours: Introduction aux lectures de l'archive.* Paris: Hachette.

Maison de la Canne. n.d. Brochure published by Maison de la Canne, Trois-Ilets, Martinique.

Mallet (avocat). 1738. *Mémoire pour Jean Boucaux, nègre, demandeur. Contre le sieur Verdelin, défenseur.* Factum 43, 1890–1945, Boucault-Bouille. Paris: Imprimerie de Cladue Simon.

Malouet, Pierre Victor. 1788. *Mémoire sur l'esclavage des nègres.* Neuchâtel, Switzerland.

Manigat, Leslie. 1977. "The Relationship between Marronage and Slave Revolts and Revolution in St. Domingue-Haiti." *Annals of the New York Academy of Sciences, 292. Comparative Perspectives on Slavery in New World Plantation Societies,* eds. Vera Rubin and Arthur Tuden, 420–37.

Marie, Claude-Valentin and Lionel Qualité. 2004. "L'Ile-de-France, region privilégiée des migrants des Dom-Tom." In *Institut National de la Statistique et des Etudes Economiques* 207, January 2002, <http://www.insee.fr./ile-de-France> (12 June).

Marsollier des Vivetières, Benoît-Joseph. 1792. *La Mort du colonel Mauduit, ou les anarchistes au Port-au-Prince.* Paris: Cailleau.

Maximin, Daniel. 1998. "1848: L'invention d'une identité." *Le Monde des Livres* 24 April.

———. 2000. "Allocution d'ouverture." In *Esclavages et abolitions,* ed. Marie-Christine Rochmann, 15–18. Paris: Karthala.

McCloy, Shelby T. 1945. "Negroes and Mulattoes in Eighteenth Century France." *Journal of Negro History* 30: 276–292.

———. 1954. "Further Notes on Negroes and Mulattoes in Eighteenth-Century France." *Journal of Negro History* 39: 284–97.

———. 1961. *The Negro in France.* Lexington: University of Kentucky Press.

Memmi, Albert. 1985. *Portrait du colonialisme.* Paris: Gallimard.

Mémorial de l'Anse Caffard. n.d. Explanatory panels at the memorial. Anse Caffard, Diamant, Martinique.

Ménil, Alain. 2000. "Les lumières à l'épreuve de l'esclavage: Entre chien et loup?" *Les Cahiers du Patrimoine* 17 and 18 (May): 249–63.

Mercier, Louis-Sébastien. 1773. *L'an deux mille quatre cent quarante: Rêve s'il en fut jamais.* London.

———. 1783. "Petits nègres." In *Tableau de Paris.* Vol. 6. Amsterdam.

Mercier, Roger. 1962a. *L'Afrique noire dans la littérature française: Les premières images, XVIIe–XVIIIe siècle.* Dakar, Senegal: Université de Dakar.

———. 1962b. "Les débuts de l'exotisme africain en France." *Revue de littérature comparée* 36: 191–209.

Michaux-Chevry, Lucette. 1998. "Cent cinquantenaire de l'abolition de l'esclavage." *France-Antilles: Supplément-Edition du 25 mai 1998.*

Miles, William F. S. "Fifty Years of 'Assimilation.'" Assessing France's Experience of Caribbean Decolonisation through Administrative Reform." In *Islands at the Crossroads: Politics in the Non-Independent Caribbean,* eds. Aarón Gamaliel Ramos and Angel Israel Rivera, 45–60. Kingston: Ian Randle Publishers, 2001.

Monnereau, Elie. 1765. *Le parfait indigotier.* Marseille: J. Mossy.

Montesquieu. [1748] 1955. *De l'esprit des lois.* In *Œuvres complètes.* Vol. 2. Paris: Société Les Belles Lettres.

———. [1721] 1990. *Lettres persanes.* Paris: Larousse.

Moreau de Saint-Méry. 1784–1790. *Loix et constitutions des colonies françaises de l'Amérique sous le vent.* 6 vols. Paris.

———. [1791] 1972. *Considérations présentées aux vrais amis du repos et du bonheur de la France à l'occasion des nouveaux mouvements de quelques soi-disant Amis des Noirs.* Paris: Hachette.

———. [1797] 1984. *Description topographique, physique, civile, politique et historique de la partie française de l'isle de Saint-Domingue.* Paris: Société Française d'Histoire d'Outre-Mer.

"Musée du Rhum, Distillerie Reimonenq." 2000–2001. In *Guide de vos loisirs: La Guadeloupe autrement.* Guadeloupe: UPAT-LANA Consultants.

Musée du Rhum. n.d. Museum displays and explanatory panels. *Distillerie Reimonenq,* Sainte-Rose, Guadeloupe.

Naipaul, V. S. 1969. *The Middle Passage.* London: Penguin.

Nora, Pierre. 1996. *Realms of Memory. Vol. 1, Conflicts and Divisions,* trans. Arthur Goldhammer. New York: Columbia University Press.

Norton, Graham Gendall. 2003. "Toussaint Louverture—French General Imprisoned by Napoleon." In *History Today,* <http://www.findarticles.com> (April).

Ogé, Jeune (Vincent). [1789] 1968. "Motion faite à l'Assemblée des Colons Habitans de S. Domingue, à l'Hôtel de Massiac, Place des Victoires." In *La Révolution française et l'abolition de l'esclavage.* Vol. 11. Paris: EDHIS.

Paquette, Robert L. 1991. "Social History Update: Slave Resistance and Social History." *Journal of Social History* 24: 681–85.

Paringaux, Roland-Pierre. 1998. "1848, la seconde abolition de l'esclavage." *Le Monde* 20 April.

Peabody, Sue. 1994. "Race, Slavery, and the Law in Early Modern France." *Historian* 56: 501–10.

———. 1996. *There Are No Slaves in France: The Political Culture of Race and Slavery in Eighteenth-Century France.* New York: Oxford University Press.

Pensey, P. Henrion de (avocat) and Poncet de la Grave (procureur du roi). 1770. *Mémoire pour le nommé Roc, nègre contre le sieur Poupet, négociant.* Paris: Imprimerie de J. Th. Hérissant, Imprimeur du Cabinet du Roi.

Pérotin-Dumon, Anne. 1991. "The Emergence of Politics among Free-Coloureds and Slaves in Revolutionary Guadeloupe." *Journal of Caribbean History* 25, nos.1–2: 100–135.

Perroud, Claude. 1916. "La Société française des Amis des Noirs." *La Révolution française* 69: 122–47.

Pétion de Villeneuve. [1790] 1968. "Discours sur la traite des noirs." In *La Révolution française et l'abolition de l'esclavage.* Vol. 8. Paris: EDHIS.

Pigault-Lebrun. 1796. *Le blanc et le noir.* Paris: Mayeur et Barba.

Pluchon, Pierre, ed. 1982. *Histoire des Antilles et de la Guyane.* Paris: Privat.

Pouliquen, Monique, comp. 1989. *Doléances des peuples coloniaux à l'Assemblée nationale constituante 1789–1790.* Paris: Archives Nationales.

Prévost, Abbé. 1735. *Le pour et le contre.* Paris.

———. 1746. *Histoire générale des voyages.* Paris.

"Proposition de loi … tendant à la reconnaissance de la traite et de l'esclavage en tant que crimes contre l'humanité, 18 février 1999," Article 2. 2000. In *De l'esclavage aux réparations,* eds. Serge Chalons et al., 153–55. Paris: Karthala.

Price, Richard, ed. 1979. *Maroon Societies: Rebel Slave Communities in the Americas.* Baltimore: Johns Hopkins.

Quétel, Claude, ed. 1996. *Histoire-Seconde: Les fondements du monde contemporain.* Paris: Bordas.

Quinney, Valerie. 1970. "Decisions on Slavery, the Slave Trade, and Civil Rights for Negroes in the Early French Revolution." *Journal of Negro History* 55: 117–30.

Raimond, Julien. 1789. *Observations adressées à l'Assemblé nationale, par un député des colons américains.* Paris.

———. 1791a. *Observations sur l'origine et les progrès du préjugé des colons blancs contre les hommes de couleur.* Paris: Belin.

———. 1791b. *Réponse aux considérations de monsieur Moreau, dit Saint-Méry, député à l'Assemblée nationale, sur les colonies.* Paris: Imprimerie du Patriote François.

———. 1793a. *Mémoire sur les causes des troubles et des désastres de la colonie de Saint Domingue.* Paris: Cercle du Social.

———. 1793b. *Réflexions sur les véritables causes des troubles et des désastres de nos colonies, notamment sur ceux de Saint Domingue.* Paris: Imprimerie des Patriotes.

———. 1793–1800. *Correspondance de Julien Raimond, avec ses frères, de Saint Domingue.* Paris: Cercle du Social. *Raimond, commissaire délégué par le gouvernement français aux îles sous le vent, au ministre de la marine.* Cap-Français, Haïti: Imprimerie Roux.

———. 1796–97. *Rapport de Julien Raimond, commissaire délégué par le gouvernement français aux îles sous le vent, au ministre de la marine.* Cap-Français, Haïti: Imprimerie Roux.

Raimond et al. [1791] 1968. "Lettre des commissaires des citoyens de couleur en France, à leurs frères et commettans dans les îles françaises." In *La Révolution française et l'abolition de l'esclavage.* Vol. 11. Paris: EDHIS.

Raynal, Abbé. [1770, 1774, 1780] 1981. *Histoire philosophique et politique des établissements et du commerce des Européens dans les deux Indes.* Paris: Maspero.

———. 1785. *Essai sur l'administration de Saint Domingue.* Paris.

Reinhardt, Catherine. 1998. "Remembering the Struggle for Freedom: The French Caribbean Slave Experience during the Enlightenment." University of California, Santa Barbara.

———. 2000. "French Caribbean Slaves Forge Their Own Ideal of Liberty in 1789." In *Slavery in the Caribbean Francophone World: Distant Voices, Forgotten Acts, Forged Identities,* ed. Doris Y. Kadish, 19–38.

———. 2001. "Forgotten Claims to Liberty: Free Coloreds in St. Domingue on the Eve of the First Abolition of Slavery." *Colonial Latin American Review* 10, no. 1: 105–24.

———. 2005. "Slavery and Commemoration: Remembering the French Abolitionary Decree 150 Years Later." In *Memory, Empire and Postcolonialism,* ed. Alec G. Hargreaves.

Resnick, Daniel P. 1972. "The Société des Amis des Noirs and the Abolition of Slavery." *French Historical Studies* 7: 558–69.

Rochmann, Marie-Christine, ed. 2000. *Esclavage et abolitions.* Paris: Karthala.

Saint-Lambert, Jean-François. [1769] 1883. *Ziméo.* In *Contes de Saint-Lambert; les chefs-d'œuvre inconnus.* Paris: Librairie des Bibliophiles.

———. 1787. *Réflexions sur les moyens de rendre meilleur l'état des nègres ou des affranchis de nos colonies.* Paris.

Saint-Ruf, Germain. 1977. *L'épopée Delgrès: La Guadeloupe sous la Révolution française. (1789–1802).* Paris: L'Harmattan.

Sala-Molins, Louis. 1987. *Le code noir ou le calvaire de Canaan.* Paris: Presses Universitaires Françaises.

———. 1992. *Les misères des lumières: Sous la raison, l'outrage.* Paris: Laffont.

———. 1998. "Le cent cinquantenaire de quoi?" *Le Monde* 16 April.

Sannon, P. 1920–33. *Histoire de Toussaint Louverture.* 3 vols. Port-au-Prince: Imprimerie Heraux.

Schmidt, Nelly. 1998. "Un homme et l'histoire: Victor Schœlcher." *France-Antilles: Supplément-Edition* (Guadeloupe) 25 May.

———. 2005. L'abolition de l'esclavage: Cinq siècles de combats, XVIe–XXe siècle. Paris: Fayard.

Scott, Julius. 1986. "The Common Wind: Currents of Afro-American Communication in the Era of the Haitian Revolution." Duke University.

Seeber, Edward D. 1937. *Anti-Slavery Opinion in France during the Second Half of the Eighteenth Century.* Baltimore: Johns Hopkins.

Segal, Ronald. 1995. *The Black Diaspora.* London: Faber & Faber.

Shklar, Judith N. 1987. *Montesquieu.* Oxford: Oxford University Press.

Société des Amis des Noirs. [1788] 1968. "Discours sur la nécessité d'établir à Paris une société pour concourir, avec celle de Londres, à l'abolition de la traite et de l'esclavage des nègres." In *La Révolution française et l'abolition de l'esclavage.* Vol. 6. Paris: EDHIS.

———. [1789a] 1968. "Description d'un navire négrier." In *La Révolution française et l'abolition de l'esclavage.* Vol. 6. Paris: EDHIS.

———. [1789b] 1968. "Lettre à messieurs les députés des trois ordres, pour les engager à nommer un comité chargé d'examiner la cause des noirs." In *La Révolution française et l'abolition de l'esclavage.* Vol. 7. Paris: EDHIS.

————. [1789c] 1968. "Lettre de la société des Amis des Noirs à monsieur Necker, avec la réponse de ce ministre." In *La Révolution française et l'abolition de l'esclavage*. Vol. 7. Paris: EDHIS.

————. [1789d] 1968. "Règlements de la Société des Amis des Noirs de Paris." In *La Révolution française et l'abolition de l'esclavage*. Vol. 6. Paris: EDHIS.

————. [1789e] 1968. "Réponse à l'écrit de monsieur Malouet sur l'esclavage des nègres." In *La Révolution française et l'abolition de l'esclavage*. Vol. 6. Paris: EDHIS.

————. [1790a] 1968. "Adresse à l'Assemblée nationale pour l'abolition de la Traite des Noirs." In *La Révolution française et l'abolition de l'esclavage*. Vol. 7. Paris: EDHIS.

————. [1790b] 1968. *Adresse aux amis de l'humanité … sur le plan de ses travaux*. In *La Révolution française et l'abolition de l'esclavage*. Vol. 8. Paris: EDHIS.

————. [1790c] 1968. "Réflexions sur le code noir, et dénonciation d'un crime affreux commis à Saint Domingue." In *La Révolution française et l'abolition de l'esclavage*. Vol. 8. Paris: EDHIS.

————. [1790d] 1968. "Seconde adresse à l'Assemblée nationale." In *La Révolution française et l'abolition de l'esclavage*. Vol. 7. Paris: EDHIS.

————. [1795–96] 1968. "Lettre de la Société des Amis des Noirs, aux auteurs de la décade philosophique." In *La Révolution française et l'abolition de l'esclavage*. Vol. 8. Paris: EDHIS.

Sorel, Albert. 1921. *Montesquieu*. Paris: Hachette.

"Supplique des citoyens de couleur des îles et colonies françaises. 2 déc. 1789." 1989. In *Doléances des peuples coloniaux à l'Assemblée nationale constituante 1789–1790*, comp. Monique Pouliquen, 151–59. Paris: Archives Nationales de France.

Suratteau, J.-R. 1995. "La question coloniale à la Constituante." *Annales historiques de la Révolution française* 299: 33–43.

Tarrade, Jean. 1989. "Les Colonies et les principes de 1789. Les assemblées révolutionnaires face au problème de l'esclavage." *Revue française d'histoire d'outre-mer* 76: 9–34.

Taubira-Delannon, Christiane. 2000 "Projet de loi." In *De l'esclavage aux réparations,* eds. Serge Chalons et al., 149–55. Paris: Karthala.

Thomas, Keith. 1983. *Man and the Natural World*. London: Allen Lane.

Tocqueville, Alexis de. 1860. *L'Ancien Régime et la Révolution*. Paris: Michel Lévy Frères.

Todorov, Tzvetan. 1985–86. "'Race,' Writing, and Culture." In *"Race," Writing, and Difference,* ed. Henry Louis Gates Jr., 370–80. Chicago: University of Chicago Press.

Toumson, Roger. 1989. *La transgression des couleurs: Littérature et langage des Antilles (XVIIIe, XIXe, XXe siècles)*. 2 vols. Paris: Editions Caribéennes.

"Tras'Mémoires commémore la lutte des esclaves ce week-end." 1998. *France-Antilles* (Guadeloupe) 22 May.

Trouillot, Rolph. 1995. *Silencing the Past: Power and the Production of History.* Boston: Beacon Press.

"Une pensée forte pour les 'neg mawon'." 1998. *France-Antilles* (Guadeloupe) 22 May.

Vanony-Frisch, Nicole. 1985. "Les esclaves de la Guadeloupe à la fin de l'Ancien Régime d'après les sources notariales (1770–1789)." *Bulletin de la Société d'histoire de la Guadeloupe* 63–64.

Vézins, Véziane de. 1998. "Les brûlots de l'abbé Raynal." *Le Figaro* 25 April.

Vidal, André-Jean. 1998. "La première abolition en Guadeloupe (1794–1802)." *France-Antilles: Supplément-Edition* (Guadeloupe) 25 May.

Vidalenc, Jean. 1957. "La traite des nègres en France au début de la Révolution (1789–1793)." *Annales historiques de la révolution française* 29: 56–69.

Viefville des Essars, Jean-Louis de. [1790] 1968. "Discours et projet de loi pour l'affranchissement des nègres, ou l'adoucissement de leur régime, et réponse aux objections des colons." In *La Révolution française et l'abolition de l'esclavage.* Vol. 7. Paris: EDHIS.

Voltaire. [1756] 1878. *Essai sur les mœurs.* In *Œuvres complètes.* Vols. 12, 13. Paris: Garnier.

———. [1759] 1973. *Candide ou l'Optimisme.* Paris: Bordas.

———. [1764] 1878. "Esclaves." *Dictionnaire philosophique.* In *Œuvres complètes.* Vol. 18. Paris: Garnier.

Walcott, Derek. 1992. "The Sea Is History." *The Star-Apple Kingdom.* In *Collected Poems 1948–1984.* London: Faber and Faber.

Welschinger, Henri. 1880. *Le théâtre de la Révolution.* Paris: Charavay frères.

Whitman, Daniel. 1977. "Slavery and the Rights of Frenchmen: Views of Montesquieu, Rousseau and Raynal." *French Colonial Studies* 1: 17–33.

Williams, Eric. 1994. *Capitalism and Slavery.* Chapel Hill and London: University of North Carolina Press.

Wimpffen, baron de. [1788] 1911. *Saint Domingue à la veille de la Révolution. Souvenirs du baron de Wimpffen.* 1788. Paris: Albert Savine.

Wood, Marcus. 2000. *Blind Memory: Visual Representations of Slavery in England and America 1780–1865).* London: Routledge.

Yacou, Alain. 1984. "Les rébellions nègres à Cuba dans la première moitié du XIXème siècle: Contenu idéologique et programme subversif. *Bulletin de la société d'histoire de la Guadeloupe* 59: 77–108.

INDEX